D0064728

The
Second Economy
in Tanzania

EASTERN AFRICAN STUDIES

Abdul Sheriff
Slaves, Spices & Ivory in Zanzibar
Integration of an East African Commercial Empire
into the World Economy 1770–1873

Isaria N. Kimambo
Penetration & Protest in Tanzania *
The Impact of the World Economy
on the Pare 1860–1960

T.L. Maliyamkono & M.S.D. Bagachwa
The Second Economy in Tanzania

Tabitha Kanogo
Squatters & the Roots of Mau Mau 1905–1963

David W. Throup
Economic and Social Origins of Mau Mau 1945–1953

Frank Furedi
The Mau Mau War in Perspective

David William Cohen & E.S. Atieno Odhiambo
Siaya
The Historical Anthropology of an African Landscape

Bruce Berman & John Lonsdale
Unhappy Valley *
Clan, Class & State in Colonial Kenya

Bruce Berman
Crisis & Control in Colonial Kenya *
The Dialectic of Domination

Bahru Zewde
A History of Modern Ethiopia
1855–1974

* forthcoming

The
Second Economy
in Tanzania

T.L. MALIYAMKONO

Professor of the Economics of Education, University of Dar es Salaam &
Director of the Eastern & Southern African Universities Research Programme (ESAURP)

M.S.D. BAGACHWA

Senior Research Fellow,
Economic Research Bureau, University of Dar es Salaam
& National Coordinator, Eastern & Southern Africa
Technology Policy Studies (EATPS)

JAMES CURREY
LONDON

OHIO UNIVERSITY PRESS
ATHENS

HEINEMANN KENYA
NAIROBI

ESAURP
DAR ES SALAAM

James Currey Ltd
54b Thornhill Square, Islington
London N1 1BE, England

Eastern and Southern African Universities
Research Programme
Secretariat at the University of Dar es Salaam
P.O. Box 35048, Dar es Salaam, Tanzania

Heinemann Kenya
Kijabe Street, P.O. Box 45314
Nairobi, Kenya

Ohio University Press
Scott Quadrangle
Athens, Ohio 45701, USA

British Library Cataloguing in Publication Data
Maliyamkono, T.L. (T Luta)
The second economy in Tanzania.
1. Tanzania. Black economy
I. Title II. Bagachwa, M.S.D. (Mboya S.D.)
339

ISBN 0-85255-122-3
ISBN 0-85255-121-5 pbk

Library of Congress Cataloging in Publication Data
Maliyamkono, T.L.
    The second economy in Tanzania/T.L. Maliyamkono, Mboya
S.D. Bagachwa.
        p. cm.—(Eastern African studies)
    Includes bibliographical references.
    ISBN 0-8214-0949-2
    1. Informal sector (Economics)—Tanzania.
2. Tanzania—Economic conditions—1964–
I. Bagachwa, Mboya S.D. II. Title. III. Series:
Eastern African studies (London, England)
HD2346.T3M35   1989
381—dc20   89-27398
                                                      CIP

Typeset in 10/11pt Baskerville
by Colset Private Limited, Singapore
and printed in Kenya
by Colourprint, Nairobi
and printed in Britain
by Villiers Publications, London N6

Contents

v

Acknowledgements

First of all, we wish to acknowledge the assistance of the Government of Tanzania for facilitating our approaches to public institutions for the information we needed. Among those with whom we held interviews we should particularly like to thank H. Kolimba, then Personal Assistant to the Premier, and P. Msekwa, then Principal Secretary to the Prime Minister and First Vice-President's Office.

The University of Dar es Salaam's Senate Research and Publications Committee spearheaded resource assistance. The National Scientific Research Council stepped in after the initial support of the International Development Research Centre (IDRC) of Canada and the Ford Foundation. Fieldwork was funded by the Ford Foundation's second grant and by NORAD. Without these two sources of financial assistance we should not have come this far.

Individual participation was equally important. The work of the Second Economy Study Group at the University of Dar es Salaam was unfortunately slowed down by the heavy work schedule of S. Rugumisa in the Prime Minister's office, and the usual academic requirements with which S. Kapunda, as a PhD student, had to contend, forcing them to pull out during the early stages of the study.

However, we continued to work closely with B. J. Humplick and P. Rwezaura, our two full-time research assistants, and we hope that the experience they gained is useful to their present employer – The Eastern and Southern African Universities Research Programme (ESAURP). Earlier, F. Stancavage assisted in focusing the proposal, and our colleagues S. Limbu, B. Mutagwaba and B. Nyagetera assisted us in the preliminary data analysis. W. Philips assisted during the last stages of the book. We are also grateful to A. Bigsten, G. Helleiner, M. Hodd, H. Lunogelo and S. Jones for reading our manuscript and providing very useful comments.

The hospitality afforded to us at the School of Oriental and African Studies, University of London, and at Queen Elizabeth House, University of Oxford, deserves mention for it enabled us to have access to academic facilities. But for regular consultations and cheerfulness, the palm must go to Michael Hodd and Frances Stewart. We owe a special debt to Todo and Alice, our greatest friends, for keeping our families happy while we worked on this book.

The study of the second economy in Tanzania has not been easy for us, although we do now feel a step closer to understanding how Tanzanians live.

T. L. Maliyamkono
M. S. D. Bagachwa

Prelude:
The 1983 Crackdown
on Economic Saboteurs

The 1983 crackdown was launched by the Government on 23 March on a broad front, not long after the second premiership of the late Edward Sokoine, and was clearly intended to administer a sharp and salutary shock to the ailing economy. There had been dire warnings of the serious straits towards which the country was heading and some corrective actions had been attempted, but with little evidence of success. Two years earlier (6 February 1981), Fili Karashani reported the President as declaring that the 'war on corruption continues' and that an ongoing committee would 'continue for some time to sweep away corrupt elements and economic saboteurs'.[1] At the same time people were sacked from the management of Air Tanzania and the Tanzania Investment Bank. For some it was a case of throwing out the gold with the dross. It was then stressed that the Government was not engaged on a witchhunt, but that 'no stone would be left unturned in the hunt for saboteurs'. In the spring of 1983 there were evidently quite a few left to be turned. The leadership described the situation as one of 'considerable strain and stress' and acknowledged that 'Tanzania is fighting for its very survival'. Elaborating on the shortages, R. Young wrote that

> The outward signs of economic deterioration seem everywhere evident. . . .
> Long lines form early each morning in Dar es Salaam outside a medium-sized
> bakery for white bread. There is a shortage of almost all consumer staples:
> flour, cooking oil, sugar, kerosene, charcoal and clothing. For the first time
> some residents speak privately of the possibility of urban violence. The

Government's policies do not seem to be able to secure a minimum level of food for the majority of the urban population. As for the rural population there is virtually nothing to buy.[2]

The Government found it difficult to explain how this disastrous situation had come about because it had introduced legislation to protect the masses. The National Price Commission had been set up in 1973. The distribution of essential commodities had been confined to the Regional Trading Companies or Government designated agents with special permits. The National Executive Council of the Party had withdrawn the right of leaders to issue special permits (*vibali*) because this concession had become out of hand and led to scarce goods being sold from private houses at exorbitant prices. A well-trained police force was guarding the diamond and gold fields, and a good number of police had been posted to the border entry points. The Government stated that 'We cannot as a people's Party sit back and watch these evil men exploit and yet have the audacity to smear the good name of the Party saying those illegal rates were Party rates.' Somehow the Government managed to convince itself that the dire shortage of goods was due to sabotage, and that it was facing a deliberate attempt to subvert public institutions to frustrate government. There was no evidence of dissatisfaction in the Army, where political education and the failure of army governments elsewhere in Africa seem to have kept morale high. But the enormous growth of the administrative apparatus following the nationalization of manufacturing, agricultural and service industries was thought to have brought about pockets of ill feeling and silent opposition to the further spread of socialism.

The hectic pace of development since independence under the leadership of a determined and highly motivated Government had concealed the emergence of new groupings in the social fabric whose welfare had been affected in different ways, and whose perceived and subjective interests by no means coincided. Increasingly these groupings polarized. First the politically powerful relied on the support of the urban and rural poor, and benefited from the public institutions they controlled, whereas the economically powerful lacked mass support and generally emerged by taking advantage of opportunities created by the new institutions. Second, the rural peasants originally benefited from higher agricultural prices and the spread of education, health and welfare services, but the size of real incomes and the lack of goods to buy led to their gradual withdrawal from participating in, for example, self-help schemes. The shortages of goods created opportunities for both rural and urban traders, many of whom became rich. Third, the state apparatus operated through newly devised institutions, whereas private institutions, whose functions had originally been curtailed, quickly took advantage of public failure and gained a large part of the service sectors through private transport, private schooling, private hospitals, private business and a fast growing informal sector in urban areas. Many of these opportunities for regaining wealth not only arose out of the internal market which was controlled by public institutions, but also came with illicit trading with adjoining countries and smuggling.

Tanzania has a very long land frontier with Mozambique, Zambia, Zaire, Ruanda, Burundi, Uganda and especially Kenya, which is almost impossible to police effectively, and many widely dispersed ports serving an extensive range of countries, as well as three major lakes with a shoreline shared by adjacent countries. Smuggling is therefore very difficult to prevent and the major routes are well known: Zanzibar and Pemba are the main exit routes for spices, cloves and fish destined for Kenya and overseas destinations; Dar es Salaam ships ivory, hides and skins, gold, diamonds and sea food to Europe and other overseas destinations; Lindi and Mtwara supply ivory, hides and skins to Dar es Salaam for onward shipment; Tanga delivers spices (particularly cardamom), fish and other sea foods, as well as coffee, to Indian Ocean ports and to Kenya; Arusha and Moshi are centres for delivering hides, skins, livestock, maize, beans, ivory, gemstones and coffee for Kenya and onward shipment; Mara is a crossing point for cattle and ivory into Kenya; Mwanza ships gemstones and gold to Dar es Salaam, Nairobi and Arusha, for transhipment. Bukoba and Kagera are centres for smuggling coffee to and from Uganda, Ruanda and Burundi; Kigoma ships ivory, skins and fish to Ruanda, Burundi and Zaire; Mbeya and Rukwa ship rice, maize, coffee and fish to Zambia.

The silent dissatisfaction and the withdrawal from official market to black market reinforced Government belief that shortages of goods had been deliberately brought about by hoarding with the objective of subverting the Government. As the nationalization measure of 1967 had particularly affected traders and businessmen, the majority of whom were of Asian extraction, suspicions were aroused that the emerging economic elite made up of successful Asian businessmen, and powerful African bureaucrats and politically dissatisfied politicians were conspiring with self-exiled dissidents, especially from Zanzibar, to bring about riots and chaos.

The immediate impact of the crackdown was dramatic. With the busy police making arrests and 'making a buck', the rather loose soldiers who had returned from the Uganda war, hooligans, thugs, thieves and robbers, all the regional capitals became terror-stricken. Although no one knew precisely what was happening, the news that something was happening spread like wildfire. The buses ran half empty because people were afraid of being caught at road-blocks. A lot of people went into hiding. Children said 'Karibu' (come in) just in case the visitor was unwanted, in order to give their father a chance to disappear through the back door. Cars were kept off the roads for fear of accidental confrontation with the police, and some headed for the borders. Bars and cinemas were empty and shops were closed. Some homes were burnt to ashes in case revealing receipts were discovered. Many houses were left empty with much evidence of having been left in a hurry. International planes were full to capacity and many charter flights zoomed to Kenya. Banknotes were paid into bank accounts by the million in order to avoid confiscation (Kigoma banked more in one week than is normally banked by rich Dar es Salaam). During the first few days of the crackdown one was likely to be offered bundles of banknotes by guilty people anxious to be rid of them. Those who were too scared to carry their money to the banks threw bags of notes on the road, but the Government hastened to create an anonymous money dumping place. Ivory waiting for shipment was buried. The rich became grave-diggers of the 'tombs of wealth' – televisions and videos which had probably been smuggled into the country. The torrential rains preceding the crackdown had made many of the roads impassable. Except for the international community – residents in Tanzania or tourists who were excluded from all this, together with *Mbifamuki* or *Kabwela* (ordinary people) – the rest of the people must have felt shock, panic, fury and misery, at least for the first few weeks.

Tanzania prides itself, with a good deal of justification, on its free press, and the following items from the *Daily News* (a daily newspaper) give a blow-by-blow account of the major events of the crackdown which extended over several months at a diminishing rate. On 1 April 1983, President Nyerere spoke to the Dodoma Elders Advisory Council; 14 April 1983, Rashidi Kawawa, the CCM Party Secretary General, announced at Mwanza that drastic measures would be taken against CCM leaders and members who failed to expose racketeers, smugglers and saboteurs. 17 April 1983, war was declared against saboteurs. In the paper's view, Government action was overdue; it was not enough to arrest people who had been hoarding goods because they must have acquired them with the help of those in high positions. The basic problem was not punishment, but to ensure that what was confiscated got to the people. On 18 April 1983, at Dodoma, Prime Minister Edward Sokoine emphasized that the crackdown was aimed at traffickers in foreign currency; smugglers of minerals, livestock, hoes and drugs; hoarders of scarce items; Party, Government and parastatal officials under investigation, and people with unlicensed arms. On 18 April 1983, Police Sub-Inspector Hashim Selena was awarded the 100,000 shillings which he was offered by a Dodoma businessman detained for racketeering. On 20 April 1983, Saidi Natape, Minister of Home Affairs, addressed the National Assembly, and the *Daily News* reported that the crackdown had netted 1,057 people so far (951 Tanzanians, 51 Somalis, 23 Indians, 10

British, 7 Arabs and 4 Kenyans). Most of those arrested were businessmen, but there were also civil servants, parastatal employees, Party employees and one MP. The goods seized included 7,892 tons of salt, 9,323 corrugated iron sheets, 792 bags of rice, 17,845 hoes, 15,828 tins of kerosene, 9,956 cartons of washing soap, 192 bags of sugar and 5,519 tins of cooking oil. Seized cash amounted to 33,835,041 shillings, $US23,147.85, £27,527, 11,900 DM, 21,975 Somali shillings and sh. 9,085.30 Kenya currency. The Economic Sabotage (Special Provisions) Bill aimed to give the President the power to decide on the law's application; to legalize retrospectively Government actions already taken; to give the President powers to authorize the police to conduct searches, and to establish the National Economic Sabotage Tribunal.

On 23 April 1983, in Dodoma, Prime Minister Sokoine outlined the saboteurs' tricks: in border regions, he said, they smuggled out goods which they then sold, and bought goods to smuggle back and sell at high prices; people registering as tour operators engaged in foreign exchange fraud; people with import permits over-invoiced them and retained the difference; those importing raw materials for manufacture did not sell the output through official channels; exporters of cash crops under-invoiced them and retained the difference; some people in Government and parastatals paid in foreign currency were paid in local currency and credited with the difference; some telephone subscribers did not pay their bills because they knew the staff; some diplomatic personnel abused the personal imports regulations; bogus contractors hoarded building materials in order to inflate costs later.

On 24 April 1983, in the Editorial of the *Sunday News* it was stated that the war against economic saboteurs and marketeers was still raging, and that the campaign was likely to prove very successful. For the last three weeks or so, the paper commented, the national news media had been carrying startling stories of hoarded goods netted by the police or surrendered by racketeers in response to the President's call. Those involved included prominent businessmen and public servants, mainly managers of regional trading corporations. They were found guilty of frustrating the nation's efforts to distribute scarce commodities throughout the country. The encouraging trend so far recorded, continued the *Sunday News*, was mainly attributable to the people's close co-operation with the Government since the launching of the campaign, for the people knew the whereabouts of the saboteurs and racketeers, and how they carried on their activities. The police force and other law-enforcing institutions should also be praised for working tirelessly to rid the nation of evil elements bent on prospering at the expense of the people. A Government statement earlier in the week had stressed that the campaign was directed at people hoarding goods, worsening the shortage of essential commodities, and Party and Government leaders colluding with racketeers by helping them to obtain goods as well as protecting them from being punished. It was therefore important, continued the statement, that people at all levels should volunteer information on suspects to trustworthy leaders and institutions as directed by the President.

On 8 May 1983, the Prime Minister told the BBC that racketeering was widespread, and that it was dominated by four major groups. The first comprised dealers who smuggled out foreign currency, especially via tourists. The second comprised those who smuggled out of the country property and goods like cattle, gold, ploughs, medicines, radio sets and batteries. The third category included hoarders, profiteers and speculators who exercised some sort of monopoly, buying large quantities of goods, storing them, and so exacerbating the scarcity of essential goods. The fourth category was a group of Government and parastatal leaders who either directly or indirectly collaborated with these economic saboteurs. The crackdown was an effort by the Government, he said, to centralize corrupt elements within the Government, and among parastatals and Party leaders. In only three weeks it had unearthed 'millions' in local as well as in foreign currency.

Eleven days later, the CCM National Executive Committee directed the Government to implement scrupulously the internal trade policy, emphasizing equitable distribution of commodities through co-operative and village shops, and on 21 May, John A. Mrosso, Chairman of the National Anti Economic Sabotage Tribunal, urged prosecutors to be well versed in the technicalities of the 1983 Sabotage Act. On 7 June, Edward Sokoine urged the speedy disposal of perishable commodities to public institutions and co-operative shops, and on 11 June, Justice Lewis Chua, at the National Anti Economic Sabotage Tribunal in Dodoma, said that people arrested under the Anti Economic Sabotage (Special Provisions) Act 1983 should be subject to the same treatment as detainees under the Preventive Detention Act.

On 21 June it was announced that by Presidential order the Economic Sabotage (Special Provisions) Act 1983 would be applied retrospectively from 25 March 1983. It would not apply to persons who surrendered gold, goods or foreign exchange, or to those depositing money with the National Bank of Commerce. On 16 July, Rashid Mohamed Hamad (Deputy Minister of Home Affairs) said that increased production of food and basic items had checked racketeering, and that 1,415 suspects had been held since the crackdown began. With the detention of the big racketeers smaller ones were phased out for lack of goods. The Human Resources Deployment Act would make small racketeers disappear.

On 17 July 1983, the Prime Minister told Parliament that regions and districts had been directed to enforce strictly the official system of distributing commodities through the distribution committees, and to write reports on the impact of the crackdown, including initiatives taken by them to rectify identified weaknesses. The crackdown had shown that regions and districts were not following the laid-down procedures of distributing commodities, because some of the distribution committees were inefficient. Assessments of the crackdown should also cover its impact on agricultural production in the villages. Meanwhile, he ordered the immediate removal of all road-blocks between the regions, but said that traffic would be confined to five bags per person. Road-blocks checking smuggling of agricultural products out of the country would be retained and strengthened.

On 8 October 1983, Zanzibar President Aboud Jumbe expressed satisfaction over the handling of the campaign against economic saboteurs in public institutions. On 27 October, in Geita, Edward Sokoine directed Mwanza regional authorities to deploy Sungu-Sungu defence groups towards weeding out saboteurs; and on the same day, the Anti Economic Sabotage Tribunal at Tabora sentenced five peasants to forty-eight years in prison for corruption and the unlawful possession of sixty-three elephant tusks. On 15 November, Rashidi Kawawa called on Party branches at places of work not to protect lazy workers and economic saboteurs. He urged TRC (railways) to find ways of checking the outflow of workers.

The actions taken during the crackdown beginning on 23 March 1983 were codified retrospectively by the Economic and Organized Crime Control Act 1984 No. 13 (Principal Legislation) which listed and defined these economic offences in the Schedule: exchange control offences; bribery and corruption; bribery of participants in sports events; hoarding commodities; leading organized crime; hoarding of money; fraudulent schemes, games and artifices, theft of public property, etc.; persons conveying or having possession of goods suspected of having been stolen or unlawfully acquired; unlawful sale of designated goods; authorization of unlawful supply of designated authority goods; occasioning loss to specified authority; cattle theft; stock theft; interfering with a necessary service (National Security Act 1970); using firearms, etc.; offences against conservation of wildlife; offences in relation to the Gemstone Industry (Development and Protection) Act 1970; unlawful prospecting, etc.; offences in relation to the Diamond Industry Protection Ordinance, and theft of mail matter.

Under this Act, arrests and prosecutions continued through normalized administrative and judicial channels. A cursory examination of press reports during the next five years suggests that of the successful prosecutions the convictions were for the following offences: corruption and hoarding, which accounted for about 60 per cent; elephant rustling and price control offences, accounting for 20 per cent; currency offences, 6 per cent; and using firearms illegally, over-invoicing and armed robberies, accounting for 13 per cent. These figures are only a broad indication, recording successful convictions; there may have been double that number of offences, simply counted as convictions under emergency regulations, and not reported. Nor do the figures give an indication of what the number of cases would have been had the crackdown not taken place.

Not surprisingly, the Economic and Organized Crime Control Act further clogged already overburdened Government machinery. Many of the procedures introduced for obtaining public goods and services, though meant to check irregularities, were complex. For example, in order to apply for a driving licence the Tanzanian citizen has to enrol with a driving school. Having completed thirty lessons the applicant has to go to the Government Revenue Office and complete a form giving his particulars. In exchange for 400 shillings he obtains a learner's driving licence valid for three months, and he must also pay the test fee. This can be renewed after three months, but if sufficiently confident an appointment may be made for a test at the Traffic Police station. But before the test the applicant has to have his eyes tested and produce a medical certificate. On the day of the practical test that certificate has to be produced, together with three passport photographs, one for the Traffic Police, one for the Revenue Office and one for the driving licence. If he survives the theoretical and practical tests, a competence form is issued, which has to be taken to the Revenue Office. For a 1,000 shillings fee, a licence is issued.

A further example of the administrative jungle is the procedure for applying for an industrial licence, clearly a key feature for a country bent on fostering self-reliance. No licence can be issued unless a company has been registered. The applicant has to take the proposed company name to the Company Registration Office where it is checked whether or not the proposed name is acceptable. If it is, the articles of association have to be drawn up and taken to the Company Registrar who extracts a variable fee according to whether it is a partnership or a limited liability company. That is only the first step, and having registered the company, an industrial licence has to be applied for from the urban authority, for example the City Council, on form TFN221. This application has to be approved by (i) the Land Officer (for urban, municipal or city residents); (ii) the Health Officer (for inspecting the proposed premises); (iii) the Ward Development Committee (for political vetting); (iv) the District Council/Ministry/Urban Authority (for planning consent); (v) the Trade Officer (for financial and fiscal scrutiny and the assessment of the licence fee); (vi) the Principal Assessor (for examining income tax for the last three years and collecting outstanding tax liabilities and provisionally assessed tax). The Assessor's tax clearance form, the application form and the registration certificate must then be taken to the Urban/District

Authority where the assessed licence fee is paid. The licence is taken to the Trade Officer where it is lodged, and the number related to the ward where the premises are located is issued, which takes up to three weeks. Finally the National Provident Office requires registration in relation to employer's liability for national insurance. It may well be that all these procedures are wholly necessary, but they certainly do not encourage initiative and enterprise. Numerous further examples of bureaucratic procedures could be described; not only do they go some way towards accounting for the remarkable increase in the percentage of GDP represented by administration in Tanzania, but their lengthy procedures have now become the fastest breeding enclaves of corruption.

The hunt for saboteurs continued for several months, although the liberalization measures introduced in the following year greatly extended the range of opportunities for committing the very economic offences that the crackdown had aimed to eradicate. The hunt continued as a major instrument of public policy and the public were encouraged to denounce transgressors to the public authorities. Regular radio programmes (*Mikingamo*) were transmitted, devoted solely to the reporting of offences against the Economic and Organized Crime Control Act, and voluntary contributors were assured of anonymity.

The crackdown was prompted by the perceived need to counter a threat to state legitimacy and organized resistance to state objectives of socialism and self-reliance. In spite of the large number of arrests and convictions among persons in positions of authority, no evidence was discovered to show any form of organization. It helped to focus attention on the real problems of the country, and convinced the Government that the shortages of consumer goods were not mainly due to hoarding. The crackdown scared off new entrants to the second economy, although five years later Arcado Ntagazwa, Minister for Natural Resources and Tourism, reported in Parliament that in 1987-8, 861 poachers were arrested and 3,109 elephant tusks, worth Tanzanian Shs 50.5 million, were confiscated.[3] On balance the crackdown reinforced faith in the legitimacy of the state and its ability to deal with illegality.

However, it may also be argued that the targets aimed at were not always hit accurately. Not only did the crackdown open wide the door to the conduct of personal vendettas and the waste of public resources following false allegations, but the draconian measures trumpeted so loudly landed tiddlers, but failed to catch the big fish. Maybe there were no big fish, for such activities did not exhibit any form of organization. The large bureaucratic apparatus which had been set up was given a virtually impossible task. This is a good example of the over-ambitious and comprehensive attempts by the state to regulate most aspects of economic activity. It has frequently been argued that the administrative machinery which had been set up was excessive for a country at this stage of development. We may also argue that the administrative machine was not adequate to discharge all the functions that were placed upon it, and that applies equally to the crackdown which straddled a very broad range of targets and probably missed a great many.

The introduction of trade liberalization may have been in response to external pressures, but the switches from centralizing Government to decentralization and back to centralization were not, nor were similar switches for the local governments and the enforcement of crop authorities to replace the co-operatives. The organization of marketing channels in several stages was partly aimed at prevention of corruption and the rise of centres of countervailing power, but all these sudden changes created uncertainties and multiplied the temptation and opportunities for corruption and/or shifted some economic activities outside the law. Added to the country's economic difficulties were real shortages of basic household needs, inflation, poor producer prices and low employment wages. All these sowed the seeds of the second economy. But not every Tanzanian was bribed or misappropriated public funds, and indeed most Tanzanians are not in positions that offer such opportunities. The question is *How do Tanzanians live?* In the rest of this book we shall try to explain how the economy deteriorated, who was responsible for what policy, what size of second economy we are talking about, and how the ordinary Tanzanian survives. Whether or not the policy options suggested at the end of the book are reasonable is a question for us all to consider.

The book is organized in five chapters. Chapter 1 focuses on the economy in general, presenting the major economic trends, from which judgement regarding the strength of the economy is made. The conclusion is that in the last few years Tanzania's economic indicators have shown a gloomy picture. It is suggested that unfavourable international trade, a succession of external shocks and some ill-conceived policies of the Government have been the major factors driving the economy into distress. Chapter 2 defines our working definition of the second economy and uses the monetary approach and the income–expenditure discrepancy method to estimate the size of the second economy.

In Chapter 3 various sectoral manifestations of the second economy are discussed. It is shown that a substantial volume of maize and rice has been bypassing the official channel contrary to Government directives, and that in general prices for Government controlled food and consumer goods traded in the second economy have been higher that those set by Government regulatory agencies. The amount of Tanzanian shillings (T.Sh) unofficially exchanged for one unit of a foreign convertible currency was on average more than twice the amount of shillings exchanged at the official exchange rate. In addition, Chapter 3 presents evidence on the volume of illegal foreign reserves entering and leaving the country.

The effects of the current trade reforms, especially on the development of the second economy, are discussed in Chapter 4. Chapter 5 presents an analysis of participation in the second economy through buying and selling on the one hand and production and sale of services unofficially on the other hand. The conclusions drawn at the end of this chapter point to improvements in the official economy as a base for reduced volume and magnitude of the second economy.

1
The Economy
in Distress

1.1 Introduction

The Arusha Declaration, passed in February 1967, some six years after the achievement of independence, instructed the Government and other public institutions to implement policies which would make Tanzania a socialist and self-reliant nation. This was deemed necessary in order to develop a locally-based economy which would bring structural changes, foster equity and hasten rural development. Twenty-one years after the Arusha Declaration, Tanzania is neither socialist nor self-reliant, but it is relatively more equitable than some of its immediate neighbours. However, the achievement of this and other well deserved social objectives is increasingly threatened by the chronic balance of payments crisis over the last few years and a prolonged and severe economic recession, pressure from the International Monetary Fund and Tanzania's aid donors, together forcing the Government to abandon some of its intermediate goals as the prospect of revival in the short term seems remote, apart from their wish and determination to remain masters in their own house.

Tanzania's development record during the first decade of independence indicates that the country was fairly successful in terms of meeting basic human needs, and performed reasonably well in terms of achieving economic growth. However, in the 1970s economic performance weakened and by the early 1980s the country had plunged into an economic crisis of unprecedented proportions. Some of the manifestations of the crisis are shown in Table 1.1 (page 139) and may be summarized as follows:

  i.   The decline in real GDP growth from an average of 5.1 per cent per annum in 1970–6 to less than 2 per cent per annum between 1977 and 1986 when population growth was 3.2 per cent per annum.

  ii. The decline in real per capita income by more than 15 per cent over the 1976–86 period.

  iii. The soaring of inflation from an annual average rate of less

1

than 5 per cent in the 1966–70 period, through 11 per cent in the 1970–6 period, to 30 per cent after 1979.

iv. The deepening external imbalance as the balance on current account deteriorated abruptly from a deficit of $US49 million in 1977 to a deficit of $US539 million in 1982, hitting an all time low of $US565 million in 1980.

v. The growing overall deficit in public finance which rose by more than 6.5 times between 1978–9 and 1984–5, reaching an unprecedented 20 per cent of GDP in 1980.

1.2 Explaining the Economic Crisis

A variety of external and internal factors led to this situation of crisis. Critical writers have pointed to the necessity of receiving food aid in a country with great expanses of arable land as vivid evidence that Tanzania's public policies have failed. More generally, they cite as evidence of a failed economy, problems of underproduction in most economic areas (food crops and industrial-based goods), heavy inter-national borrowing, and dependence on foreign aid to support social welfare programmes. They have generally blamed Tanzania's economic problems on its socialist policies – nationalization of the major means of production, the establishment of a state-directed economy, and the attempt to rely on central planning, policies which they say have dampened individual initiative by denying a fair reward for efforts spent. However, they have also noted that the problems are not entirely of Tanzania's making, and that 'Western assistance has also inadvertently compounded the crisis'[1] by investing too heavily in the building of capacity – capacity that the country does not have the foreign exchange to keep supplied with inputs.

Another group of writers has focused its remarks on Tanzania's political stability over two decades; land democratic practices; its contri-bution to the liberation struggle in Southern Africa; it adherence to a position of non-alignment in international politics, and its success in promoting literacy, preserving its ecology, and providing homes for the homeless. Indeed, Tanzania has been singled out for praise of its extremely workable programme for dealing with refugees, and the country's public policies have been said to reflect the nature of the Tanzanian people. Both of these views, which differ not so much in fact, but rather in emphasis and choice of values, have been discussed in detail by Kahama *et al.*[2]

Those who have been closely involved with the Tanzanian situation recognize that the present economic problems are partly the result of international conditions beyond the control of the Tanzanian people. Although there is controversy about the long-term trend in terms of the trade of primary producers, there is a general consensus that it has been generally unfavourable since the early 1970s. As a relatively unindustrialized country competing in the international market, Tanzania has had to face the fact that its exports are basically agricultural (accounting for 79 per cent of total exports in 1986) and, consequently, highly subject to the volatile forces of supply and demand. Since the mid-1970s Tanzania has traded in an environment of escalating world prices for oil and manufactured good, while, simultaneously, a global recession has dampened the demand for primary commodities in the wealthy countries that are the traditional customers for Tanzania's exports. For example, the cost of a seven-ton truck rose by more than 1.8 times (from T.Shs 66,500 to T.Shs 123,500) between 1977 and 1985, whereas the price of mild coffee per kilo dropped by 40 per cent (from T.Shs 40 to 24.40) between 1967-77 and 1981-2.[3] There has been no change for the better in recent years. Recently President Mwinyi was quoted by the *Daily News* as saying that while in 1983 one tonne of coffee fetched US dollars 3,000, in 1989 the same tonne would fetch only US dollars 1,000. Equally, while a tonne of cloves sold at US dollars 9,000 in 1983 it was being sold for 1,000 dollars in 1989.[4]

High import prices and low export earnings have led to the drastic worsening of Tanzania's terms of trade. In 1985, for example, the purchasing power of Tanzanian exports was just one-third of their purchasing power in 1977 (Table 1.1). In 1978-82, the loss of income purely on account of terms of trade movements amounted to 12 per cent of GDP.[5] Furthermore, the oil import bill, as a proportion of total export earnings, rose sharply from 26 per cent in 1978 to 56 per cent in 1982, with quantities remaining fairly constant.[6] As the country's import capacity became severely constrained, imports were drastically cut and by 1982 import volumes had fallen by 32 per cent below the 1978 level.

Increases in world petroleum prices first experienced in 1973-4 and further price doubling in 1979-80 have been key contributors to Tanzania's economic crisis, for both its newly developed manufacturing base and the more modernized aspects of its agriculture are highly dependent on adequate oil supplies. In 1980 oil imports accounted for 23 per cent of total imports, while 57 per cent of total export revenues went for the importation of oil inputs.[7] Between 1974 and 1979, the nation had to decrease its fuel consumption to 2.8 per cent of GNP. This may be compared with an average annual usage of 9.4 per cent of GNP during the 'good times' between 1960 and 1970. The decrease in fuel consumption cut heavily into Tanzania's infant industrial and distribution systems and adversely affected agricultural production.

As Tanzania's economy has contracted, and as the price it has had to pay for industrial inputs has increased, the country has inevitably been plunged into trade deficits which rose to the order of about $US359 million in 1985. Although a substantial percentage of the deficit has been taken care of by short- and long-term loans and grants, this has resulted in a rising foreign debt both overall and as a percentage of GNP (debt as a percentage of GNP was up from 19.9 per cent in 1970 to 27.6 per cent in 1980). Further, Tanzania has increasingly found itself in the unenviable position of incurring debt for costly and technologically sophisticated building projects established under the Basic Industry Strategy (BIS), which are favoured by Western aid and loan donors. Naturally the procurement of inputs for the aided projects has affected adversely the availability of intermediate inputs for the domestic industrial sector, resulting in high rates of underutilized capacity. Some Western money donor institutions, foreseeing further problems ahead for Tanzania, began to be hesitant to extend additional loans fearing that they may never be repaid. Although claiming to be ideologically neutral, these lenders have tied many of their objections to Tanzania's socialist policies, asserting that the policies are economically unworkable and should be abandoned.

Military spending occasioned by the war with Amin's Uganda was another factor in depleting Tanzania's domestic savings, and severely affected foreign exchange during the late 1970s. In addition to disrupting economic activity and causing loss of life, the war, 'although applauded by many African states as having rid the continent of one of the worst tyrants',[8] caused severe budgetary strains on Tanzania's economy. Just before the war (in 1978), Government spent 14.6 per cent of its total spending on defence. During the fiscal year 1979, however, the share of defence in total expenditure rose sharply to 23.3 per cent. This was the main reason for the increase in the budget deficit from about 10 per cent of GDP in 1977 to 20 per cent in 1979. Official estimates (by the Ministry of Finance) put the cost of the war at T.Shs 4.1 billion (about $US500 million) – the equivalent to Tanzania of one year's total export earnings. Moreover, the geographical location of Tanzania and its support of indigenous independence movements in adjacent countries has involved the country in incurring considerable extra military spending.

The other exogenous shock came from the breakup of the East African Community in 1977, which not only ended Tanzania's legitimate trade with its partners, but also caused the country to incur unexpected start-up costs for the new structures of civil aviation and telecommunication systems.

To add to Tanzania's problems there were natural calamities which had a particularly marked impact on an economy where a high proportion of the population depends on subsistence farming and has only limited access to the cash economy. Droughts were particularly severe in 1973–4, 1981–2 and 1983–4, affecting both food and export crop yields, while occasional floods caused severe damage to roads and bridges. The shortfall called for large-scale food imports which were mainly met by foreign aid, in the case of wheat and rice and about two-thirds of the cost of maize imports in 1981–2, falling to 29 per cent in 1984–5. The 1981–2 drought revealed Tanzania's dependence on imported food. Until 1972–3 food imports were marginal except in a drought year like 1973–4. After 1981–2 food imports rose rapidly to deal with famine relief and continued at about 10 per cent of total imports to 1985. R. Green has estimated the total foreign exchange costs of these events to Tanzania to be approximately $US1.5 billion,[9] which, according to A. Singh implies that the country has lost three years of its export earnings.[10]

Despite the validity of many of the arguments presented above, it would be unrealistic to believe that the Tanzanian economic crisis is entirely external in origin. Certain macro-economic decisions made by the Government during the 1970s also seem, in retrospect, to have had a deleterious effect on the country's economic performance. The first of these was the decision to emphasize industry over agriculture in an unsuccessful effort to make the country more self-reliant. Agriculture is the dominant sector in the economy, accounting for nearly half of the GDP, generating over 75 per cent of foreign exchange, and supporting 90 per cent of the population living in rural areas. Despite its enormous importance, between 1977 and 1980 agriculture received, on average, only 13 per cent of the development budget, while industry was allocated 18.5 per cent of the total development budget annually. Equally, for the period 1977–85, the share of agriculture in fixed capital formation averaged 8 per cent per annum, compared to 25.8 per cent for manufacturing.[11] Government discrimination against agriculture has also assumed more subtle forms such as low prices for agricultural products relative to prices of industrial products, lack of access to public socio-economic services, inadequate and irregular supply of agricultural inputs, poor extension service, poor marketing facilities, and scarcity of basic consumer goods.[12] Indisputably, the agricultural sector in Tanzania has been starved of adequate incentives, financial, technical and managerial resources. By withdrawing resources from agriculture, and emphasizing an economic sector which also happened to be heavily dependent on foreign oil and other foreign inputs, the Government cut export earnings and worsened the balance of trade.

The second costly Government decision was to allow the central bureaucracy to proliferate, ostensibly to faciliate the decentralization of development planning. As a consequence, administration became the fastest growing sector of the economy in the 1970s, more than doubling its contribution to GDP between 1971 and 1982. In fact, as can be seen for Table 1.1, the little expansion in overall output that has taken place recently has mainly been attributed to expansion in administration and other services. Between 1977 and 1986 agricultural output has stagnated while industrial output has experienced continuous negative growth rates.

The Tanzanian version of collectivization 'Ujamaa' began in agriculture. In 1973, villagization, to be in line with decentralization, became compulsory. It was regarded as essential for social as well as economic transformation and it was also seen as facilitation for the provision of education, health and water services throughout the country. Additionally, villagization was intended to achieve positive effects through better organization, more economies of scale, more technology dissemination and greater use of inputs.

The villagization programme was part and parcel of Tanzania's version of socialism – *Ujamaa*. Conservative critics have pointed out that such a policy is bound to fail because it stifles personal initiative and interferes with the 'smooth' operations of the invisible hand – i.e. the free interplay of market forces. Yet liberal and left opinion points out that the Tanzanian state has not acted as a 'going concern'. Rather, the state bureaucracy has been labelled as irrational and inefficient, and its incessant desire for short-term political pursuits and control have bred corruption, and contempt of peasants as being irrational and inert.[13] This has made the peasants produce less agricultural surplus and sell a large proportion of their output to unofficial marketing channels.

What is certain, however, is that the villagization programme which began as a voluntary movement to villages after the Arusha Declaration in 1967 expanded rapidly (in some areas through compulsion) during the 1970s. While there were 2 million people living in *ujamaa* villages in 1973, the picture changed dramatically to 9 million in 1975 and then shot up to 13 million in 1977.[14] This rapid villagization programme caused immense disruption at least in the short run, involving loss of output especially as it coincided with the drought of 1973–4 which made large-scale food imports necessary, accounting for 23 per cent of total imports in 1974. Moreover, there was growing uncertainty among peasants regarding the marketing of their produce as this was also the time when the Government instituted a new marketing arrangement.

Agricultural co-operatives 'which were instrumental in upholding values of Tanzanian society, which stressed equality and participation'[15] but were later accused of corruption and of emerging as a political force, were dissolved in 1976 and replaced by crop authorities, which became parasitic over the years and dependent on huge Government subsidies, largely because of inefficiency and malpractice. Eventually this led to their reorganization, and the reinstatement of co-operative unions as marketing agencies a decade later.

Tanzania's policy of providing for the basic needs of its 23 million inhabitants, though desirable equity-wise, has been yet another drain on its resources. Tanzania raised its adult literacy rate from 10 per cent to 60 per cent between 1961 and 1977, doubling that of any other low-income country. At independence Tanzania was behind other low-income countries in the percentage of its children entering school, with 25 per cent enrolment compared to 37 per cent for low-income countries on the average. By 1977, Tanzania had reversed this situation, making primary education available to all, while other low-income countries averaged only 64 per cent primary school attendance. Higher education also increased so that, for example, by 1984 there were 1,800 engineers as compared to only 2 at independence. Impressive records were also set in health, with life expectancy increasing from 43 years at independence to 52 years now. By comparison, equivalent countries increased their life expectancy only from 40 to 48 years on the average. During the same period, Tanzania's infant mortality rate also fell, from 152 to 103 per thousand births (compared to average decreases from 164 to 130 per thousand in other low-income countries), and its mortality rate was cut from 33 to 19 per thousand. All of these education and health improvements, however, meant heavy spending by Government. Social welfare spending has also been increased by the misfortune of long periods of successive droughts.

Finally it is important to note that the intensity of the economic crisis in Tanzania has been exacerbated by different forms of economic mismanagement and inefficiencies. It is important to distinguish two broad types of mismanagement: misappropriation of resources and wrong choice of development policies and strategies. The first type involves all sorts of malpractices including illegal transfers of resource (for example, fraud, theft, kickbacks on contract, smuggling of goods, etc.), and constitutes an important aspect of this study. In general illegal transfers tend to stifle work effort by imposing an unnecessary burden on the productive members of the official economy, and may therefore adversely affect savings and investment. However, the magnitude of their adverse impact on economic growth cannot be assessed with certainty because, by their nature, they are difficult to quantify. But the yearly report by the Auditor-General, and evidence revealed during the 1983 crackdown on economic saboteurs, clearly attest that corruption in the public service is rampant.

Apart from misguided economic policies mentioned earlier in relation to agricultural development and over-ambitious and unrealistic target setting in the provision of basic needs, another type of inefficiency has been associated with the system of organizing production and the mechanisms used to regulate the economy. In particular, as we will show later, the public sector in Tanzania has expanded beyond its technical and managerial capacities and has invariably been associated with proliferation of unproductive bureaucracies and financial losses. Furthermore, the regulation of the economy mainly through excessive centralized economic decisions, quantitative restrictions, licensing and price- and interest-rate fixing by governmental agencies during a prolonged period of shortages has fuelled the growth of parallel markets – the second economy.

To sum up, Tanzania's economic problems are basically typical of countries which stand in the metropolitan – satellite relationship noted by J. F. Rweyemamu who likened their integration in the world capitalism market to satellites, involving foreign ownership and control of the periphery's resources and commercial institutions.[16] The declines in domestic savings, foreign exchange earnings, cash and food crop production; the costly wars and long periods of drought; as well as the high price of petroleum and manufactured goods and the heavy subsidies required until very recently by the crop authorities and parastatals have all had immense negative impact on the present economic situation. Tanzania's industries are consequently working very much under capacity while the necessary inputs and spares (mostly requiring foreign exchange) are lacking. Perhaps Glenn Frankel exaggerates the story, but he has a point to make when he says: 'The schemes have littered Tanzania's rural landscape with remains of factories, farm machinery, roadways and water pumping systems that the country lacks the money, spare parts and expertise to operate and maintain.'[17]

Finally, because the industries are not producing to the demand levels, shortages are rampant, and the Government has been forced into rationing mechanisms, price controls, and interference in business activity. Agricultural production is also adversely affected. Not only do the peasants lack necessary agricultural implements like hoes and ploughs, but they have no incentives to produce more for cash when there are severe shortages of basic manufactured goods such as soap, salt, sugar, cooking oil, two-wheel bicycles and clothes.

1.3 Reforms Introduced to Deal with the Crisis

1.3.1   Structural Adjustment Programme, 1983–1985

Government's first major attempt to redress the deteriorating economy was the adoption of the Structural Adjustment Programme (SAP) in 1982.[18] The programme was to cover a three-year (1983–5) period and was primarily an independent effort seeking to restore output to the 1978 pre-crisis level, to improve public sector finances, reduce inflation, and to improve both external and internal balances. The SAP also aimed at restructuring economic activity through a system of incentives to producers, rationalizing Government spending, introducing measures to improve capacity utilization and labour productivity, and strengthening the planning system by instituting more effective budgeting, monitoring and enforcement of priorities.

Subsequently, in order to stimulate expansion in agricultural output and hence increase export earning potential, the Government increased the level of investment in agriculture and incentives to producers. The share of agriculture in the development budget was raised from 11.7 per cent in 1982 to 23 per cent in 1983, and then to 28.5 per cent in 1985. The recurrent budget to agriculture was increased by 4.7 times between 1982 and 1985. Producer prices were increased by 40 and 80 per cent for export and food crops respectively during 1983–4, and by 46–50 per cent in nominal terms (an increase of 5 per cent in real terms) during the next fiscal year. The Tanzania shilling was devalued by 32 and then by 40 per cent in 1983 and 1985 respectively. Government also sought to rationalize the marketing and distribution systems by removing restrictions on inter-regional trade, abolishing pan-territorial pricing for agricultural commodities, abolishing crop export taxes, reducing the number of price controlled items, and restoring co-operatives with the primary responsibility for procuring crops from farmers and villages, storage and delivery to marketing centres.

B. J. Ndulu has examined in detail the adjustment efforts under SAP and found that (i) although the real level of GDP rose from zero growth in 1983 to about 3 per cent in 1984 and 2.3 per cent in 1985 this was below its 1978 peak, and in per capita terms represented negative growth; (ii) only 35 per cent of the SAP targeted foreign capital inflow actually came; (iii) export earnings fell short of programme target by 33 per cent; (iv) the level of imports was only 64 per cent of that anticipated while the overall external balance worsened by 80 per cent between 1982 and 1985; (v) money supply grew at 19.1 and 21.1 per cent between 1983–4 and 1984–5 respectively instead of the targeted 13.8 and 13.0 per cent growth.[19]

The anticipated success of SAP reforms hinged crucially on the assumption that foreign capital inflow would be forthcoming in sufficient amounts. Since this was not the case, the effectiveness of these reforms was seriously undermined by the very low level of import capacity. Certainly the SAP measures recorded some limited success, particularly in reducing costs and increasing the efficiency of Government operations, and therefore constituted a good foundation for future growth. However, the observed real positive growth in GDP recorded during 1983–5 reflected increases in output of the services sector. As Table 1.1 shows, the SAP measures did not halt the declining growth in the productive sectors of agriculture and industry. Inflation continued to run at 30 per cent per annum and shortages of both consumer and food stuffs were rampant.

1.3.2   Economic Recovery Programme, 1986–1989

The programme generally refered to as the Economic Recovery Programme (adopted in July 1986) represents on organic extension of the Structural Adjustment Programme implemented during the years 1983–5. The objective of this set of measures was the gradual attainment of sustained growth in real incomes and output. This called for higher levels of production of food and cash crops through appropriate incentives, improved marketing structures, and increasing resources available to agriculture; the carrying out of deferred maintenance to stem the rapid deterioration of the physical infrastructure required to distribute higher outputs; and a major effort to procure additional imports of raw materials so as to improve the level of capacity utilization in the industries set up after independence. In addition the ERP aimed at correcting the external imbalance, reducing budget deficit, cutting down inflation and providing incentives to all types of producers.

The ERP measures were deemed necessary by the Government at this juncture because the results of the adjustment effort under the SAP were slow in coming, and because actual performance fell short of programme targets. It had become obvious, for example, that a severe cutback in the level of imports in order to replenish rapidly dwindling foreign exchange reserves threatened declining agricultural and industrial output and failure to collect and move exports to the ports. The ERP measures and much of the previously enacted SAP measures were subsequently incorporated in the agreement Tanzania signed with the International Monetary Fund (IMF) in August 1986. Policy actions undertaken by the Government in pursuit of the ERP reform have included regular monthly adjustment in the exchange rate and introduction of a crawling peg; consolidation of the partial import liberalization measures; measures to improve agricultural marketing structures, further relaxation of controls, and a more active role of increased producer incentives to stimulate agricultural output. These measures were to be accompanied by reforms in the fiscal, monetary and interest rate structures in order cut down inflation and to instil discipline and improve efficiency in the allocation of domestic resources.

(i)   Exchange rate policy

During the 1980s there were persuasive and demonstrably good reasons for adjusting the exchange rate. Indeed even during the early years of the decade the controversy between the Government and the IMF did not centre on the principle of devaluation but on the extent and timing of devaluation. As pointed out earlier, even before Tanzania signed the agreement with the IMF, the Government had since 1982 frequently used exchange rate action as a policy for economic management. As shown in Table 1.2 (page 141) the shilling had depreciated from 8.32 to 16.32 to the US dollar between 1981 and 1985, a devaluation of 96 per cent in shilling terms or 42 per cent in dollar terms.

Adjustment of the exchange rate was needed because between 1982 and 1986 the annual rate at which Tanzanian prices were rising was on average four times higher than the rate of inflation in Tanzania's major trading partners. Moreover, the shilling was traded on the black market at a rate between two and four times the official rate. Export incentives had declined, and as Table 1.1 shows (page 139), the country was experiencing massive budget deficits as well as increasing deficits on the external trade account especially since 1978. All these indicate that the real exchange rate must have appreciated. Odegaard estimates that by 1981 the exchange rate was already overvalued by 53 per cent.[20]

The overvalued exchange rate posed severe problems to the adjustment effort. First, it meant that a significant portion of the much needed foreign exchange leaked out through smuggling and other black market deals. Secondly, since the producer price was being set as a residual between the expected world market price net of export taxes and the marketing margins of the marketing boards, an overvalued exchange rate had a depressive effect on producer prices and hence acted as a disincentive to increased production of cash crops. This is obvious since the world market price of cash crops in Tanzania shillings is simply the product of the exchange rate and the world market price in any of the internationally convertible currencies. Indeed, as Odegaard has observed, 'The taxation of agricultural exports via an overvalued exchange rate apparently was substantially higher than the direct tax on cash crop exports.'[21]

Thirdly, if not adjusted, increasing overvaluation of the exchange rate would progressively price Tanzania out of foreign markets since her exports would be relatively expensive compared to similar exports from other countries. In turn, this could have led to reduced foreign exchange earnings and hence increased import pressures, leading to further deterioration in the balance of payments. On the other hand, the artificial cheapening of imports might encourage increased importation of nonessential imports.

Devaluation, it was argued, was needed to improve the country's competitiveness in exports, to provide remunerative prices to cash crop producers, to reduce leakages of foreign exchange through black market channels, to improve the balance of payments and to facilitate the restoration of Government budgetary balance.

Yet the Government consistently resisted pressures from the IMF for massive devaluation on the grounds that it would not lead automatically to export growth because of agricultural time lags, low output response elasticities, and increased price effects on agricultural inputs and industrial goods that farmers buy. In particular, it emphasized that a substantial element of agricultural marketing costs, especially transport, comprises of tradables (vehicles, fuel and spare parts) which tend to increase in price proportionately with devaluation. Thus the full extent of devaluation might not be passed to the producer partly because the marketing boards might cream off part of the price increase, and partly because the inflationary consequences of devaluation could further erode the nominal producer price. On the other hand, if the margins of official marketing agencies were to be squeezed or kept constant in order to allow increased cash receipts to farmers, the income of the marketing agents would fall making them incapable of marketing crops and hence resorting to Government subsidies.

Furthermore, it is often pointed out that being a small commodity exporting country Tanzania is a price taker and therefore can sell whatever it is able to at internationally determined prices. Devaluation in such a case would have a neglible impact on the volume of exports. The argument that devaluation could discourage the importation of non-essential goods by raising the domestic price for imports is considered as less convincing because the Government, through the Bank of Tanzania, already controlled the allocation of foreign exchange and has to ensure that licences are granted only for the most essential imports. Thus non-essential goods have already been eliminated. In the circumstances, devaluation would raise the prices of essential imports, and because its impact on raising output would be neglible, it would contribute to inflationary pressures in the country. In the medium term these inflationary pressures would raise the cost of marketing food, thus raising food prices. Rising food prices, in the absence of subsidy, would depress real urban wages reducing further the demand for food products. It was the possible political implications of urban violence prompted by the rise in the cost of living following devaluation that Nyerere (then President) feared most.

With respect to the parallel market for foreign exchange, the Government believed that this problem could be solved with strict enforcement of foreign exchange regulations. Besides, the black market exchange rate was primarily determined by reasons of capital flight and not the health of the economy or current account considerations.[22]

The timing of devaluation of the shilling was considered crucial because if it were to take place after the harvest had been sold, low-income peasants with insufficient cash reserves and had no access to credit would be worse off because they could not afford the increased prices of food and agricultural inputs immediately following devaluation.

Nevertheless, the Government finally decided to use actively the exchange rate action as a tool for economic management to provide incentives for farmers, as a way of correcting overvaluation in the shilling and to attract more donor support. Subsequently, since 1986, the Government has made major changes to its exchange rate policy by introducing monthly adjustments designed to keep the real exchange rate or purchasing power more or less constant. Thus from March to June 1986, the shilling fell from T.Shs 16 to the US dollar to T.Shs 30. This was followed by a shock devaluation of 37 per cent against the US dollar in the 1986/7 budget. Since then the shilling has been substantially devalued through the crawling peg (Table 1.2), especially following the realignment of the values of the major currencies in 1987. In November 1988 the shilling was brought down from T.Shs 98 to 120 to the US dollar, followed by a downward crawl. Since 1986 the devaluation of the shilling has been even more pronounced against the pound sterling and the deutschmark (Table 1.2).

(ii) Partial liberalization of trade

The first attempted liberalization of imports was in 1976–7 on the advice of the World Bank, prompted by the combination of expanded coffee production and a large increase in coffee prices on the world market. Unfortunately that liberalization occurred at the time of the breakup of the East African Community, the Uganda war and a drought. It helped to bring about the foreign exchange crisis from which the country has not yet recovered. The basic argument in favour of trade liberalization is that it exposes import substitution industries to healthy competition and promotes industrial efficiency and balanced growth. Nyerere's wish was that the surplus would be ploughed back in increased investments. But the effect on struggling industries and the balance of payments was disastrous. Table 1.1 shows that between 1976–7 and 1977–8 the trade account deteriorated by 185 per cent, the current account balance of payments account dropped sharply from a surplus of $US137 million to a deficit of $US319 million. Since this happened at the time the East African Community was breaking up and in the wake of the war with Uganda, which in turn were partly responsible for the worsening external balance, there was a severe squeeze on domestic and external resources available to sustain output and productive capacity.

Government reaction was to tighten controls on both internal and external trade, which resulted in massive import cutbacks. The scarcity of imported inputs resulted in extremely low levels of capacity utilization in industry, leading to a sharp drop in industrial production. It became increasingly difficult to transport agricultural produce from villages to marketing and processing centres or ports because the roads had deteriorated due to lack of repair and maintenance, shortages of transport facilities and low levels of vehicle availability. All these factors contributed to more declines in exports, eroding further the country's capacity to import.

So when the Government decided to embark on liberalizing the trade regime again in the early 1980s, it proceeded cautiously, partly to avoid counterproductive repercussions similar to those experienced after the 1977–8 liberal regime; but also not to upset current socio-economic political thinking which had long been opposed to such liberal moves, at least in principle. In order to ease transport bottlenecks, to increase the supply of consumer and intermediate goods in the country, Government first allowed individual residents to import commercial vehicles (particularly pick-ups) whenever they could secure foreign exchange outside the official allocation system. Then in the 1984–5 budget, the Government extended this provision to cover the importation of a specified range of consumer, intermediate and capital goods by introducing the own-funded import scheme. In addition it established the 'export to import' scheme which allowed exporters to retain varying proportions of their export earnings in order to import basic inputs required to sustain operations in their productive activities. Export taxes were abolished and farmers were promised that they would receive 75 per cent of the world market price for their export crops.

As the *Tanzanian Economic Trends* (*TET*) notes, however, Government measures to liberalize external trade were partial in the sense that:

(i)   Exchange controls were *not* withdrawn and in principle have been only mildly relaxed. Foreign exchange receipts are still *in law* to be handed over to the Central Bank;

(ii) The list of imports allowed under the own-funded imports scheme is *not* completely open; in principle definite restrictions on the list of permissible imports remain in place;

(iii) Own-funded imports remain subject to tariffs and as the exchange rate has adjusted the shilling value of *ad-valorem* tariffs should have increased in proportion.[23]

In fact the Government thinks that these measures are temporary and that they will be phased out as soon as the external balance is restored. It was also originally believed by the Government that the own-funded imports scheme would not last long because residents would soon exhaust their foreign exchange holdings. This, however, was an underestimation of the potential of the unofficial economy as a source of foreign exchange, and as we will show in Chapter 4 own-funded imports are increasingly becoming more important than those secured under the import support scheme from donors.

As far as internal trade is concerned partial liberalization measures undertaken by the Government aim at reducing the gap between official and parallel market prices, facilitating the smooth flow and more efficient distribution of food and industrial goods to deficit areas at required times, and providing more incentives to producers of food crops. Measures undertaken to implement these policies were initiated under the SAP and were to be consolidated under the ERP. They include (i) raising producer prices at the rate of 5 per cent per annum in real terms over the next 3–5 years; (ii) abolishing pan-territorial pricing for agricultural commodities; (iii) reducing the number of essential goods under price control to 12; (iv) removing restrictions on inter-regional trade and allowing private traders in the retailing of maize and other minor grains, and (v) removing consumer subsidy on maize and agricultural inputs (especially fertilizers). The impact of these measures on the performance of the economy are discussed in more detail in Chapter 3.

(iii) Streamlining crop marketing and distribution

A major factor accelerating inflationary trends was the accumulation of vast operational deficits by the crop marketing parastatal organizations set up in 1975. In order to bale them out the Government was forced to resort to the banking system and increase the money supply. The parastatals took over as monopoly marketing agents from the co-operatives whose functions were greatly enlarged following the nationalization of the wholesale trade. The functions of the agricultural co-operatives were transferred to crop authorities which are parastatal institutions partly because co-operatives were thought to have ceased to act as socialist institutions and it was feared that control could pass to financially successful farmers who might achieve too much political influence. The crop authorities set up to take over from them were given additional responsibilities for supplying agricultural inputs, storage and processing facilities and the provision of extension services. This involved an increase in bureaucratic intervention and control. The cost of the extra services provided widened marketing margins and reduced producer returns. Prices fixed took into account the cost of the services provided and yet the parastatals built up huge marketing deficits.

For example, in 1982 eleven agricultural parastatals lost over T.Shs 2.2 billion and accounted for 80 per cent of the total overdraft facilities of the National Bank of Commerce.[24] Certainly, both the magnitude and the high interest burden of these loans has put a considerable strain on Government budget (which has to subsidize their operations), leading to increased borrowing and expansion of money supply and hence aggravating inflationary pressures.

In the case of food crops, where the National Milling Corporation had the monopoly power over domestic and external processing, transportation, distribution, storage and marketing of food crops the situation was even worse. NMC had been notorious for providing inefficient and ineffective transport services for moving crops from villages to marketing centres, failing to collect crops and to provide payments to farmers on time, and accumulating large trading losses.[25] These problems, coupled with lack of producer incentives – especially low official prices for agricultural products – gave rise to three unfavourable trends. First, it led to the growth of the parallel market which in the case of food grains extended well beyond the purely traditional market transactions of the rural markets. Secondly, as a consequence, it led to increased per unit transport and marketing costs as the share of officially marketed agricultural surplus declined. Lastly, food shortages multiplied particularly in urban areas.

Apart from other reforms already mentioned, the Government reacted by restoring co-operatives which took over some of the functions of the crop authorities and those of NMC in procuring, storing and delivering goods to marketing centres with a view to transforming the crop authorities into marketing boards. Since NMC used to purchase, collect, mill and distribute food grains at a substantial loss it was believed that its reorganization, by reducing its role in favour of co-operatives, would result in substantial savings. Subsequently, in 1984, the ban on inter-regional movement of food was lifted. In 1987 the issuance of special permits to move food within the country was abolished allowing anyone to move food without the prior permission of NMC. At the same time Government decontrolled the pricing and marketing of drought staples (millet, sorghum and cassava) at Co-operatives Union level. By 1988 NMC was no longer the buyer of last resort but was left to act as a commercial concern. Maize trade was decontrolled at the Union level and private traders were allowed to market maize from the Union level onwards.

These institutional changes, however, should not disguise the continuity of monopolized marketing control as a means of state control and revenue collection. Indeed the Government is still heavily involved in agricultural marketing, continues to set the producer prices for the major staples, and consumer prices for maize grain, rice and wheat flour. Only maize trade is decontrolled at the Union level, rice and wheat trade are still controlled. The Government's reluctance to institute more liberal reforms in the marketing of agricultural crops stems mainly from its socialistic ideological commitment to socialize internal trade and hence the need to eliminate the potential for exploitation implicit in the licensed private trader system. It also stems partly from the Government's desire to extract resources from agriculture for capital formation and state consumption, and the need to secure low cost food supplies for the urban population. But as we will show in Chapter 3, Government-controlled parastatals and co-operatives do not always achieve these objectives effectively.

(iv) Reducing budget deficits

Although Tanzania is a relatively highly taxed country and has received a large amount of foreign aid, the budget has been in chronic and rising deficit. The IMF insisted on large reductions in public expenditure in order to reduce deficits. After the publication of the Structural Adjustment Programme of 1982, IMF discussions led to the issue of a new agricultural policy document. The 1984 reform package was introduced with the June 1984 budget and the following budget was a standstill one because of the elections due in October 1985. The chronic deficits can be traced back to the final implications of the coffee boom which had led to higher Government expenditure. Earlier, in an attempt to reduce the growing budget deficit, higher crop export taxes were introduced which had the effect of reducing producer returns from crops and hence contributing to the fall in the volume of exports.

Under SAP and later ERP the Government has made bold attempts to reduce budgetary deficits by adopting measures to increase revenue generation and cut down growth of both recurrent and development expenditures. Government revenue was to be increased through improved efficiency in tax collection, expanding the tax base by raising the general level of economic activity, reducing overvaluation in the exchange rate and hence increasing revenues from import duties, and making special efforts to bring the self-employed into the tax-net using presumptive incomes estimation methods. To reduce recurrent spending the Government committed itself to selective reduction of over-manning in the public sector; freezing recruitment of employees in this sector; reducing defence expenditure to peacetime levels; cutting transfers to parastatals and limiting total recurrent expenditure growth to 15 per cent or less per annum in nominal terms. The Government also announced the transfer of some responsibility for education, health services and small roads from central Government to urban and district councils which have been empowered to raise local revenue.

The development budget was to be largely restricted to financing rehabilitation and the completion of ongoing projects. New investment could only be undertaken where there was a potential for directly generating foreign exchange or where it involved the distribution of essential goods or services.

(v) Money and credit

In order to stimulate financial savings and to facilitate more effective utilization and allocation of resources, the Government promised to make periodic adjustment in the interest rate structure with a view to making them positive in real terms during the recovery period. Subsequently, annual interest on savings deposits rose from 7.5 per cent in 1985 to 24 per cent in 1987, while interest on 20-year Government stock rose from 10 to 29 per cent during the same period. Interest on medium- and long-term lending has risen from 10 to 29.50 per cent. However, in the absence of well developed financial markets in Tanzania, positive interest rates alone cannot be expected to have a substantial positive effect on savings mobilization unless they are accompanied by a conscious programme of expanding the financial infrastructure in terms of geographical coverage and the range of financial instruments.[26]

During the crisis period, Government financed the growing budget deficit mainly through borrowing from the banking system. But given the low level of economic activity resulting from severe import cuts and extremely low levels of capacity utilization, monetary expansion was bound to be inflationary. Thus in order to reduce the budget deficit and to cut down inflation, Government aimed to limit the rate of growth of money supply and overall expansion of credit within the range of 15–20 per cent per annum during the recovery period.

The success of this programme for restraining expansion in money supply and credit crucially depends on the mobilization of external inflows of resources to support the recovery effort. In particular it will depend on Government's attempt to convince aid donors to redirect aid flows to finance rehabilitation and completion of ongoing projects so as to increase the overall level of capacity utilization.

To sum up, it is important to emphasize that the ERP reform measures and the subsequent Tanzania–IMF agreement package were an organic extension of the SAP measures implemented over the period 1983–5. Indeed much of what was incorporated in the agreement with the IMF had been enacted previously. Slight differences between the SAP and ERP reforms relate essentially to the speed and intensity of adjustment and to the extent to which various policy instruments were relied upon to influence economic activity. Adjustment under SAP was more gradual with less emphasis on the use of prices and exchange rate policies to effect the desired changes in the economy than during the ERP period. For example, during the three years of SAP, the shilling depreciated from T.Shs 9.52 to the US dollar in December 1982 to 16.50 in December 1985, a change of 73 per cent. During the first two years of the ERP period, however, the shilling fell by 191 per cent from T.Shs 40.43 in June 1986 to 119 in December 1988. Thus the ERP period was associated with more active use of exchange rate adjustment as a tool for economic management. It was also associated with shock devaluations of larger magnitudes than those under SAP. In addition the ERP period has witnessed deeper and more far-reaching institutional reforms, especially in the reorganization of crop marketing institutions, the increasing role of the private sector in the various sectors of the economy and the scaling down of the quantity of public sector services, than those experienced under SAP.

1.4 Achievements and Prospects of the ERP

The speech of the Minister of Finance, Economic Affairs and Planning in the National Assembly on 16 June 1988 to introduce the Annual Development Plan and Revenue and Expenditure Estimates for 1988–9 provides a convenient summary of current plans and policy developments.

The 1988–9 Annual Plan is the first stage in implementing the decisions taken at the Party National Conference in Dodoma. The Economic Recovery Programme begun in July 1986 had the objective of marshalling national resources, augmenting foreign exchange earnings, rehabilitating infrastructures, increasing industrial capacity utilization and restoring fiscal balance and the balance of payments. The measures introduced were concerned with macro-economic policies, the allocation of priority to agriculture, transport and communications, industrial energy and social sectors, but above all the availability of foreign exchange. The programme is generally on track and GDP has risen by 3.9 per cent from 1986 to 1987, exceeding the 3.2 per cent population growth for the second consecutive year; but further effort is required to attain the Programme's 4.5 per cent annual growth rate target between 1986 and 1991. Capital formation in 1987 declined by 5.5 per cent against 1986 mainly because of foreign exchange shortages for building materials required for roads, bridges, irrigation and land development. However, capital formation in the shape of buildings increased by 27 per cent.

The target for reducing credit and growth in the money supply was missed due to substantial credit requirements of the National Marketing Corporation and the marketing boards for cotton and tobacco. These were largely caused by increases in the production of cotton and maize and problems caused by transportation, storage and insufficient cotton ginneries (Table 1.3, page 141).

Government borrowing from the banking system has declined from T.Shs 5.6 billion in 1985–6 to 1.7 billion in 1986–7 and is targeted to fall to 0.236 billion in 1987–8. The budget continues to rely heavily on external grants and loans which provide 30 per cent of the total recurrent budgetary costs, indicating the distance from a self-sustaining economy. Provisional out-turn figures of Government revenue and expenditure indicate revenue collections largely on target, mainly as a result of intensified collection efforts, and recurrent expenditure exceeded target by 3 per cent. Development expenditure fell short of target by over T.Shs 2 billion, but total budgetary expenditure still amounted to over one-third of GDP.

The rate of inflation continued to fall from 33.3 per cent to 32.4 per cent in 1986 and 29.9 per cent in 1987 but is still well above the target figure of 25 per cent in the Economic Recovery Programme. The scarcity of foreign exchange continues as the major constraint although the declining trend in export earnings which persisted until 1985–6 has been halted and reversed. Exports increased by 12 per cent in the first year of the ERP and 9 per cent in the second, only just missing the target. Non-traditional exports like cardamom, pigeon peas, beeswax, marine products, kapok, carvings, textiles and other industrial products rose by 83 per cent over the previous year. Traditional exports have disappointed and only tea and tobacco are expected to show any increase over the previous year. Cotton exports are expected to fall from 46,730 to 45,000 tons due to ginning and transport bottlenecks and cashew nuts from 11,560 to 9,000 tons.

The fall in export volume has been amplified in its impact on the balance of payments by a continuing fall in commodity prices. Coffee prices have fallen by 39 per cent, sisal prices by the same proportion and clove prices by 14 per cent against the previous year. Cashew nut prices, however, nearly trebled. Import prices rose substantially – for example oil by 26.7 per cent, and the average increase in the prices of industrial imports was 13.4 per cent. The 'retention' and 'own' funds schemes for privately financing imports are estimated to have brought in $US250 million worth of extra imports, about half of which were for agriculture, transport, medicines and construction and electricity plant. Additional efforts were made, with some success, to increase loans and grants from donor countries in support of the ERP, but by the end of 1987–8 only two-thirds of the amounts pledged had been drawn. Exports, external assistance and debt refinancing taken together paid for 93 per cent of the programmed import target in 1986–7 and 96 per cent in 1987–8, leaving only a small gap in financing imports at a considerably higher level than from 1982–3 to 1984–5. Nevertheless the servicing of its national debt continues to represent a heavy burden on Tanzania, as it does for most developing African countries.

In the ERP programme to improve performance in production and in providing services, first priority has been given to agriculture. In 1987–8, 15 per cent of all commodity imports were agricultural inputs and total demand should have been met. It is expected that agricultural output bought through official channels in 1987–9 will have increased as against 1986–7 by 13.7 per cent for cotton, 51.5 per cent for cashew nuts, 10.0 per cent for sisal and 10.4 per cent for food crops.

For manufacturing industry the ERP programme aims at at least 60 per cent capacity utilization. Industrial goods accounted for 27 per cent of the total import bill but well over one-half of what was procured under import support. In spite of shortages of raw materials, spares, transport and power and water supplies, the industrial sector staged some recovery and enhanced its contribution to GDP by 4.2 per cent. Transport and communications continue to represent a serious bottleneck in the economy which will take some years to remedy. Exports in 1987–8 are expected to pay for only one-third of the total value of imports. To sustain the growth in the export sector various measures will be taken, including improved agricultural producer price incentives and improved supplies of agricultural inputs. 'Duty drawback' and 'export to import' schemes will be continued.

Development expenditure has increased by 39 per cent, of which 57 per cent will be contributed by grants and loans. Recurrent expenditure in 1988–9 is scheduled to rise by 50.3 per cent over the previous year. Recurrent revenue in the current year is estimated to meet 53.7 per cent of forecast recurrent expenditure and 38.2 per cent is expected to be available in 1988–9 from grants and loans.

This budget speech affords an opportunity to examine to what extent there has been a departure from established development policies. There is certainly no explicit reference anywhere in it to a deliberate change of direction, but it conveys the Government's intention to adopt temporary measures to redress the severe economic crisis through which Tanzania has passed and which threatened a downward spiral of economic contraction, putting at risk all the positive achievements since independence. It attempts to foster a spirit of shared responsibility and to spread the sacrifices called for with reasonable equity. The administrative reforms outlined are principally addressed to curtailing parallel markets, domestic and cross-border smuggling and the associated widespread tax evasion. A central feature of the announced policies is the continuation of the struggle against high inflation rates. It is recognized that growth of the marketed output is an essential condition of recovery, and to that end incentives by way of tax concessions are provided both to agricultural producers and wage earners.

1.5 Some Emerging Concerns

It is not the intention of this study to make a full assessment of the performance of the ERP. In any case it would still be too early to arrive at a conclusive statement about the likely output performance of the programme because of adjustment time lags characteristic of certain structural features of the economy. However, it is instructive to use the already discernible short-term trends to highlight the future challenges likely to be faced in managing the economy. While we reserve the analysis of the effects of the ERP on specific sectors of the economy for Chapter 3, it is important to make the following general statements.

Certainly, there have been positive signs in the revival in output. Overall production of export crops has recovered significantly after trending downwards for more than a decade. For example, between 1985 and 1986 official purchases of export crops which roughly reflect production levels (with the exception of coffee and cardamom where there is some smuggling) have increased by 109 per cent for cotton, 38 per cent for sisal, 20.7 per cent for tobacco, 9.7 per cent for tea and 6.4 per cent for cashew nuts. Production in food crops has also increased substantially. Maize production increased by 14.1 per cent and paddy by 51.5 per cent. Official purchases by NMC rose to a record level, by 103 per cent in the case of maize, and 113 per cent in the case of rice.

It should be pointed out, however, that the peaking up of agricultural output cannot be attributable solely to increased producer incentives. In Tanzania, where smallholder farmers who account for about 90 per cent of marketable agricultural output depend mainly on rainfed agriculture, weather is an important factor in influencing supply responsiveness of peasants. In particular, the observed increased production has also been associated with good weather in most parts of the country for the period 1985-8. In fact there exist sufficient historical data which suggest that long periods of drought as far back as the beginning of this century had similar adverse effects on overall agricultural output, particularly on the availability of food, necessitating the importation of food stuffs.[27]

Furthermore, increased agricultural production has failed to lead to a peak up in the dollar value of exports, partly because of ginning problems for cotton, processing difficulties for tobacco, cashew nut diseases and the general poor state of marketing and transportation for all crops. Partly it also reflects the fact that world commodity prices were generally depressed, with the exception of cotton and sisal. In addition, many farmers are still complaining about the poor services they receive, especially the considerable delays experienced in selling their produce to official marketing agents and in payment for their crops. Thus increased producer price theory as being the necessary and sufficient measure for production increases is being questioned more closely. Evidence seems to be pointing to greater investments in agricultural inputs and infrastructure.[28] The 1973-4 villagization programme, formerly held to have been a strong contributory factor to low agricultural performance, seems to have been overtaken by time.[29] Perhaps this affected food supply in the short run.

An equally important and positive impact of the economic recovery reform has been the revival in trade. As noted in the quarterly review of the economy, *Tanzanian Economic Trends*, 'While ERP targets for imports have not been quite achieved, the very considerable build up of imports has been sufficient to ease the veritable "goods famine" of the early 1980s and to provide the incentive goods and inputs for the revival of agricultural production.'[30] However, accessibility to the increased flow of inputs and consumer goods is made difficult by the relatively high rate of inflation which continues to erode nominal incomes, particularly of those with fixed incomes. The excessive depreciation of the shilling has been important in reducing the extent of overvaluation (Table 1.4, page 142), but it continues to impose severe burdens on industry which finds it difficult to finance purchases of imports which are becoming increasingly expensive in Tanzania shillings. Industries producing for exports also face problems since imports are necessary inputs for their export products.

Moreover, it is important to note that while the ERP reforms have been essential in triggering off donor funding for imports, which as a percentage of GDP rose from its low point of 13 per cent in 1983 to 38 per cent in 1987 (Table 1.1), a larger part of the increase in imports is a result of the own-funded imports scheme which allows the repatriation of foreign exchange illegally held within and outside the country. This raises some concern about the income distribution consequences of this policy, which seems to favour the private merchandizing sector. It also raises concern about state legitimacy – namely, the fact that the state can guarantee amnesties to those agents it had previously labelled as economic saboteurs, and even allow them extended benefits in the form of profits accruing from sales of imports obtained through previously stolen public funds and assets. The last concern, which is indeed part of the subject of this study, is the effect this policy is likely to have on the growth of the underground economy.

Table 1.4 shows that the Government has also experienced considerable difficulties in attempting to reduce the level of the budget deficit which was equivalent to 16.8 and 15.7 per cent of GDP in 1986 and 1987 respectively, compared to 17.8 per cent of GDP in 1980. Failure to reduce overall budget deficit partly reflects the slow growth in public revenue which is a result of a combination of low tax base, inefficiency in tax collection, growing incidence of tax evasion and the general low level of economic activity during the recession period. Partly, it also stems from Government's reluctance to reduce recurrent spending which consists largely of wages and salaries of public workers whose incomes have already been severely eroded to bare minimums by the adverse economic situation. Massive layoffs of public workers is politically sensitive and might result in political instability. In addition there has been the growing debt interest payment which in 1987–8 accounted for 17.6 per cent of recurrent expenditure. As a result, recurrent expenditure in real terms was, in 1987, 23 per cent higher than its 1980 level.

On the other hand, Table 1.4 suggests that the burden of expenditure cut has fallen almost entirely on the development budget, which in 1987 fell by 47 per cent (in real terms) below its 1980 level. This reduction in capital spending is not entirely attributable to deliberate expenditure cuts, however. It is due partly to low rates of disbursement of external assistance and the low rate of project implementation. Overall, the long-term implication of this massive reduction in development expenditure raises serious concern in that it may prejudice long-term growth. There is even more concern when such cuts are not directed at unproductive sectors such as military spending and administration, but are taken from expenditure on education and health. For example, military spending which was reduced to peacetime levels in 1982 rose again in the mid-1980s as Tanzania increased solidarity military assistance to Mozambique to check the advance of MNR forces in northern Mozambique. In 1987–8, Tanzania's military assistance to Mozambique was estimated by Green as falling between $US125 and 150 million, with two-thirds of the expenditure involving direct or indirect imports.[31] Shifting the financing of primary education from central Government to local governments has led to a dramatic decline in the quality and quantity of education because local governments have failed to raise sufficient revenues to finance primary education. As a result primary school enrolment dropped by 16 per cent between 1983 and 1985 (from 99.7 to 83.5 per cent respectively).[32]

Government spending on education as a percentage of total expenditure dropped from 7.5 per cent between 1976–8 to 5 per cent between 1983–6. For the same period expenditure on electricity and water declined from 6.4 to 3.5 per cent; while for roads and bridges the fall was from 5.5 to 3.5 per cent.

It should also be pointed out that deterioration in physical infrastructure, and underutilization of investments have been brought about in part by inadequate recurrent and development spending. In turn this has led to higher production and marketing costs and hence higher prices, but also to real production declines. For example, cotton production increased by more than 50 per cent between 1986–7 and 1987–8. However, due to deteriorating road and rail conditions, shortage of vehicles and rail wagons, and poor processing capacity, 39 per cent (93,458 tons) of seed cotton purchased from peasants during the 1987–8 season could not be transported to ginneries. Of the 39,301 tons ginned, 18,200 tons (46.3 per cent) were stranded at the ginnery godowns and railheads (Table 1.3).

In such circumstances some of the IMF prescriptions ought not to be taken without medical advice. In particular public expenditure cuts ought to be made with care if the result is not to threaten further deterioration in economic performance. Cuts in education, welfare, wages and general public infrastructure would undermine further the morale and productivity of workers and boost second economy activity. Cuts in military expenditure could be defended on both economic and moral grounds, but there are always political reservations prompted by the fear of being invaded and/or an armed forces rising as in the Sudan. It seems therefore that a more sensible way of reducing budget deficits is not through expenditure cuts, which are politically difficult to implement, but through strengthening the tax base, improving revenue collection, and reducing the incidence of tax evasion.

Lastly, there is growing concern about the increasing burden of external debt. Despite initiatives since late 1986 to reschedule part of the debt, the country's debt service ratio has risen from 17 per cent in 1981 to nearly 81 per cent in 1987. The sharp deterioration in the external debt problem continues to frustrastrate all efforts to mobilize foreign exchange and is a potentially major constraint to the recovery programme, unless cancellation of some debt or further rescheduling under softer terms is effected.

2
The Size of the Second Economy

2.1 Defining the Second Economy

The complex phenomenon referred to here as the second economy has meant different things to different observers. Indeed a plethora of concepts and terms have been coined to describe the economic transactions which are not captured and/or are under-reported in official GNP statistics. The International Labour Organization (ILO), for example, popularized the concept of the 'informal sector' to describe all 'activities that operate largely outside the system of government benefit and regulation';[1] Peter Gutmann has used the term 'subterranean economy' to define all transactions 'that escape from taxation'.[2] Writing on the same phenomenon, Feige defines the 'hidden economy' as the one that 'escapes the purview of our current societal measurement',[3] whereas Tanzi defines the 'underground economy' as 'gross national product that, because of unreporting and/or underreporting, is not measured by official statistics'.[4] Del Boca and Forte define the 'paralled economy' as those activities that are characterized by lack of formal transactions.[5]

In Tanzanian official quarters, the concept of *Ulanguzi*, which is an aspect of the second economy activity, is interpreted as being synonymous with the illegal production and distribution of both illegal and legal goods and services (for example, dangerous drugs, pornography, poaching, illegal mining, currency trafficking, commodity hoarding, smuggling of commodities, unlicensed arms, and so on). It also includes illegal transfers such as fraud and public theft. Elsewhere, this phenomenon has also appeared under a host of alternative terms including black market, submerged, moonlight, unofficial, twilight and shadow economy.

As this phenomenon has meant different things to different observers, it is necessary to develop a working definition at the outset. For operational and analytical convenience we shall analyse the second economy at two levels – the aggregate (macro) and disaggregate (micro) levels. At the aggregate level, we are particularly concerned with the size, trend, causes and overall impact of the second economy. At the micro

26

level we narrow our focus and concentrate on the nature of roles played by different economic agents (institutions and other occupational groups, classes, gender, etç.) in the production and exchange of tradable commodities. At both levels we shall define the second economy to engross all production and exchange activities which, given current conventions, are not measured by national accounts statistics.[6] At the macro level such a definition is instructive in several ways. First, it serves as a necessary precondition for the measurement of the size of the second economy. Second, as the concept implies, the second economy is defined in relation to the first or officially recorded economy, which permits a comparison of its size with that of the officially measured economic activity.

In practice, the second economy comprehends a vast and varied set of activities, too broad to be studied in a single research effort. It is possible, however, albeit with some degree of overlap, to group second economy activities into two broad categories according to the society's social conventions which define what is legal and what is illegal. The two categories consist of:

(a) Production and distribution of market and non-market goods and services that according to social convention are considered as legal in themselves but have not been included in the official estimate of national income data. These activities include: household or broadly informal sector activities; barter exchange; moonlighting or clandestine employment which involves having concealed paid work during or outside official regular working hours; off-books business which involves incorrect reporting of revenues and expenditures to evade taxes and other charges; rent-seeking activities which realize capital gains from illegal price rise which is due to no factor activity.

(b) Production and distribution of market and non-market goods and services that are inherently illegal and strictly forbidden by Government statutes – for example narcotics trafficking, illegal transfers (thefts, bribes, etc.) and the like.

There are various reasons why these activities are sometimes omitted from the national income data. In some instances omission is deliberate because of accounting convention. For example, with the exception of own-house construction, rents from owner-occupied dwellings and food production for own use where official staticians impute values, much of the productive unpaid household or informal sector activity work such as domestic work and self-service activities is not included in the value of recorded GDP as defined by the National Accounts of Tanzania. Neither do the Accounts impute values for bartering through exchanges. In addition, the National Accounts of Tanzania do not distinguish between illegal and legal activities, which suggests that illegal income-generating activities are presently excluded from GDP estimates.

Omission from National Accounts may occur by chance or oversight. In certain cases, omission or under-reporting is caused by deficiencies in estimation methods (especially in the informal sector). It may also,arise from difficulties in data collection particularly where activities are not easily accessible. Often, however, the required information is deliberately concealed from public authorities either because the agents are involved in forbidden illegal activities or, where such activities are legal, there is a deliberate intention to avoid paying taxes, to evade price controls, or to avoid paying social security and medical insurance contributions and suchlike charges. Concealed legal production and undeclared incomes are often associated with clandestine employment, off-books business and rent-seeking activities. .

Underestimation of economic activity is potentially important in three main areas: private construction, smallholder production and subsistence consumption, and the urban informal sector. National Accounts estimates on rural own-account construction are based on the outdated information on construction generated by the Statistical Training Centre and the general 1969 household budget surveys, with the latter providing bench-mark data for the sector. Since then the number of rural housing units constructed has been estimated to be increasing at the same (2.6 per cent) annual rate of growth as that of the rural population. The cost of construction is estimated on the basis of 'mud houses' at that time and updated annually by applying half of the growth rate in the consumer price index. Yet casual evidence suggests that there has been a significant change in the quality of housing for the past two decades as reflected, for instance, in widespread use of burnt bricks, tiles, corrugated iron sheets and cement blocks.

Equally, in urban areas, data on the volume and value of private residential construction have been extremely unreliable, especially after 1972 when the Town Councils which used to issue permits for construction of new buildings and/or extensions were abolished. The values of private buildings in urban areas are currently estimated by marking up the 1976 value by the increase in cement consumption. But in a recent review of capital formation in Tanzania, the *Tanzania – Economic Trends* observed that

> The estimates of residential construction (around T.Shs 200 million in current prices 1978–80, T.Shs 500 million plus 1985–7) hardly seem consistent with the evident urban population growth and what is known about typical construction costs, nor do recent estimates seem in line with the value of cement sales. It is possible that urban residential construction is significantly underestimated.[7]

The value of goods produced in the official economy that goes into private construction – paint, cement, and corrugated iron sheets, for example – is certainly included in the official GDP. Some locally produced materials like self-help burnt bricks, own-grown timber and informal value added (for instance labour costs for unlicensed contractors) are likely to be omitted from official GDP estimates, however.

In the case of rural smallholder production, serious sources of error stem from problems associated with estimating the value of labour spent on tending cash crops with long gestation periods such as coffee, sisal, cashew nuts and tea; from the development of locally traded crops such as coconuts and fruits of all kinds; from estimating the utilization of labour spent on non-farm activities and from estimating subsistence consumption.

Finally, it is difficult to provide accurate estimates for the informal sector mainly because it is unregistered. Moreover, given the high rates of urbanization in recent years, the widely observed phenomena of high growth of informal sector activities during this period of economic retrenchment and the relatively high degree of labour intensity of these activities, it is feared that this sector is grossly underestimated in the official GDP.

2.2 Conceptual Approaches

The second economy is a widely known yet imperfectly studied phenomenon. But despite its universal prevalence it appears that no general theory which would explain the behaviour of the individuals acting in the first and second economy has emerged. It is difficult to say precisely why such a theory has not emerged. Intuitively, however, one can speculate about five possibilities. First, it is apparent that though this phenomenon is an old problem, it is only recently that it has been subjected to serious empirical scrutiny.[8] Hitherto it has always been the subject of talk based on anecdotal information, stories in newspapers and magazines. Second, as already pointed out, no single commonly accepted definition of the second economy exists. As a result, the problem of what constitutes the second economy continues to be conjecture. Third, partly because of the definitional variations and partly because those concerned with the phenomenon come from diverse disciplines, no dominant conceptual approach has emerged. The subject has thus been approached from different frames of reference. Fourth, although there is some consensus as to what causes the second economy, disagreement abounds over the impact of the second economy on the overall development process within a given country. Lastly, there has been the difficulty encountered in gathering reliable information to be used in moulding together the diverse behaviour of the many agents involved, particularly when actors attempt to conceal their actions. In other words, 'the attempt to measure what is by nature unmeasurable is bound to create serious methodological confusion'.[9]

Given these definitional and conceptual variations, it is not surprising that the two dominant hypotheses often advanced to explain the functioning of the second economy are widely divergent. One hypothesis points to its dysfunctional aspects by postulating that the existence of the second economy is necessarily antipathetic to the healthy development of modern economic and social service structures. This view emanates from the belief that the second economy activities represent departures from established economic and social norms or equilibrium.

Some social scientists view activities in the second economy as reflecting moral decay or the disintegration of standards of proper behaviour. Wiles, for example, contends that all economic systems – whether capitalist or socialist – are guided by a practical morality besides a larger theoretical ideology. This practical morality, which preaches love (not hate), obedience (not breach of norms) and hard work, is the same everywhere. Second economy activities, however, breach this morality.

> Indeed in the writer's opinion the opportunity cost to the official economy, in terms of stolen labour time, stolen materials, the shrinking tax base and the consequently high tax rates, the general damage caused by dangerous drugs, the expense of theft and fraud prevention is very big indeed. He questions strongly whether the 2E is even a net economic advantage to the nation.[10]

Similarly, a number of economists view such activities as departures from equilibrium: departures that are prone to be performing neither the economic function of increased productivity nor the equitable distribution of national wealth.[11] According to this view, the second economy is conceived as irrational when compared with the economic rationality of the first, self-equilibrating economy. Such an economy represents a passing phenomenon; a phenomenon that lacks the potential to recreate and sustain itself.

The dysfunctional view of the second economy was shared by the Tanzanian Government until the mid-1980s. All along, the Government strongly believed that one of the fundamental problems arising from the second economy is that it does not add directly to productivity. Rather, it is merely exploitative, adding a surcharge to goods and services produced (albeit in short supply) by the official economy. A second major problem is that the second economy distorts societal objectives. An egalitarian society is characterized by small income disparity among its workers and peasants, and Tanzania has succeeded relatively well in closing known or legal nominal income gaps within its labour force – cutting the disparity in nominal wage earnings from 1:50 at the time of independence (1961) to 1:7 in the 1980s. This was done at a cost of some social discontent, through a highly progressive tax system and periodic increases in minimum wages. Now, however, the second economy cuts away at these gains by allowing some citizens to enrich themselves unjustly at the expense of others and by undercutting the Government's goal of goods at fair prices available to all.

Thirdly, the second economy was also seen as threatening Tanzania's desire for a classless society. In Tanzania like any other young, poor country, those in power – politicians and bureaucrats – belong to a class, not necessarily homogeneous, but different from workers and peasants who are the majority. The second economy increases the number of those in the powerful class, and, worse still, creates a different type of class – one which owes no allegiance to the goals of the society. The *walanguzi*, or marketeers, buy corruption, using their economic power to purchase the co-operation of some parastatal managers who divert goods from the official economy; customs officers who allow smuggled goods into the country; Party and Government officials who arrange various 'favours'; and police and magistrates who look the other way so that the second economy can operate smoothly.

In the fourth place, it was believed that second economy activities also interfere with the country's legal system and encourage tax evasion. Finally, the informal economy system fosters centre – periphery types of relationships by encouraging some sophisticated Tanzanian residents to join with overseas business partners in carrying out foreign currency transactions and transfers of goods that in one way or another cheat the Tanzanian Government and the Tanzanian people.

These reasons tied in well with Tanzania's *Ujamaa* political rhetoric with its emphasis on egalitarianism, communalism and self-reliance as opposed to '*ubepari* and *ukabaila*' or 'imperialist and capitalist exploitation'. Government's belief that exploitation and class differentiation were perhaps the principal ways in which the second economy threatens the state legitimacy is clearly reflected in various attempts by the state to counter the growth of the second economy.

As early as 1967 the Government enacted the Party Leadership Code which prohibited all leaders of the only ruling Party (TANU), including their spouses, from having extra sources of income other than those earned from their official regular jobs. The Code also prohibits all Party members from hiring employees of any sort. At the time of writing this book, the Leadership Code is in principle still in force. In practice, as we will show in Chapter 5, the majority of Party leaders and their families receive a significant portion of their incomes from informal income generating activities. This has prompted a series of discussions between the Party and Government organs with a view to trying to strike a workable balance between the existing economic realities and the Party's ideological principles. The discussions followed Government's loosening of 'its stance in May of last year [1987] when [President] Mwinyi said that since the Government could not afford to pay people adequate salaries, they should be free to do various income generating activities to support themselves'.[12]

In another attempt to check the advance of what Government labelled clandestine employment, and unfair competition to more established formal trading concerns, in 1973 it abolished the issuance of urban trading licences to self-employed urban traders. This was followed later in 1976 by Government's attempt to resettle the self-employed and the unemployed residents of Dar es Salaam into neighbouring farming villages. The campaign failed, however, as most of those who were moved into villages shortly returned to the city. In 1983 the Government made another move by enacting a Penal Code amendment which branded all the self-employed and unemployed as 'unproductive' and 'idle disorderly persons' who were to be banned from towns.[13] In the same year, the crackdown on the so-called 'economic saboteurs' was launched.

A year later, the Human Resources Deployment Act, also known as *Nguvu Kazi*, was hurriedly passed. Under this Act those who could not produce officially recognized identification cards were to be rounded up and resettled into the countryside. At the same time, the activities of the crackdown on 'economic saboteurs' which had begun on 23 March 1983 were codified retrospectively by the Economic and Organized Crime Control Act of 1984. Both Operation *Nguvu Kazi* and the crackdown on 'economic saboteurs' clogged the already overburdened Government machinery. In the latter case, we have already noted (in the Prelude) the limited success of the Government's war on 'economic saboteurs'. As for *Nguvu Kazi* which sought to rid towns of 'idlers' and 'loiterers' (mainly unlicensed self-employed persons), 'The campaign was not successful. No sooner were truckloads of people dropped off in rural areas than the same people returned to the city to resume their small-scale enterprises.'[14]

The dysfunctional approach to the study of the second economy has one major shortcoming – that is, the failure to distinguish elements within the second economy that constitute a potential asset to the development of the nation from those that are socially and economically harmful to the healthy development of the economy. This limitation has in turn prevented the emergence of a selective and creative policy analysis that would have sought to promote the positive aspects of the second economy and limit the multiplication of its negative aspects. Instead, what one tends to observe is the clamping down on all forms of second economy activities, a rather unfortunate act which perhaps largely explains the failure of such policies.

The realization of this limitation has led to the emergence of an alternative view which regards the various institutions harbouring the second economy activities as fulfilling, at least in part, positive functions which are not adequately fulfilled by existing social and economic structures. Accordingly, second economy activities are seen as adaptations to social or market forces working towards societal harmony or equilibrium. For example, an activity such as smuggling might be seen as having some positive influence on welfare since it constitutes evasion of tariffs which for a small country would signify a sub-optimal policy. Similarly, it has been argued that the bulk of the informal sector activity in Tanzania represents truly innovative and self-reliant schemes striving to meet the basic needs of daily life. In addition, informal activities possess the dynamism of upgrading artisanal skills, mobilizing the otherwise idle domestic resources, especially through provision of additional employment, and utilizing economic resources productively.[15] If such activities were to be promoted, they could become an important factor in the development of Tanzania which aspires to build a self-reliant economy. However, the rapid growth of the informal sector during the early 1980s has not been due to Government's promotional efforts, but reflects independent survival efforts by informal entrepreneurs to sustain livelihood of the low-income earners following the failure by the official economy to provide sufficient supplies of commodities.[16]

According to this view the second economy is not a pathological fact but rather a kind of 'nature's revolt', a sort of healthy reaction to the pathology of the state.[17] Such a phenomenon is clearly not a passing one, but a vibrant and steadily rising economic sector. This view may explain the apparent paradox that although certain aspects of the second economy are considered illegal, they are conspicuously public and it would seem they are officially tolerated. By recognizing that not all aspects of the second economy are socially undesirable, this view offers a better perspective in that it encourages the search for more appropriate policy instruments commensurate with particular behaviourial aspects of the second economy. This is why we have found it instructive to situate our inferred hypotheses in this context.

2.3 Origins of the Second Economy

In Tanzania and indeed in Africa in general the second economy is not a new phenomenon but the latest manifestation of the older economic dichotomies. In development literature such sectoral dichotomies as 'subsistence–urban', 'traditional–modern', 'subsistence–market', or 'rural–urban' were already receiving scholarly attention in the 1950s and 1960s.[18] These concepts were essentially used to convey the idea of two parallel sectors which coexisted in the framework of the same economic system. According to this schema the two sectors were assumed to be different in several aspects, for instance in the way production was organized, the degree of participation in both capital and labour markets, and technologies utilized. In all these aspects the first sector (urban, modern, market, etc.) is always considered as developed, organized and dynamic while the second sector is seen as underdeveloped, unorganized and stagnant. But even within African economies the dual economy perspective was misguided in at least three respects. First, the relationship between the two sectors was far more fluid than implied by the dualist theories. The traditional sector linked up within the modern sector through consumption linkages (provision of food) and through the labour market. Secondly, the colonial policy had radically transformed the traditional sector into a commercial (cash) crop economy. Lastly, the dual sector concept failed to capture an increasingly emerging group of activities within the modern, urban-based sector which had attributes akin to the traditional sector but which was not adequately covered in official statistics and hence fell outside the purview of Government regulation.

The emergence of these groups of semi-organized and unregulated activities, which were largely undertaken by self-employed persons, and which became popularly known as the 'informal sector', caused a sharp shift in thinking about sectoral dualism and soon became a centre of attraction. This was partly due to a growing disenchantment with the capacity of the large-scale, capital-intensive modern sector for meeting the employment and consumption needs of the masses. But also, it was in part due to the realization that a large segment of the urban population in developing countries was not that which was openly unemployed (in the sense of lacking paid work or actively looking for wage employment), but consisted of people involved in disguised tasks or underemployed. For many observers therefore, in view of its small-scale and labour-intensive operations, the informal sector seems to offer viable and flexible employment opportunities for the unemployed.

Contrary to the classical theories of development, which view the informal sector as a passing phenomenon destined to phase out with time, giving way to the large-scale, more organized modern sector, experience in developing countries shows that this sector has considerably increased both in its level of production and the number of persons engaged in it.[19] The informal sector is said to engage more than 50 per cent of the urban population in developing countries and this section of society is growing at a higher rate than the overall population of these countries.[20] In India, for example, the informal sector GDP is said to be of the same order as that of the formal sector.[21] In Africa the informal sector accounts for 60 per cent of the urban labour force and it is quite likely that it contributes between one-quarter and one-third of urban incomes.[22]

The second economy may then be seen as the outgrowth of the informal sector. The increasing use of this term seems to reflect the broadening and intensification of informal sector activities in almost every aspect of economic life. Second economy activities are not confined to the urban economy, but extend to the rural areas. They are almost everywhere: in direct production, distributive services, communication and transportation. Second economy activities are not just the usual informal self-help activities often initiated with honest (legal) objectives in the face of bureaucratic indifference or outright hostility; they also now cover activities with illegal objectives such as drug trafficking, smuggling and poaching.

Although the informal sector has always been viewed by most governments with a critical perspective (largely because of what they consider to be unfair competition with the formal sector, and because of its ability to escape standards of workers' health and safety), it has always been regarded as non-threatening. In its new and excessive form, however, the over-expansion of the informal sector poses a challenge to the state legitimacy of many African countries.

It might be useful at this stage to explore the possible causes of the emergence and pervasiveness of the second economy. But since we have hypothesized that the second economy has it roots in the informal sector, it will be instructive to start the discussion by highlighting the origins of the informal sector. Conventional wisdom has it that the informal sector is a product of two broad developments. It is considered that on the one hand there is a demographic explosion in the modern (urban) sector, and on the other hand an agricultural crisis in the traditional sector. It is pointed out that because much of the development effort in the LDCs has gone into the cities, living conditions there have improved much faster than those in rural areas. Until recently, as a result of the improvement in sanitary and health conditions, mortality rates have decreased significantly, shifting the labour supply curve to the right. At the same time forces of stagnation in the traditional sector have resulted in mass migration into cities. Partly because of these developments and partly because expansion of industrial activities in the modern sector is increasingly assuming a capital-intensive bias, the demand for labour has fallen. The result has been the observed high levels of unemployment which have forced a significant portion of the urban labour force to earn its living in low productivity 'informal' activities.

This explanation seems to be consistent with empirical evidence gathered from Africa where internal migration, combined with stagnating formal wage employment opportunities, has been found to swell the ranks of the urban informal sector.[23] Certainly, the explanation is also consistent with available evidence on Tanzania where simple estimates of formal wage employment trends indicate bleak prospects. For example, according to the 1978 national population census the working population age (15–64 years) constitutes about 48.5 per cent of the total 17.5 million population, and is estimated to be growing at 3.5 per cent per annum. At this rate, the average annual increase of the potential labour force is about 380,000. However, between 1983 and 1986 only 27,083, 15,130 and 1,129 new jobs respectively were created.[24] Given this historical trend the formal wage employment sector cannot be expected to perform miracles. Furthermore, the ILO/JASPA study estimates the rates of unemployment for Dar es Salaam and Tanga to be respectively 17.6 and 29.9 per cent in 1984.[25] The unemployment situation is likely to worsen with full implementation of the Economic Recovery Programme (1986-9), which among other things advocates drastic cuts in public sector employment. The recent survey of informal sector activities in Arusha and Dar es Salaam towns also confirms the predominance of migrant workers as a proportion of total informal sector workers (84 per cent in Arusha, 90 per cent in Dar es Salaam), suggesting that the rural–urban drift could be a major factor in explaining the origin of the urban informal sector.

This statement needs to be qualified, however. The predominant status of migrants in the labour force profile of the informal sector seems to reflect its youthful character since the majority (about three-quarters) of the workers are aged between 20 and 45 years. A breakdown by age clearly indicates that 65 per cent of those aged 15–20 years were born in the respective urban places. This is consistent with the general migration trend in Tanzania which shows highest rates of rural–urban migration in the 1960s and 1970s with a sharp decline in the 1980s. With such a sharp decline in migration one would have expected contraction in the informal sector activity. That this did not happen suggests that there are other factors behind the expansion of the informal sector economy.

Writers like Bromley and Gerry[26] point to the flexibility of working hours, location and greater job mobility of self-employment, and increasing job insecurity in the formal sector as reasons drawing an increasing number of people into the urban informal sector. In addition Cornuel and Duriez[27] list a number of advantages which help informal enterprises to minimize costs, including absence of taxes, social security contributions, obligatory deductions and work regulations. While such explanations are relevant in explaining the existence of the urban informal sector, they fail to answer four important questions relating to the dynamics of the informal sector and the emergence of the second economy.

In the first place, the traditional view seems to suggest that the informal sector, or more broadly the second economy, is basically an urban phenomenon. This perspective, however, fails to explain the existence of a substantial number of activities and economic transactions that operate outside the official net in the agricultural or rural sector. Secondly, as Hernando de Soto has argued,[28] even the high rates of unemployment in the modern urban sector may only explain why people are not employed in traditionally established business activities, but not why new businesses operate outside Government regulation. Thirdly, what accounts for the emergence and pervasiveness of the second economy? And lastly, if the second economy (which operates outside Government regulation) is sufficiently large then it should be obvious that the Government is aware of its existence, raising the question of why the Government does not eliminate it.

The failure of the traditional approach to explain the emergence and pervasiveness of the second economy prompts us to explore new sets of hypotheses. In the Tanzanian context it appears that apart from internal migration and declining formal employment opportunities, the expansion of the informal sector and hence the growth of the second economy are a result of four interacting forces: (i) failure of the agricultural sector to support adequately the rapidly growing rural population; (ii) excessive and inefficient Government regulations which have generated costly barriers and stifled formal economic activity; (iii) Government's failure to institute adequate legal and institutional control mechanisms which could have backed up and supervised its interventionist programmes, and (iv) the economic crisis.

A point which is sometimes overlooked is that in the Tanzanian context it is not only the formal (enclave) sector which has failed to support adequately the growing population, but also the agricultural (traditional) sector. About 88 per cent of the total population of Tanzania lives in rural areas. Natural population growth in the rural areas is relatively high and averages about 3 per cent per annum. Yet agriculture, which provides employment for more than half of the total labour force in the country and over four-fifths of the rural labour force, offers low returns to labour and is growing so sluggishly (Table 1.1, page 139) that employment opportunities are expanding little if at all. Only some 4–5 per cent of the total cultivable land area is cultivated, suggesting that in principle land, which is a decisive factor in the determination of agricultural employment, could possibly support a higher agrarian population than at present. However, much of the area is infected by tsetse flies which pose a health hazard to the local population and animals. In addition, the rainfall pattern in many places is not adequate to give the cultivators a reliable food harvest.[29] Thus, given the pressure of the rising population and the limited technological options currently available to most farmers, land is already becoming a limiting scarce factor in many areas of rural Tanzania. That this is so is demonstrated by declines in the fallow period and the extension of cultivation into less fertile areas.[30]

A combination of rising population pressure, environmental deterioration, and lack of appropriate innovation on the one hand, and the low level of investment in agriculture, lack of agricultural research, lack of accessibility to credit by small farmers, inadequate and irregular supply of inputs, scarcity of consumer goods and poor transportation and marketing facilities on the other hand, have led to declines in output per unit of land, landlessness and under-employment. This has forced a sizeable segment of the rural population either to migrate to towns or to involve themselves in all sorts of non-farm (informal) income generating activities.

To some extent, excessive Government intervention and controls seem to underlie the recent expansion in second economy activity. For a peasant, trader or potential entrepreneur, the legal requirements for obtaining formal services, access to official marketing channels, property rights or business licences have been quite burdensome so that even a hardworking citizen with honest motives is forced to operate outside the law. Government's excessive regulation and red tape have tended to raise costs of operation and administration, thus stifling personal initiative and increasing risks among different sectors in the economy.

Active Government intervention in the management of the economy can be traced back to the Arusha Declaration (February 1967). Hitherto much of the economic development that took place was largely the result of private sector initiative. But it soon became clear that private (mainly foreign) sector initiative could not be relied on to bring about structural change. The inflow of foreign private capital fell short of what was expected, and the little that came was more than offset by the corresponding capital outflows in the form of profits, interest payments, management fees and so on.[31] According to the Tanzanian leadership at the time, economic development could only be meaningful if it were to bring about equity, self-reliance and development of the broad rural masses. This belief incidentally coincided with the intellectual climate at the time, which held that economic growth did not necessarily bring about economic development. These broad development themes were later spelled out in the Arusha Declaration. In particular the Declaration stipulated the need for public control of the major means of production so as to facilitate the achievement of national objectives of socialism, self-reliance, equity and rural development. It is quite clear then that the need for state intervention was not prompted solely by the ideological commitment to socialism. There were other, genuine, underlying forces – such as the past failure of the private economy to implement development, the search to bring about structural change, and the need to develop an indigenous entrepreneurial class. What ought to be questioned, however is not the very act of state intervention but its capacity to intervene, and the manner and speed with which it was implemented.

The immediate result of the Arusha Declaration was the nationalization of the strategic activities of the economy. Thereafter,

Government intervention has increasingly assumed the form of promoting new public institutions and the active use of a wide range of economic policy instruments. The overall result has been the dramatic proliferation of public sector institutions. For example, the number of public organizations (parastatals) increased from about 43 in 1966 to 380 by 1979, and was about 425 by the mid-1980s. As the World Bank observed, 'Only in countries as large as Brazil (six times the population and 50 times the GDP of Tanzania) and Mexico (3.6 times the population and 35 times the GDP) does one find more than 425 parastatals.'[32]

In the rural areas state intervention was partly manifested in a rather hastily planned massive operation in 1972–5 to resettle the hitherto scattered population into villages in order to encourage communal production and control peasant production. Crop marketing was also controlled by the state, and in 1976 co-operatives were abolished and replaced by monopsonic (single buyer) crop parastatals. Although co-operatives were reintroduced in 1982 their independence was sharply curtailed.[33]

The rapid growth and multiplicity of public sector institutions has been accompanied by a complex host of regulatory procedures with a strong leaning towards quantitative controls. The most important control mechanisms have included (i) central control of investment planning; (ii) administrative allocation of foreign exchange through import licensing; (iii) price controls administered by the National Price Commission; (iv) credit rationing according to the Annual Finance Plan; (v) wage regulation administered by the Permanent Labour Tribunal; (vi) confinement policy whereby wholesale and retail trade for some imported and domestic commodities is restricted to specified parastatal organizations, and (vii) other forms of direct controls.

Ideally one would have expected that, given such an elaborate set of regulatory controls and a sizeable public sector, the major economic decisions would increasingly have reflected Government priorities rather than the decisions of the private sector. But the existence of the second economy belies this notion, suggesting that Government's genuine intentions towards public intervention have not been carried out. In turn this prompts us to ask why the genuine intentions of Government controls have not been realized. It appears to us that this is largely due to the Government's failure to strike a workable balance between the roles played by public and private sectors in economic development. In particular, Government intervention in the management of the economy has been too excessive to implement and co-ordinate, given the existing institutional capacity. But in an important way, Government capacity to monitor and supervise its intervention programmes has been further undermined by the economic crisis.

There are important theoretical as well as practical reasons to explain the tendency of the second economy to grow strongly during periods of economic retrenchment. The onset of the macro-economic crisis in the early 1970s resulted in deterioration in the terms of trade, output declines in both domestic and export sectors, and hence the tightening of the foreign exchange constraint. For Tanzania, this meant a sharp contraction in real imports per capita, and given the increasingly import-intensive structures necessitated by the need to build basic industries, this imposed a tremendous squeeze on real resource availabilities. Government reacted by introducing exchange and import controls and imposing price controls on key consumer items with a view to protecting urban real incomes. But it is obvious that price controls amidst scarcity constitute a potential rent as the unsatisfied market would be willing to pay above the controlled price. This would then permit those in possession of the commodity at the controlled price to reap rents if they sold to the unsatisfied consumer. This is what happened in Tanzania, and although a system of rationing was introduced to check the situation it never worked well because it was not effectively policed.

It should be emphasized moreover that the impact of the economic crisis affects not only the supply of tradable commodities but also the life-style and standard of living of the people. The economic crisis erodes the real value of public salaries and wages, and for the peasant the real producer prices. When this happens in a situation where most commodities cannot be obtained at official prices, formal incomes reach a point where they can no longer provide the basis for minimum subsistence. For example, while in 1973 one day's minimum wage could buy either 10 kg of maize or 4.8 kg of rice, in 1985 it could earn only either 2 kg of maize flour or 1.6 kg of rice at the prevailing official prices. In practice, however, since most purchases were made in the second economy markets this meant that a day's minimum wage could earn only either 1.3 kg. of maize or 0.8 kg. of rice.[34]

The precarious situation of the wage earners in Tanzania is vividly revealed by the ILO study and other independent surveys. According to the ILO study, Tanzania experienced a 65 per cent drop in real wages from 1979 to 1984, one of the sharpest declines in real income in Africa.[35] At the low levels of incomes obtaining in Tanzania, such a drop in real incomes would have entailed massive starvation had it not been cushioned by (informal) supplementary incomes.[36] Tripp's recent survey lends further support to the plight of urban wage earners in Tanzania. Her study, which involved a cluster survey of 287 people in two of the most heavily populated parts of Dar es Salaam (Tanzania's largest city), revealed that the average size household of 6 persons can feed itself for only 4 to 6 days of the month if it relies solely on the formal wage.[37]

The extremely low levels of real wages and salaries at all skill levels are partly a result of small, usually infrequent wage revisions and annual increments, high rates of inflation (Table 1.1), a relatively high and progressive income tax structure, and partly of overstaffing. According to the 1986 report by the National Productivity Council, the take-home pay ratio between the minimum wage and the top salary fell from 1:19 in 1962 to 1:6 in 1985. If we disregard fringe benefits which normally accrue to top salary groups and on which data are not easily available, the report shows that between 1980 and 1985 nominal minimum wages rose by 113 per cent, but in real 1977 constant shillings they represented about one-half of their 1980 level. In 1985, top level public sector employees earned 21.5 per cent more than they did in 1980; but in real terms their 1985 earnings were 66 per cent less than those received in 1980.[38]

Even for the topmost executives in the Government and parastatal sectors formal salaries fall short of providing for the minimum wage requirements. After the 1987 budget rise in salaries, the most senior executive in a large parastatal earned a gross monthly salary of about T.Shs 7,500. Typically 25 per cent of this is tax, 12.5 per cent is house rent, and 5 per cent is contributed to the Provident Fund. Disregarding the fringe benefits, many of which are provided in the form of services rather than money, the net monthly take-home pay can hardly keep the family running for more than two weeks of the month. It is not surprising therefore that moonlighting has become an important source of supplementary household earnings, particularly in urban areas.

As for the peasants, while consumer prices increased tenfold from 1976 to 1986, the 1985 real producer prices for maize and rice were almost at the same level as those prevailing during the early 1970s.

All of the foregoing economic hardships hit abruptly in the late 1970s, following more than a decade of high expectations in which Tanzanian society had aspired to build a socialist and egalitarian nation. How then have Tanzanians responded to these socio-economic hardships? Certainly individual responses to the crisis vary widely. However, certain patterns of responses are distinctly discernible and therefore warrant special attention.

Some peasants in the rural areas reacted, for example, by changing both the composition of output and the sales destination of their marketable surpluses. Ellis[39] and Odegaard[40] have shown that the raising of export taxes during the late 1970s and the overvalued exchange rate had a marked depressive effect on the producer prices for export crops, resulting in substantial income transfers from cash crop producers. This led to farmers shifting from the production of export crops to production of food which offered relatively higher returns for their efforts. The switch to food production was not entirely prompted by the supremacy of familial and social obligations over the cash nexus as Hyden[41] has argued, but it was also prompted by pure economic considerations. Unlike export crops which are mainly sold abroad through Government agencies, food crops were in high demand domestically and could be traded easily in the parallel market at prices well above official prices. As farmers became increasingly reluctant to sell their output through official marketing channels and instead chose to produce more for subsistence and for sale in the parallel market, the official economy shrank as a result of reduced volumes of crop exports and the subsequent reduction in revenue from export taxes and export receipts.

Some farmers seeing their agricultural incomes shrinking day after day responded by seeking part-time employment in non-farm activities. In some instances this meant a revival of traditional skills (for example, blacksmithing). From our survey of rural households (reported in detail in Chapter 4) it is clear that the proportion of farmers involved in non-farm income generating activities had increased substantially during the mid-1980s compared to the mid-1970s. Rural non-farm activities are particularly important for farmers with little plots of land, the landless and the youths who have recently graduated from primary schools.

Hyden[42] has documented in detail a more subtle peasant response to the ever-increasing state control over peasant production. By resorting to a non-violent strategy of day-to-day non-compliance, the Tanzanian peasants have managed to evade Government pressure to collectivize their activities, so making it difficult for the Government to maximize surplus extraction from the rural peasants. 'The effect of people's "evasion of the state" was the state's retreat away from villagization in the 1980s and even an admission on the part of some top Government and Party leaders in recent years that the policy was ill- conceived and poorly carried out.'[43]

In urban areas responses to the crisis took various forms. Some urban residents discovered new productive ways of becoming truly self-reliant by getting involved in sideline activities (for example, food vending, operating small kiosks, repair and maintenance services, furniture making, shanty eating places, tailoring, shoe-making and repair, local beer brewing, hair braiding, urban farming). On average every productive urban household member is involved in one way or another in a *mradi* (sideline project). Typically when wage earning members of the family return from their regular jobs they get involved in one or more of the above mentioned activities. Those who remain at home are usually engaged in urban farming or food vending, besides performing their routine domestic tasks. Some children even sell buns and peanuts after school hours. Because of the extremely low levels of formal wages and salaries, others have found formal employment unattractive and unrewarding and have left it to be self-employed or to engage in full-time urban farming. Tripp's survey[44] has revealed that of those respondents who had left formal employment, 30 per cent did so during the pre-crisis period in the 1970s, while 70 per cent left after 1980.

This trend is consistent with the pattern of the age structure of urban informal activities which reveals that most are of recent origin. In their study of urban informal sectors in Arusha and Dar es Salaam, Bagachwa and Ndulu[45] found that about three-quarters of the informal enterprises in Arusha Town and four-fifths of those surveyed in Dar es Salaam had been established between 1980 and 1987. Table 2.1 (page 143), which is reproduced from their study, indicates the skewed distribution of informal sector firm age towards recent years.

Rapid expansion in the number of establishments, as well as being a recent phenomenon, occurred mainly in activities producing or distributing wage goods, especially in food vending, tailoring and carpentry. Similarly, in her 1987–8 survey of Dar es Salaam,[46] Tripp found that 64 per cent of the self-employed had begun their enterprises within the past five years, while only 15 per cent had started in the previous five years. Tripp's survey also reveals the increasing role of women in self-employment. While earlier studies had described Tanzanian women as 'relatively inactive' in terms of seeking self-employment opportunities,[47] Tripp's survey showed that 66 per cent of urban women were self-employed and most of them (78 per cent) had started their business in the past five years.

Partly, the quantitative insignificance of old firms in the sample reflects the inherent instability of the informal sector and hence its short-lived character. But it is also true, and perhaps most importantly so, that the expansion of informal activity in the 1980s reflects attempts by informal operators to pursue survival strategies after the formal sector failed to provide the population with basic goods and services. This was strongly reflected in responses to questions seeking respondents' reasons for establishing their firms.

Those who have studied in detail the operations of the informal sector in Tanzania are unanimous on four important points relating to the structure and potential of this sector. First, the sector consists of semi-organized and unregulated activities undertaken largely by the self-employed. This provides latitude and flexibility for a broad range of decisions in terms of personal initiative and innovation, the size of the enterprise, the choice of technique, and the utilization of incomes. Secondly, there are minor barriers to entry in any of these activities, creating a potential base for rapid expansion once opportunities and incentives are present. Thirdly, these studies consistently find that the sector is relatively more labour-intensive, more efficient, more profitable, saves more on skilled labour and foreign exchange, and can generate more jobs with smaller capital outlays than large-scale formal sector activities. This reduces its vulnerability to external shocks compared with the level faced by the formal sector. Finally, there is also considerable evidence that informal sector entrepreneurs can mobilize their own savings.[48] Thus from a dynamic perspective it appears that informal sector activities have the potential capacity to respond to future increases in demand provided the policy environment does not discriminate against them.

Most of the informal sector activities mentioned above represent mainly legitimate survival strategies adopted in the face of declining incomes, growing unemployment and under-employment. They explain one important motive people have in engaging in second economy activities – namely, to raise incomes for their own support so as to alleviate hunger and poverty. To the extent that these unrecorded informal sector activities are legitimate and are associated with disadvantaged groups (the landless, jobless, women and low income earners), the employment and incomes generated tend to have a stabilizing and equalizing effect.

While some people resorted to legitimate informal sector activities, others resorted to illegitimate activities. As the crisis intensified ideals were not abandoned, but they lost their hold on some individuals. Consequently, significant indicators of illegalities in Tanzania's economic system became more conspicuous for the first time since independence.

Much of this illegal activity was spurred by the overall shortages of goods. For example, housing shortages became acute as scarcity of building materials ground the entire building industry to a halt. As the shortages intensified, rents for existing housing were raised in circumvention of state regulations by demanding advance payments – or key money – from renters. Landlords went a stage further in giving preference to tenants with foreign exchange access. The buying and selling of real estate developed into land speculation around and within the big cities, and, ultimately, tendering bribes to National Housing and Registrar of Buildings officials started to became the only viable means of obtaining a house to live in.

Real shortages were made worse by artificial shortages created through the hoarding of goods and services, and sometimes by mismanagement. But Government policy was also to blame. As already pointed out, in a situation of goods famine, and in the absence of formal rationing and effective policing, Government control on prices below clearing rates constituted a potential rent which speculators could reap if the frustrated purchasers were willing to pay above the controlled price. On the other hand, with both inputs and outputs prices controlled by the National Price Commission through a cost-plus pricing methodology, there is a built-in incentive for a production manager, whether in the private or public sector, to inflate costs, lobby directly or corrupt price-fixing officials so as to qualify for price increases. This is indeed rent seeking.[49] Thus another important reason for engaging in the second economy is profiteering through price control evasion.

Tax evasion is certainly an important source of illegitimate profit and hence an important, but not the only, cause of the second economy in Tanzania. The country's narrow tax base has always been the excuse for constant increases in tax rates. For example, in order to provide incentives for exporters while maintaining revenue flows from custom duties, Government had gradually abolished export taxes but significantly raised import duties (between 1981 and 1983) to offset the decline in the volume of imports. As will be shown in Chapter 3, high tariff rates have been an important cause for under-invoicing of imports. In addition, tax rates on net corporate profit generally average 50 per cent. So understating net corporate profits can significantly raise profits, while not declaring them can more than double profits accruing to the firm.

Historically personal income tax rates in Tanzania have generally been progressive and relatively high, ranging between 20 and 95 per cent for the 1974–84 period. In 1981, for instance, a person earning a monthly income of T.Shs 4,000 paid a quarter of the income in taxes, while one earning a monthly income of T.Shs 25,000 paid three-quarters of the earnings in taxes. In 1984, Government took the initiative and reduced personal income tax rates to between 20 and 75 per cent. These were further reduced to a range of 15–55 per cent in July 1988. Furthermore the minimum taxable income was increased from T.Shs 1,200 per month to T.Shs 1,500 per month. Even with the current reforms, which include a moderate rise in wages, income tax rates are still relatively high given the general low income base and the high levels of inflation. There is no doubt that a combination of inflation and high income tax rates has further eroded the purchasing power of most fixed income earners, acting as a disincentive to increased production in the official economy.

Of particular importance as far as the second economy is concerned has been the increasing tax burden from indirect (sales and excise) taxes. Since the mid-1970s, tax revenue has accounted for slightly over 90 per cent of the total revenue. A larger share of total revenue now consists of sales and excise duties which have risen from an average of 40 per cent between 1977–8 and 1981–2 to about 57 per cent between 1982–3 and 1987–8. As a proporportion of GDP, revenue from indirect taxes increased from 7 per cent in 1977–8 to 12.5 per cent in 1982–3, and then declined slightly to 11.2 per cent in 1987–8. Since this increase occurred when industrial output was declining, it can be plausibly explained in terms of higher tax rates per article. For example, between 1977–8 and 1983–4 the tax rate on beer was increased by about 6 times, on cigarettes by 11 times and on sugar by 2.2 times. In the 1988–9 budget sales tax rates on beer were increased from 241 per cent to 250 per cent, and on soft drinks from 115 to 130 per cent.

In general, given the inefficiency of many industries in Tanzania, tax rates per product are higher than net profit rates per item. This encourages tax evasion in order to offset trading losses and/or to reap illegitimate profit. It has also been suggested that the steep rise in the price of bottled beer after the mid-1970s was largely due to increases in sales tax, and it is held by some that it induced some substitution to locally brewed beer.[50] Increased local brewing created additional demand for grains which were already in short supply nation-wide. In turn the widening excess demand pushed up the parallel market prices for food grains, creating incentives for more production for sale in the parallel markets. Moreover, the incidence of indirect taxes is relatively regressive since they are levied on consumption and the majority of low income people spend a large share of their incomes on consumer goods.

Overall, high tax rates combined with the deteriorating economic situation have tended to shift production towards those activities that are difficult to tax (i.e. informal sector activities).

Other examples of people's evasion of excessive controls may be seen in the thriving illegal foreign currency transactions, and the then illegal importation of restricted luxury goods such as saloon cars, televisions and video recorders. In addition, the administrative control and allocation of foreign exchange and import licences created incentives for firms to overstate their foreign exchange requirements and/or to physically lobby for higher allocations of foreign exchange.

As the crisis deepened and as the real purchasing power of wages declined continuously some public servants lost hold of their work ethics. They began to use the public office as a market contact for their personal business, and spent a substantial part of the official working day attending to such business, justifying their absence under the pretext of searching for scarce essential commodities in various shops. In essence this amounts to stealing wages since such wages are paid for work which is partially performed or not performed at all. Some went to the extent of using not only the employer's time for personal business, but also employer's assets and office space during or after office hours. This is what Wiles[51] has labelled 'stolen services of capital' and is, quite frankly, illegal.

In such a situation it becomes increasingly difficult to distinguish between a legal and an illegal economic transaction. On the one hand there is the private sector which can now easily escape Government controls by bribing the very persons supposed to implement them; and on the other there are public servants who use state assets in ways that are socially undesirable, such as soliciting payments for access to what is socially considered a free public service. This paradoxical behaviour is sarcastically summarized by the man in the street in Dar es Salaam who refers to the unofficial price as the (national ruling) 'Party's sanctioned price', and to the National Economic Survival Programme (NESP) as the 'Personal Economic Survival Programme' (PESP).

Quite clearly this situation reflects extreme forms of moral decay among public servants, and their use of official allocation mechanisms is bound to result in public disillusionment and demoralization. A good example of declining social controls over the economy is the Government's lack of trust in the formal legal machinery to handle corruption cases uncovered during the 1983 crackdown on 'economic saboteurs'. As the President put it:

> We have a problem on what to do with these people. The normal procedure would be to take them to court. However, we have not yet decided what action to take in the present circumstances. Magistrates and judges forgive us if we hesitate to take the culprits to courts of law.[52]

The President further remarked that past experience had shown that many racketeers and corrupt persons were set free or given only light sentences by the courts. It was his belief that the culprits used their ill-gotten gains to engage lawyers who were 'experts in twisting the facts', or to influence the courts to decide in their favour. In such a situation it was very difficult to secure the conviction of those arrested for offences which later came to be known as economic sabotage offences.

Table 2.2 (page 143) gives statistics on corruption offences prosecuted by the authorities before the April 1983 crackdown, and appears to support the view that the ordinary legal machinery was having difficulty disposing speedily of cases involving sabotage offences. The table shows that the number of cases involving corruption remained substantial for the period 1980 to 1983, but that convictions were few and continued to decrease. The number of cases pending before the courts was also large and rising every year, mainly due to the small number of magistrates and poor records. Cases which remained pending for a long time tended ultimately to be withdrawn and the suspects discharged.

The same observations about the inadequacy of the legal machinery could be made in relation to several other sabotage offences, including thefts committed by public employees in public institutions, cattle rustling, hoarding, and other allied offences. Consequently, it was decided that persons arrested during the crackdown operation should be detained under the Preventive Detention Act of 1962, a law which empowers the President to detain persons conducting themselves in a manner prejudicial to the security of the state. The detention of saboteurs lasted until 1984 when the Economic and Organized Crime Control Act 1984 No. 13 was passed.

Economic problems in neighbouring countries also contributed to the shortages of commodities and to the promotion of the second economy in Tanzania. Uganda under Amin was desperate for agricultural implements and consumer goods from Tanzania and Kenya. Apart from reducing industrial production to an extremely low level by the late 1970s, Amin had appropriated most of what was available for his army, resorting to hoarding and even ordering commodities overseas for this purpose. The illegal trade – *Magendo* – described by Green[53] therefore grew strong during Amin's tyrant rule in Uganda. A portion of the little that Tanzania had left after its own declining production found its way into Uganda, where it was paid for in Tanzania shillings smuggled out of the country or where it was bartered for coffee.

This second economy trade across the borders must be analysed in its historical perspective. The three East African British colonies (Kenya as a colony, Uganda as a protectorate, and Tanganyika as a trusteeship territory) were administered commercially from Nairobi. A number of private companies representing those in the centre had their main East African branches in Nairobi. Dar es Salaam and Kampala were Nairobi sub-branches. Even after the breakup of the East African Community, this relationship of sub-centres remained. A number of businessmen in Dar es Salaam and Kampala still maintained old relationships with their counterparts in Nairobi who could help them co-ordinate their efforts in illegal trade. Since Nairobi was more industrialized than either of the other two cities, it is no wonder that it became a trading centre for Ugandan and Zairean coffee and gold, and for Tanzanian beef cattle, to mention only a few of the best selling commodities in the illegal trade. Further, when Amin expelled Asians from Uganda, most of them went to England, where they were in an even better position to arrange foreign trade deals with their old associates back in Dar es Salaam and Kampala.[54]

From the foregoing discussion it is instructive for both analytical and policy purposes to distinguish three important aspects of the second economy: (i) that which involves legitimate, self-reliant and productive household or more broadly informal sector activities. These activities belong to the second economy because they lie outside Government regulation and control; (ii) that which involves illegitimate activities and which originates and takes place in the genuinely parallel circuit outside the official system, and (iii) that involving illegitimate activities originating from the official system. In other words, a clear understanding of how the second economy operates in Tanzania requires a systematic analysis of the official and unofficial private and public sectors of the economy. Central to the operations of the second economy is the state, which defines what is legal and what is illegal, what is private and what is public. It is the state which regulates economic activity through policy directives and administrative machinery. Thus the very authority, legitimacy and credibility of the state depends on its success in regulating and enforcing its policy directives.

It is against this background that the emergence and subsequent growth of the second economy in Tanzania is seen as a reflection of the weakening of state control, and not only the inability of the state to provide the basic needs of the masses but also its ineffectiveness in controlling and co-ordinating its excessive interventionist programmes.

2.4 The Need for Estimating the Second Economy

There are three important reasons which make the study of the second economy compelling, particularly in the Tanzanian context. First, it enables us to understand the response of Tanzanian society to the hardships imposed by the economic crisis. For even a casual observer, the way people in Tanzania survive is very much at variance with the picture painted by official statistics. The extent of the disparity between economic statistics and observed economic reality needs to be examined.

Secondly, the second economy is of policy relevance from the macro-economic point of view. Since much of the macro-economic policy is based on variables derived from national accounts, if the national acccounts give erroneous information, the policies based on them would definitely be misleading. In particular, the predominance of second economy activities would imply that GNP, and the observed levels of savings, consumption, productivity, growth, inflation and unemployment are grossly distorted.[55] In such circumstances any monetary or fiscal policy manipulation through these variables is bound to fail. If such policies were introduced to correct perceived adverse economic trends, they are bound to be ineffective.

Thirdly, the study is very timely. Since the mid-1980s Tanzania has instituted and implemented a number of liberal reform programmes intended to check the advance of the economic crisis and its attendant adverse side effects, including expansion in second economy activities. Of particular interest are the recent trade, finance and exchange rate policies that provide alternative outlets for capital accumulated in the second economy. It is useful to determine whether in fact the second economy declines or not as liberalization increases, and also whether or not Tanzanian society is any better served as a consequence.

2.5 Estimating the Second Economy in Tanzania

There are no consistent estimates of the overall size and growth of the second economy in Tanzania. Evidence of its existence has been sparse, primarily circumstantial and anecdotal. Even then, the limited evidence available relates mainly to the various partial manisfestations of the second economy without necessarily establishing the relative magnitude of its activity flows in relation to official activity flows.

Some of these studies have made use of the observed discrepancy between official and unofficial commodity prices and exchange rates as indicative evidence of the existence of a second economy.[56] Others, like Odegaard,[57] have pointed to a noticeably large unexplained residual between total production and officially marketed agricultural output after allowing for subsistence consumption as a clue to the size of the second economy. It has also been suggested that the high incidence of corruption and other related illegal transactions such as poaching, hoarding and smuggling as revealed by the Government's 1983 crackdown on *walanguzi* (the so-called saboteurs) indicates the existence of a second economy.[58] In some cases, circumstantial evidence on the existence of the second economy in Tanzania has been inferred from the artificial contraction of supply in relation to demand.

Although these studies have been important in shedding some light on the different forms in which second economy transactions take place, more systematic analyses are needed in order to (i) establish the overall size of this sector; (ii) study its causes and establish its effects on Government regulation and policy, and (iii) develop methodologies which allow for more, and consistent, empirical research. This study is therefore an attempt to generate additional material under these three headings.

2.6 Methods and Empirical Results

Perhaps the most difficult area of analysis in the second economy is measuring the monetary value or magnitude of the transactions involved. Yet such a measure is necessary to permit, for instance, comparisons of the size of the second economy relative to the size of the official economy. Apart from figures advanced in media reports on the basis of speculation and educated guesses, a giant step forward has been made to establish more well-defined methods for estimating the size of the second economy.[59]

Some analysts, mostly economists, rely on monetary statistics to establish discrepancies between currency normally needed and that which is actually observed in the monetary sphere as a means of measuring indirectly the size of the second economy. This method is known as the monetary approach and we shall comment on its application shortly. Another approach is to attribute the 'residual' between the reported income and visible expenditure sides of the total economy to the second economy. Normally this is derived from a survey of a sample of households and extrapolated to the whole economy to give a clue to the size of the second economy. We shall also turn to this method shortly.

Another way of understanding the volume of the second economy is to analyse the labour force statistics. The labour force participation approach attributes an 'unusually' low rate of labour force participation to the existence of clandestine employment in the second economy. The difficulty with this approach, which measures people and not money, as Wiles points out[60] is to quantify the adverb 'unusually'. Estimates of the second economy have also been obtained by first estimating the value added of each activity and then aggregating these estimates to arrive at the overall total. In practice, it is difficult to identify and measure precisely the value of each second economy activity. So what is usually done is to estimate the value added of the most important activities in the second economy. The contribution of other less important second economy activities may then be guessed as a residual.[61]

An important contribution to the measurement of the second economy is that made by anthropologists and sociologists who generate useful information about the nature and organization (but usually with no overall size figures) of the second economy by living for some time and pretending to behave like second economy operators, i.e. through participant observation. In this study we shall use both the monetary and the income–expenditure discrepancy approaches to estimate indirectly the size of the second economy in Tanzania. In addition we shall provide partial and indirect estimates of the magnitudes of selected second economy activities.

2.6.1   The Monetary Approach

The basic premise of this approach is that in order to avoid Government detection, all second economy activities avoid the use of cheques or credit cards and rely on currency for transactions. Relative changes in currency holdings are thus interpreted as reflecting volume movements in the second economy activity. Following Tanzi[62] we may distinguish three variants of this approach: the denomination of currency method, the currency–demand deposit (C–DD) ratio, and the demand for currency equation variant. The denomination of currency method hinges on the assumption that as the second economy increases the need for currency (or cash) increases; and in order to facilitate payment, the high denomination notes in circulation are preferred and hence their number rises.

The currency–demand deposit (C–DD) ratio method was first used by Cagan,[63] but was made popular by Peter Gutmann.[64] Feige[65] used a similar method, but instead of the C–DD ratio he adopted the MV–GNP ratio, where M is money supply defined as currency plus demand deposits, V is transaction velocity of money, and GNP is the officially estimated gross national product. This method assumes the following: (i) the second economy is cash based; (ii) an appropriate bench-mark period in which second economy activity is negligible can be identified; (iii) the ratio of currency to demand deposit associated with the bench-mark period would have prevailed up to the terminal period were it not for growth in the second economy, and (iv) the volume of GNP supported by one unit of currency in the second economy is the same as that supported by one unit of the same currency in the official economy.

Given these assumption, an increase in the amount of currency relative to the amount of demand deposits is interpreted as an increase in the share of the second economy. The relative increase in currency observed is then transformed into a GNP estimate of the second economy by assuming that the velocity of currency circulation is the same in the second and official economies. When using the demand for currency approach it should be borne in mind, therefore, that the major underlying assumption is that second economy transactions are paid for strictly by means of currency in order to minimize the probability of detection by public authorities.

The demand for currency equation method measures the effect of a change in the variables that influence the informal behaviour of economic agents on the demand for currency. From the estimated equation, an estimate of the currency held in the second economy is made, and with the assumption that currency is used primarily in effecting second economy transactions an estimate of the overall size of the second economy may be made. First, we will examine over time the level of currency (cash) in circulation outside banks. As can be seen from Table 2.3 (page 143) the nominal total value of currency in circulation increased by 27 times between 1970 and 1986. At the same time, nominal currency holdings per capita (Figure 2.1, page 145) have increased by almost 15 times, rising from T.Shs 42 in 1967 to T.Shs 625 in 1986. This implies that an average Tanzanian household of five persons needed to hold T.Shs 3,125 in cash in 1986 compared with T.Shs 210 two decades ago. Evidently, the jump is astronomical.

Second, we examine changes in the composition of currency notes in circulation. Here, we observe that the number of T.Shs 100 (highest) denomination notes has risen sharply by 70 times between 1967 and 1986 (Table 2.3). As a result the per capita holdings of the T.Shs 100 notes has risen from 15 to T.Shs 578 in the same period (see Figure 2.1). This is an increase of 38 times which exceeds by far the rise in the total value of currency held by a single person (23 times) and that of the total value of notes (19 times). Furthermore, the ratio of T.Shs 100 notes to all other notes in circulation rose astronomically from 35.5 per cent in 1967 to 88.3 per cent in 1986, implying a corresponding fall in the share of notes with denominations smaller than T.Shs 100 (Figure 2.2, page 145).

Third, we look at movements in the ratio of currency to demand deposits (Figure 2.3, page 146). This ratio has moved from an average of 85 per cent between 1967 and 1972 through 69.3 per cent between 1973 and 1979, and then up to 100 per cent for the period 1980-6. One would have expected this ratio to decline over time, as the economy became increasingly monetized. In other words the economy ought to have moved out of currency and not into it. Furthermore, we note from Figure 2.3 that the two currency money ratios $C-M_1$ and $C-M_2$ have fluctuated marginally around 0.5 and 0.33 respectively, suggesting that the increase in the C-DD ratio, particularly after the mid-1970s, is most likely not due to shifts in portfolio holdings of individuals from demand deposits to other financial assets.

All these monetary movements indicate that the level of cash in circulation has not fallen as might have been expected, given the steady rise in bank-cheque transactions. The Tanzanian economy has therefore not moved into a cashless or credit society. One plausible explanation for the unusual increase in the amount of cash held by the public could be the rise in second economy transactions which use currency to escape detection.

Using Gutmann's[66] approach, it is possible to get some clue as to the overall size of these second economy activities by tracing movements in the ratio of currency in circulation to demand deposits as outlined earlier. Accordingly, we assume that 1977 was the year in which the ratio of currency to demand deposits was 'normal', in the sense that second economy activities were negligible in that year.[67] It is further assumed that the cash–demand deposit ratio (C-DD) of 59 per cent associated with 1977 would have prevailed were it not for the growth of the second economy. However, this ratio has increased slowly but steadily since then, as shown in Figure 2.3.

If the 1977 C-DD ratio had been maintained at the 1986 level, the volume of money supply (M_1) required to produce the officially estimated GDP of T.Shs 131.346 billion should have been T.Shs 19.980, made up of T.Shs 7.414 billion of currency and T.Shs 12.566 billion in current deposits. The actual figure for M_1 for 1986 was T.Shs 26.245 billion, however. If we go by Gutmann's assumptions, the difference of T.Shs 6.265 billion is attributable to currency held by participants in the second economy. Given that the level of official GDP for 1986 was T.Shs 131.346 billion and the volume of money (M_1) T.Shs 19.980 billion, the income velocity of money was 6.574. Since we have assumed the income velocity of money to be the same in the official and second economy sectors, the T.Shs 6.265 billion would produce T.Shs 41.187 billion of GNP in the second economy. The size of the second economy in Tanzania is thus estimated to be 31.4 per cent of the officially estimated GNP in 1986.

An important advantage of Gutmann's approach is that it permits the calculation of a time series of second economy activity. We report in Table 2.4 (page 144) the second economy gross national product (SECGNP), calculated on the basis of this methodology for the period 1977–86. It is interesting to note that between 1978 and 1986 the second economy has been growing extremely rapidly at an annual rate of 30.1 per cent as opposed to the 19.4 per cent annual growth in official GNP. This has resulted in an increase from 9.8 per cent of GDP in 1978 to 31.4 per cent in 1986. It seems, therefore, that during the slowdown in economic activity of the late 1970s and early 1980s, the second economy has picked up rather rapidly. This was expected as individuals attempted to alleviate the economic hardships by seeking income outside the official economy.

The trend indicated in Table 2.4 is quite consistent with the evolution of the Tanzanian economy in the past decade. The low level of second economy activity in the period 1975–8 reflects the picking up of the economy and relaxation of physical controls during the short-lived coffee boom. However, the worsening economic situation following the war with Uganda, the impending drought, and another round of oil price shocks imposed a tremendous squeeze on real resource availabilities. But as the Government tightened import controls and embarked on commodity rationing and a system of confinement in a situation of serious resource scarcity, there was a dramatic increase in unlawful activities as people sought alternative means of sustaining their livelihoods. Thus the unprecedented economic crisis which faced Tanzania between 1979 and 1984 was at the same time accompanied by an explosive increase in the second economy activities, obliging the Government to intervene more forcefully in 1983 through the crackdown on illegal economic activities. This intermittent intervention probably explains the slowdown in second economy activity in that year.

Estimates of the second economy for various countries arrived at by using the monetary approach are summarized in Table 2.5 (page 147). These estimates suggest that the second economy is generally significant. Although the Tanzanian estimate of the second economy appears to be relatively larger than those reported for the USA, the UK, Canada and Australia, it compares well with that reported for Ghana, but is definitely much lower than those reported for Uganda and Zaire.[68]

However, caution is necessary when interpreting these results as there are several problems associated with this approach. First, the assumption that transactions in the second economy are strictly paid for by currency alone introduces a downward bias in the estimates. We know for certain that both open and crossed cheques may occasionally be used to effect payments of covert transactions in the second economy. Equally, the assumption of having the same velocity of currency in the official and second economies oversimplifies reality and can only be verified empirically.

In the second place, the monetary approach to the measurement of the second economy does not impute values for transactions involving barter exchange and where goods and services are exchanged for foreign money. It would certainly be an error to assume that such transactions do not exist in Tanzania. Indeed as we will show in the next chapter, the 1983 crackdown uncovered a substantial amount of illegally held foreign currency equivalent to $US1.99 million. Consequently, estimates of the second economy derived from monetary statistics are bound to be biased downwards.

Third, the choice of an appropriate bench-mark period, where the ratio of currency to demand deposits is assumed to be 'normal', entails an element of arbitrariness. Ideally, no second economy activity is supposed to exist during the bench-mark period. Operationally such an ideal period is difficult to identify. At best, this assumption can be interpreted as implying that the volume of the second economy activity in the base year period was negligible. And yet, as some studies have shown, the choice of base period crucially determines movements in the currency–demand deposit ratio and hence the size of the second economy.[69] Certainly, the choice of a bench-mark period other than 1977 would in our case have yielded different results.

In the fourth place, an increase in the C–DD ratio cannot be attributed solely to a rise in currency. It can also result from a decline in the demand deposits. This could happen if, for example, people shifted their holdings from demand to time deposits which earn interest. In Tanzania it is certainly evident that demand deposits have been growing at a decreasing rate. While they grew at an average annual rate of 18.5 per cent between 1970 and 1977, growth declined to 8.6 per cent per annum in the 1978–86 period. In relation to currency growth, demand deposits grew by 2.7 per cent faster than currency in circulation between 1970 and 1977 on a per capita basis. But this situation was reversed in the years 1978–86. During this period, currency growth was 10 per cent faster than growth in demand deposits on a per capita basis. It does not appear, however, that the slowdown in the expansion of demand deposits was a result of depositors shifting their portfolio holdings from demand to time deposits. In fact, there was a slight decrease in the annual rate of growth of time deposits from 18.8 per cent to 18.4 per cent during the 1970–7 and 1978–86 periods respectively. This suggests that the observed increase in the C–DD ratio cannot be fully explained by a decline in demand deposits. Indeed this is clearly seen when we replace demand deposits by total deposits. The resulting ratio does not fall, but rises gradually, following more or less the pattern shown by the C–DD ratio.

It seems probable, then, that the increase in the C–DD ratio is due more to a rise in currency than to a fall in demand deposits. But since it is also possible that the rise in nominal per capita currency holdings can be explained in terms of the rapid inflationary build-up characteristic of the period, it is worth exploring this possibility. Thus when we adjust for price changes (Figure 2.4, page 146) the evidence becomes somewhat less convincing. As Figure 2.4 shows, the amount of currency per capita in constant 1970 shillings has risen gradually from T.Shs 46.30 to a peak of T.Shs 79.50 in 1979. Thereafter real per capita currency holdings have been falling at a rate of 8.9 per annum, and by 1986 it was 66 per cent of its 1970 level. An almost similar trend may be observed in the large T.Shs 100 notes. However, real per capita holdings of these notes have risen more sharply than the increase in the real per capita total currency holdings. For example, real per capita holdings of T.Shs 100 bills more than doubled their 1960s level for the period between 1979 and 1982. It is this disproportionate increase in the use of large denomination notes that is indicative evidence of the existence of second economy activity in Tanzania.

Increased cash holdings outside the banking system is also revealed by the decline in the velocity of currency below its historical level in the 1979–84 period (Table 2.3). The velocity of currency in circulation, which had remained constant at about 9.5 between 1970 and 1978, dropped to about 7.5 between 1979 and 1984. Under normal circumstances one would have expected this ratio to rise as the economy became more monetized.

Indeed the 1983 crackdown on *Ulanguzi* revealed many cases involving possession of local currency in inordinate amounts. The records show that many people were found with hundreds of thousands of Tanzanian shillings in their homes, some even moving about with it in their vehicles.[70] Clearly, even under conditions of inflation nobody would have expected a typical family of five to hold cash to the tune of T.Shs 100,000. Individual cash holdings had increased so much that during the 1983 Government crackdown on economic crimes, due to panic Kigoma, a small town of less than 25,000, banked more money in one week than was banked during the same period by the more rich one million plus residents of Dar es Salaam.[71]

The fact that possession of money in large quantities was a practice well spread over the whole country deserves explanation. It is strongly felt that, due to the highly unpredictable market situation, traders and others in search of essential commodities had to keep cash readily available to take advantage of opportunities as they arose. The abnormally large amount of cash uncovered in the course of the crackdown was not actually 'hoarded' in the sense perceived by the Government (i.e. hoarded with the clear intention of interfering with and disrupting the circulation of money to the prejudice of the country's economic stability). Rather, it was kept handy in order to pay for the high prices and other transactions in the second economy market. We shall show in more detail in the next chapter that, as the crisis deepened, the supply of essential commodities went underground and black market prices for these commodities more than doubled the official price ceilings.

We should hasten to emphasize that such evidence is only indicative and not conclusive. Indeed there might be some explanation to currency hoarding which is quite unrelated to the growth of second economy activity. We may cite, for example, the lack of alternative currency substitutes such as the absence of credit cards, the lack of confidence in personal cheques, distrust in banks, general economic and policy uncertainty, low interest rates on deposits and some people's desire to conceal wealth. Additionally, as another explanatory factor for hoarding currency, O'Higgins[72] explains the substitution of large currency notes for small ones in official transactions in terms of higher prices. That is, large bills become more useful as the average price level increases.

In view of the shortcomings inherent in Gutmann's method, a more flexible econometric approach developed by Tanzi[73] has also been tried. This approach is flexible in the sense that it does not assume constancy in the currency–money ratio, and in addition the results are not sensitive to the choice of the initial period. This method has been explained in detail by Tanzi.[74] Briefly the method consists in specifying a demand for currency equation in order to quantify the effect on that demand produced by changes in the variables considered important in influencing economic agents to behave informally. The underlying assumption of this approach is that currency is used mainly for carrying out transactions in the second economy or for storing wealth. In this sense then, the second economy activities are regarded as being the direct consequence of the variables that encourage such informal activities. In a generalized form, the demand for currency equation may be stated as:

(1) $\text{Log } D_c = f(X_1, X_2 \ldots \ldots X_n; X_{n+1}, \ldots \ldots X_t) + \log u$

where D_c is any of the C–DD, C–M_1 or C–M_2 ratios; and $X_1, \ldots X_n$ are the logarithms of variables traditionally considered to be the major determinants in the demand for currency; the $X_{n+1}, \ldots X_t$ are the logarithms of the proxies for variables that stimulate second economy activity; and u is the stochastic disturbance term. When the variables that stimulate second economy activity disappear, i.e. $X_{n+1} = \ldots X_t = 0$, then the regression equation yields the estimate of the D_c ratio of the formal economy. It is then possible to estimate currency holdings with or without second economy activity. The difference gives an estimate of the currency held in the second economy which when multiplied by the income velocity of money gives an indication of the size of the second economy.

Using data obtained from the Bank of Tanzania and the National Accounts Statistics, the following conventional explanatory variables were tested in the econometric estimations: real per capita income and the annual rate of (both nominal and real) interest on time deposits. A number of proxies were also tested to capture the variables that induce informal behaviour. These included a tax evasion variable (average tax burden; top-bracket statutory tax rate) and the second economy activity variable (domestic currency traded in the maize parallel market; number of workers in the public sector as a percentage of the active labour force). Several regression equations were estimated using various functional forms for each of the three ratios combining the variables listed above. The estimation of the formal economy ratios was carried out by assuming that the second economy activity variables were zero (i.e. the variables are replaced in each case by a yearly figure plus one).

The overall results were quite uninformative as regards the sources of influence in the determination of demand for currency. Although in most regressions the real per capita income and the real rate of interest variable had their expected negative signs, they were in all cases not statistically significant at even the 20 per cent level of significance. In all cases the overall fit was very poor (R^2 was less than 0.20), rendering individual coefficients insignificant. Apart from the problems of multicollinearity and serial correlation, the fundamental problem lay with the dependent variables. The three ratios (C–DD, C–M_1 and C–M_2) used separately to measure the dependent variable do not exhibit sufficient variations over time and hence statistically there is little variation to be explained by the explanatory variables. In other words valid application of the demand for currency equation method requires availability of good time series data with substantial variation in the currency–money ratio over the years. Since the precision of the results obtained by this method crucially depends on the accuracy of the fit of the regression equations, we have refrained from estimating the size of the second economy using this method.

2.6.2   The Income–Expenditure Discrepancy Approach

National income can be compiled from either aggregate expenditure or aggregate income sources. Since income earned by an individual will later show up as expenditure, aggregate income and expenditure should in theory be equal. According to the income–expenditure discrepancy approach, the discrepancy between income and expenditure is attributed solely to the second economy activity. Thus another way of estimating the size of the second economy is to compare National Accounts estimates of income sources and expenditure outlays (at the macro level). Alternatively, a micro-level approach can be used to assess the income–expenditure discrepancy of particular individual households or groups. If the sample is reasonably representative the results can be extrapolated to constitute an estimate of the second economy for the whole economy.

Unfortunately, it has not been possible to use the income–expenditure discrepancy approach at the macro level to estimate the size of the second economy in Tanzania. This is mainly because there are no actual figures for private final consumption expenditure. An estimate for private final consumption expenditure is derived as a residual between GNP at market prices on the one hand and a sum of total Government final consumption expenditure, gross capital formation, increase in stocks and net exports, on the other hand. The discrepancy, therefore, does not arise because it is lumped together with the private final consumption expenditure.

Even if figures on private final consumption expenditure were available the use of the income–expenditure approach at the macro level would still be questionable. There are two major shortcomings of the comparison between income at the national accounting level: (i) there are bound to be errors in both the income and expenditure aggregates, which may arise from non-reporting and under-reporting of factor incomes such as income from bartering, illegal activities and in-kind activities which are not fully counted; and (ii) errors may also arise due to differences in time and statistical coverage.

Thus both the monetary approach and the macro-level version of the income–expenditure approach are best suited to the analysis of second economies in developed countries where nearly all economic transactions are monetary and where considerable resources have been committed to the maintenance of accurate national statistics. In Tanzania, however, subsistence and barter arrangements are important economic strategies for large segments of the population. In such circumstances national statistics are known to offer only limited coverage of informal income and production, factors which account for a sizeable fraction of the economy. Due to these limitations, we propose to utilize household surveys in representative communities throughout the country to yield micro-level data on income and expenditure in household accounts, on participation in the underground labour market, and on the mechanisms by which food and household goods reach the consumer.

There are several reasons for our decision to include micro-level data wherever possible. First, as has been suggested above, macro-level data may be less reliable, due to the many problems associated with compiling accurate national statistics in a country with limited data management resources. Secondly, national data, even if accurate, may be of limited utility in analysing the second economy due to the existence of major regional and urban/rural differences in the ways in which households satisfy their daily economic requirements. (The transitional nature of Tanzanian society and the imperfect penetration of official economic institutions to remote regions both contribute to such differences.) Thirdly, the micro-survey methods are desirable because they allow us to focus on the economic experiences of the different social classes, and particularly the rural peasants and urban proletariat who constitute the majority of Tanzanians.

In this section we report the results of the household survey which relate only to the magnitude of the overall activity in the second economy as estimated by the income–expenditure discrepancy approach. In the next chapters we look more closely into the sectoral manifestations of the second economy, participation in the underground labour and product markets, and the mechanisms by which food and household goods reach the consumer. The survey covered 1,200 households scattered in ten regions of Tanzania and covered both rural and urban areas. The ten regions were purposively selected to reflect the diverse patterns of income levels, surplus and deficit food supply and consuming areas, locational conditions and overall regional economic potential. The main purpose was to establish a representative sample of households for the whole country. In each region, the selection of the villages in which the households were located, and that of the specific households, was random. In urban areas the selection of the household was specific, with the intention of capturing different occupational groups (i.e. wage earners, self-employed and traders), and also a representative economic and area distribution.

Briefly, the estimation method consists of identifying and listing all sources of factor incomes for each private household and ascertaining their values. These values are then compared with the household's expenditure on goods and factor services. In each case both monetary and non-monetary sources and disposal of incomes were considered. The major income sources and expenditure categories are listed in Table 2.6 (page 148). The corresponding income and expenditure figures have been computed separately for rural and urban locations. The results show that among urban households 39 per cent of their total expenditures could not be explained. In rural areas the income–expenditure discrepancy among households was 36 per cent. When these estimates are extrapolated the resulting national income discrepancy is 36.5 per cent. When our estimate of private consumption expenditure for 1986 is compared with the official estimate for that year, the results show that the official private consumption estimate is understated by 30 per cent. It may then reasonably be generalized that on average 30 per cent of the economic activity is not accounted for in the official statistics and hence, for 1986, about T.Shs 39 billion worth of economic activities took place in the second economy.

It is important to note, however, that such an estimate of the second economy is very conservative and should be regarded as the lower boundary for unreported income. This is true despite our estimate including some imputed income from bartering activities. There is definitely some unreported income that does not show up as expenditure (for example, income from criminal or immoral earnings and spent on such related activities). The results, however, are quite remarkably similar to those arrived at using the monetary approach, further reinforcing our belief that the second economy is thriving in Tanzania.

Nevertheless, the information presented in Table 2.6 should be interpreted with caution. The observed averages mask important variations in income sources and expenditure outlays by individual households involved in different occupations. For example, the relatively high share of wages and salaries (59 per cent) in total urban household incomes is partly attributed to the large number of full-time formal wage earners (73 per cent) in the sample. Partly, it is also attributed to the inclusion of informal wages and salaries.

A more detailed breakdown reveals that, in 1986, an average full-time self-employed person earned a monthly income of T.Shs 7,300; an average full-time formal wage earner received T.Shs 2,000 per month; while a full-time wage earner also involved in part-time informal activity earned about T.Shs 4,500 per month. Considering a typical urban household of six members, with the household head working full-time in formal employment, the spouse taking care of domestic tasks and four school-going aged dependants, the monthly wage of T.Shs 2,000 could hardly meet the minimum monthly expenses of about T.Shs 5,000. At most, the formal wage could only keep the family going for 12 out of the 30 days in the month. Consequently, supplementary incomes from second economy activities had of necessity to be resorted to if massive starvation was to be averted. This basically explains why most formal wage earners have more than one job, why an increasing number of wage earners are turning to self-employment opportunities and, as we will show in Chapter 3, why there is an increasing role of barter whereby foodstuffs brought from villages by visiting relatives are reciprocated with gifts from the city.

3

Sectoral Manifestations of the Second Economy

Chapter 2 attempted to measure the importance of the second economy focusing mainly on its relative size in relation to the official economy. In this chapter we shall try to establish the various manifestations of the second economy in three important sectors of the economy – in agriculture, industry, and in the internal and external trade sectors. The objective is to establish not the relative sectoral magnitudes of the second economy, but the various forms in which the second economy may reveal itself. Once these forms have been identified it is then possible for policy makers to design specific policies directed at correcting the particular imbalance or distortion.

The previous chapter has already identified two macro-level manifestations of the second economy – namely, discrepancies between income and expenditures, and evidence visible in monetary aggregates. To these we shall add three other forms: (i) evidence in the form of discrepancies between what is produced, consumed, and officially marketed; (ii) evidence in the form of a discrepancy between official prices or exchange rates and unofficial prices or exchange rates, and (iii) evidence revealed by differences in official and unofficial marketing channels. Our analysis will have to take into consideration the behaviour and decisions made by producers, buyers and sellers in the whole economy – that is, in the private official sector, the public sector and the second economy.

3.1 Agriculture

This section focuses on the various manifestations of the second economy in the agricultural sector. Partly because of the importance of food in the basic needs basket and partly because of availability of comparable data, our analysis draws mainly on evidence concerning the production, distribution and consumption of food crops, particularly the major preferred staples of maize and rice. Maize is the most important food crop grown by more than 50 per cent of Tanzanian peasants for both subsistence and commercial use. Maize is also the dominant source of calorie intake in the country, accounting for 61 per cent of total calorie intake. Rice is also an important subsistence crop in Tanzania, and second only to maize in terms of volume and value of crops marketed officially. Rice contributes about 10 per cent of the total (nationwide) calorie intake. It is, however, much more important in urban areas where it provides almost a quarter of total calories.

Various manifestations of the second economy in the food crop sub-sector relate to pricing, procurement and crop distribution systems as well as to overall production and consumption patterns.

It is crucial that we look at how much the crop produced is consumed on-farm, how much is sold through official (Co-operative Unions and National Milling Corporation – NMC) channels and at what prices, and how much is marketed through alternative (thereafter parallel) market channels and at what prices. The existence of second economy transactions will be indicated by (i) the unexplained residual between the quantity of crop produced, what is consumed on-farm and what is officially marketed; (ii) the difference between official and parallel market prices, and (iii) the existence of parallel marketing channels.

3.1.1   Government Intervention Mechanisms

Government intervention mechanisms in the agricultural sector have operated at three levels: at the level of production, marketing and distribution, and price setting. At the level of production Government intervention dates back to colonial times. The German and British colonial administrators in Tanzania used brutal force and taxation to compel subsistence peasants to switch to commercial agriculture. The major aim of the colonial Governments was to maximize surplus extraction (in the form of foreign exchange earned through cash crop sales), and to get the necessary raw materials for their home-based industries.

After independence there was a series of Government attempts to mobilize individual peasants into *ujamaa* (communal) villages in order to develop backward agriculture by exploiting economies of scale; to search for the most cost-effective way of providing social services to hitherto scattered rural populations, or to encourage communal production and more grass-root participation in the decision making process. In addition, there was also the usually hidden motive: to facilitate the extraction and appropriation of surplus, from subsistence agriculture to state consumption. However, the actual implementation of such programmes has been plagued by planning, financial, administrative and organizational problems.

First of all, some peasants were certainly not happy with Government's action of abandoning its earlier strategy of voluntary inducement to move to specially designated villages in favour of compulsion, which began to be exercised early in 1974 through 'Operation Sogeza'. Sites for the new villages were in most cases centrally and hastily selected without consulting peasants, and were often chosen on such general criteria as being near roads and having sufficient land to support at least 300 families.[1] No serious considerations were given to soil fertility, potential natural hazards or availability of pasture.

Peasants were further frustrated by exhortations from the Government, especially during the 1973–5 economic crisis, which decreed that peasants plant at least three acres of food crops and a minimum of one acre of cash crop. Moreover, once peasants were settled in the new villages they faced a situation of increasing risk and uncertainty. Over time there has been pressure on land which could only be offset by intensive farming methods. But as already mentioned, fertilizers and other key agricultural inputs have not been forthcoming and a situation of labour involution has set in. Increased risk also arises because labour time is sometimes diverted to communal activities that are less productive than household activities. For individual farmers, the absence of land leases has meant increased insecurity of land tenure and has acted as a disincentive to further investment in agriculture.[2]

That the peasants in *ujamaa* villages were dissatisfied is clearly reflected in their gradual withdrawal from participating in communal production. In fact the level of communal production in the villages was so low that as early as 1972 Government issued a directive which permitted and thereafter popularized block farming in addition to individual and communal farming. At that time block farming was considered more acceptable to peasants than communal farming because it combined the tapping of individual efforts and initiatives (for example, during weeding and harvesting) with advantages of large-scale co-operative farming (for instance, using a communally rented or owned tractor for land tilling). Later on, especially after 1973, the idea of communalization was shelved, and, for instance, was not considered as a necessary condition for the establishment of the new development villages. This is categorically stated in the 1975 'Villages and *Ujamaa* Villages Act' which specifies certain levels of communal activity to be achieved before a village legally qualifies as an *ujamaa* village.

Thus the villages established after 1973 were 'development villages created to facilitate infrastructure delivery rather than socialist villages undertaking collective production'.[3] Collier *et al.* quote a Government communiqué issued in January 1978 which announced that of the 7,400 villages in the United Republic of Tanzania not one of them was *ujamaa*.[4]

Although in the short run villagization might have caused disruption in peasants' production schedules, possibly resulting in short-term output declines, its long-term effect on aggregate output and productivity is not clear to us. We have a strong feeling, however, that Government's failure to stimulate communal production and services was one of the causes which facilitated the growth of the second economy. In the first place, the de-emphasis on communal production has provided a loophole for relatively wealthy peasants to acquire administrative powers in the organizational structures of the villages. And as Coulson[5] has pointed out, this group has behaved as an elite, fostering personal and individualistic interests and thus thwarting further efforts towards egalitarianism. For example, although the Village Council is legally empowered to redistribute land in accordance with the interests of the village members, Putterman[6] argues that in practice private claims to land override village land rights. Given the high rates of growth of rural population and the fact that some villages were badly situated in areas with little suitable arable land, land shortage is increasingly becoming a major constraint. This is indeed a potential source of land speculation in the rural areas.

Secondly, as peasants concentrated more on individual and block farming it became increasingly difficult, particularly for the less interested village governments, to monitor what was being produced by individual peasants, and even more difficult to ensure that the agricultural surplus was being marketed through the officially established marketing channels. Government's failure to implement fully the *ujamaa* programme is another clear indication of its declining social controls over the economy. When these factors are put together with those mentioned earlier regarding lack of appropriate incentives to farmers then the incentive for farmers to continue participating in the official economy becomes weaker and weaker.

Official intervention in the marketing, distribution and pricing of cereal grains in Tanzania can be traced back to the colonial period. During the Second World War, Cereal Boards were established in Kenya, Tanganyika (now Tanzania) and Uganda with the objectives of guaranteeing stable prices to producers, to rationalize internal trade, to achieve food self-sufficiency, and to build surpluses for meeting post-war shortages in other countries of the sterling bloc. When the war ended control continued to be exercised through the marketing boards. These boards had monopoly power to buy and sell specific crops at fixed prices. In Tanganyika the Cereals Pool operated from 1945 to 1949. In the latter year Tanganyika withdrew from the Cereals Pool and set up its own food crop control agency known as the Grain and Storage Department (GSD). Apart from having monopoly in purchasing and marketing of food crops the GSD was also to ensure provision of storage facilities for holding working and surplus food stocks. However, following successive bumper grain harvests in 1953 and 1954 Tanzania attained food self-sufficiency and the GSD was made redundant and was formally abolished in 1955. From 1955 to 1962 the produce control policy was abandoned in favour of a free market policy.

Following independence (1961) the Party and Government, seeking to exert their influence, became increasingly involved in checking further advance of private sector entrenchment in agricultural trade. This was made even more urgent following the poor grain harvest in 1961, followed by a complete crop failure in 1962. Subsequently, Government designed a new marketing structure which gave the newly (1963) established National Agricultural Products Board (NAPB) monopoly powers in the pricing and marketing of agricultural crops. In order to encourage the development of the co-operative movement, NAPB appointed co-operative unions as agents with exclusive privilege (through their respective co-operative societies) in purchasing crops from peasants. Through this marketing arrangement, Government intended to eliminate private wholesalers, retailers and brokers in the agricultural trade.

The milling function and other food processing activities still remained the monopoly of private enterprises. However, within the Arusha Declaration spirit (1967), the milling function was also brought under state control. The eight major milling companies were nationalized and placed temporarily under NAPB until February 1968, when they were amalgamated to form the National Milling Corporation (NMC). Initially therefore, NMC was established primarily as a manufacturer, processor and importer of agricultural products.

By the early 1970s, the co-operative movement had established itself firmly – both politically and economically – particularly in the cash crop growing areas of the country. This, however, attracted the Party and Government attention which began to monitor and direct the hitherto spontaneous movement. As a first step, Government issued compulsory marketing orders which instructed that co-operatives be set up in those areas which had not developed them voluntarily. This move was intended partly to eliminate private traders, and partly to achieve parity between the more advanced and the less privileged parts of the country.

Over time however, it became obvious that the rural elite who controlled the co-operative movement were the primary beneficiaries (through corruption, fraud and mismanagement of funds) of the system. This was seen as leading to increased social differentiation – an undesirable element which jeopardized the Party and Government's aspirations for rural equity. More important, however, was the realization that the rural elite who dominated the co-operative movement posed a potential challenge to local political control.[7] Partly as a result of this and partly in order to be consistent with the 1972 policy of decentralization, agricultural marketing boards including NAPB were abolished in 1973 and replaced with semi-autonomous parastatal crop authorities. The crop authorities assumed much broader powers being responsible for supply of agricultural inputs, research, extension, purchase, sale, transport, storage and processing.

As a result, the newly (1973) established crop authorities eroded away some of the co-operatives' jurisdiction over crop collection and processing activities. The NMC, for instance, assumed crop procurement from NAPB. It was to be responsible for purchasing, processing and distributing staple grains countrywide. Additionally, NMC was also given responsibility for managing the strategic grain reserve and became responsible for imports and exports of food grains. In May 1976, the co-operative unions were finally abolished. Their previous economic functions were transferred and shared among Crop Authorities, Regional Trading Companies (RTCs) and District Development Corporations (DDCs). The primary co-operative societies which had served as procurement points for the unions were replaced by the newly established villages. These were legally instituted to act as multipurpose co-operative societies.

It was during this wave of change that, in 1975, NMC's already overextended functions were expanded through enactment of a revised NMC Act and the dissolution of NAPB. The new functions of NMC were to include the purchase, distribution and storage of all general grains and staples offered for sale. The new Act thus gave NMC monopoly power over control of maize, rice, wheat, cassava, millet, sorghum and beans. Under this legislation, private trade in these cereals beyond direct use by one's family or for small retail sales directly by farmers was illegal and punishable if detected. Road-blocks were established between districts and regions to ensure that no unauthorized inter-regional transactions in food grains took place.

In principle, NMC has little room for financial flexibility because Government determines the official prices for the crops it purchases and sells. Producer price control is another important form of Government intervention. In the early 1960s, official into-store and out-of-store prices for maize, rice and wheat were set by the marketing boards and were the same throughout the country. At that time, producer prices were set as a residual after deducting the handling charges by the co-operatives. Consequently producer prices for maize, rice and wheat were different in each region reflecting differences in the marketing margins of various co-operatives. In 1967 Government took a more active role in the pricing of food crops by transferring the authority to set into-store prices to the Economic Committee of the Cabinet. This was also considered essential in order to ensure that producer prices conformed with the country's newly announced overall wages, incomes and prices policy.

Beginning in the 1970s Government adopted a pricing methodology which set the marketing margin as a residual in order to improve the efficiency of the co-operatives. In addition, Government abandoned the practice of setting pan-territorial into-store prices and introduced a system of setting pan-territorial producer prices. According to this policy a uniform price is set for each scheduled crop, irrespective of the location of growing areas or transportation costs. Government hoped that by subsidizing transportation costs for producers located in high transport cost regions relative to the local market or export point it would encourage farmers in these remote areas to produce more for the market. In this way inter-regional income differentials would also be reduced.[8] Pan-territorial prices were to be set for maize, paddy, wheat, tobacco, cashew nuts, pyrethrum and cotton. Only cotton had had a uniform price since the mid-1960s. The policy of pan-territorial pricing was also extended to cover basic industrial consumer goods. In addition, the number of scheduled food crops was increased from maize, rice and wheat to include the drought-resistant crops of millet, sorghum and cassava. The latter move followed the poor harvest of 1973–4 and the need to guarantee peasants a fair price and market outlet for these less preferred staples. Thus in principle the policy of pan-territorial pricing was consistent with Tanzania's goal of equal development of all regions.

Overall the official agricultural price policy has sought to foster an increased supply of marketed grains by subsidizing agricultural inputs and remote producers with a view to achieving food self-sufficiency and even regional development. At the same time Government has sought to protect low income earners in urban areas by keeping food prices low through subsidies.

In practice agricultural marketing and pricing policies in Tanzania have had limited results. In the first place the efficiency of the monopolistic crop marketing parastatals including NMC has been discouraging. Odegaard has examined in detail the official crop market-ing system which operated between the mid-1970s and early 1980s and found it to be grossly inefficient in terms of (i) ensuring timely collection of peasants' produce; (ii) prompt payment of peasants for their produce; (iii) ensuring timely supply of agricultural inputs to peasants, and (iv) effectiveness in reducing collection, handling, transportation and overhead costs.[9] These inefficiencies were partly due to organizational problems such as overmanning, centralized bureaucracy, inadequate take-home pay, misappropriation of public resources and the general low morale of workers which resulted in low productivity. Part of the inefficiency was rooted in the institutional set-up, however. For example, the use of pan-territorial pricing, maintenance of an overvalued exchange rate and lack of appropriate incentives to producers have resulted in overall output declines. These inefficiencies largely explain the huge accumulated financial losses of agricultural parastatals alluded to earlier.

It is quite clear that the structure of parastatal costs between 1976 and 1984 did not provide any incentive to maximize marketed output. The cost of this inefficiency was borne not by the parastatals but directly by the farmer (through reduced producer prices) and indirectly by the general public because at times Government had to subsidize parastatal losses and consumer prices. For example, during the three-year 1981–2, 1982–3, 1983–4 period, Government subsidy to NMC alone amounted to T.Shs 939 million. NMC marketing losses were aggravated by the increasing unit cost of marketing and handling a declining volume of officially marketed output. As these subsidies were mainly absorbed by the Government through running a budgetary deficit, there was a tremendous squeeze on real resources as the Government deficit widened every year, further aggravating inflationary pressures. The strained liquidity position of NMC largely explains why peasants were not paid cash upon delivery of crops – a major factor contributing to their lack of trust in the official marketing system. Indeed in 1984 President Nyerere publicly admitted that the dissolution of co-operatives in 1976 was one of the wrong decisions made by his Government.[10]

Secondly, given the relatively high level of inflation in the 1980s the increases in nominal producer prices have been more than offset by increases in the rate of inflation, resulting in a marked decline in real prices received by producers. Producer price indexes for various categories of agricultural products are summarized in Table 3.1, page 149. The overall index for all agricultural crops declined from the mid-1970s until 1982–3. Since then it has been rising consistently. Between 1976 and 1984 producer prices for the major staples have been strongly influenced by the need to protect the cost of living of urban consumers. Thus nominal increases in producer prices were usually associated with increased subsidization of consumer prices. Hence, final producer prices for the major staples were politically determined and were largely dependent on revenue available for subsidies and the cost of living among urban wage earners. The substantial decline in real producer prices of the predominant staples partly reflected the growing difficulties of the Government in subsidizing urban consumer prices.

Since 1984, real prices for the predominant staples have been substantially increased reflecting Government's desire to stimulate food production and to encourage the sale of grains into the official marketing system. Yet real producer prices for both exports and domestic crops still remain below their 1977–8 peak levels.

Lastly, Government policy of subsidizing agricultural inputs, especially fertilizers, did not generally result in increased output, except in a few regions such as Rukwa, Ruvuma, Iringa and Mbeya. Even there the beneficiaries of input subsidization have been the few large-scale farmers – a factor which prompted Government to remove the subsidy on fertilizers in 1986. It should be emphasized that the ineffectiveness of the agricultural input subsidization policy was largely due to the absence of an effective system of enforcing official subsidized prices. The result was that many peasants obtained such inputs in the parallel market at abnormally high prices.

An important effect of Government's attempt to enforce monopolistic marketing and producer price control has been the development of the parallel markets. A combination of acute food grains shortfalls, deterioration in the official marketing system reflected in its failure to collect peasants' produce in time and to effect their cash payment promptly, and unfavourable producer prices, coupled with Government's failure to effectively enforce the monopolistic marketing and price control programmes, led to the development of the parallel (thereafter second economy) food markets, particularly for the predominant staples of maize, rice and to some extent wheat.

3.1.2   The Second Economy Food Markets

How then have Tanzanian peasant households reacted to the various Government control policies? First it must be recognized that there is now sufficient evidence – casual, anecdotal and empirical – to show that the conventional paradigm which treats smallholder peasants as being passive, inert, and irresponsive to change, innovation and incentives once they have achieved the minimum psychological levels of consumption does not hold in the Tanzanian context. For example, the results of our survey show that in a sample of 500 smallholder producers scattered in ten regions of Tanzania, when peasants were asked why they had not expanded their farm acreage for the past two years, 85 per cent of the respondents indicated that it was not profitable to do so. Odegaard[11] has also shown that remote and high transport cost regions such as Rukwa and Ruvuma have benefited significantly from inter-regional crop subsidization made possible by the policy of pan-territorial pricing. He points out that such revenue gains have been crucial in explaining why these regions have increased their share of official purchases of maize from about 2 per cent prior to 1973 to about 30 per cent after that period. Also, a number of studies have found a significant positive response of the marketed surplus to own and relative price changes.[12]

There are probably very few farmers who produce purely for subsistence consumption. Most smallholder peasants consciously plan production partly for household consumption and partly for sale in the market. They therefore participate in the market by choice. This choice depends mainly on three things: prevailing market prices (in conjunction with household preferences as they relate to both farm and consumer goods), risk and uncertainty, and ease of access to the market. Ease of access to markets is important because delays imply extra storage costs, additional losses due to pests and shrinkage, and non-availability of cash to purchase farm inputs and basic consumer goods. Producer prices are crucial because farming is risky in that returns in any given year can be much above or below the average levels. Typically, however, farmers tend to be moderately risk-averse in the sense that they prefer stable income streams (even though these might be at a lower level) to unstable ones. Since a major source of farmers' income is derived from the sale of crops, measures that stabilize producer prices should encourage farmers to produce more. Risk and uncertainty are also important in determining the amount of crop to be sold in the official market. Sales in the second economy (parallel) markets involve risk. Both buyers and sellers face the risk of penalties if they are caught and a loss of income if they have to bribe their way out. These two aspects imply that generally a higher price prevails in the parallel market than in the official market.

Although there were price controls on maize, rice and wheat, and the distribution of these cereals is confined to public institutions, this study found that private trade in scheduled cereals is significant throughout the country. According to Odegaard[13] trade in scheduled crops outside the official marketing system became much more pronounced after the mid-1970s. Prior to 1983, price control enforcement was fairly successful. Temporary grain shortfalls (which were rare) were easily met by imports and did not significantly affect the administratively set prices. Grain surpluses (which were not uncommon) were either used to build up modest reserves or were exported. However, the situation changed after the 1973–4 drought and the concurrent oil shock. These resulted in critical grain shortfalls which could not be adequately covered by imports because the country's foreign reserves were insufficient. The emerging excess demand exerted a tremendous upward pressure on official prices and second economy markets began to develop. This is clearly reflected in Table 3.2 (page 149) which shows a declining share of scheduled cereals marketed through NMC, particularly for the 1978–9 – 1984–5 period.

For example, for the period 1974–5 to 1979–80, the capacity of NMC to meet urban food demands was on the average 72.8 per cent for mainland Tanzania. This average veils important regional variations, however. Whereas it was 80 per cent for Dar es Salaam and 40 per cent for Mwanza it was only 13.6 per cent in Mbeya town.[14] Because NMC's purchases of maize and rice were falling, this meant that urban demand was largely met from imports which constituted 70 per cent of its sembe sales, 68 per cent of wheat and 81 per cent of rice sales for the 1981–2 marketing year. Nevertheless, the 20–30 per cent shortfall in urban food demand suggests that it was met from parallel markets and own source (food grown by urban households and some bartered food with the rural or up-country areas).

The structures of the second economy food markets show important differences in terms of space and organization. This study has found that apart from the official marketing channels (i.e. through NMC), there are at least five other food marketing arrangements. First, there is the 'traditional' food market. This involves trade in both scheduled controlled and non-scheduled food crops (such as pulses, starches, fruits and vegetables) between members of one village or nearby villages. Transactions in this trade are carried out primarily for compensating shortfalls in particular farm households. They may thus be regarded as part of the subsistence consumption. In the 'traditional' food market transactions may take place at the farm as direct sales by peasants or at an established local market place (and hence involving other family members). Traditional food markets have existed in most villages for a long time. Although trade in scheduled food crops in the traditional food market is primarily meant for meeting personal consumption needs, some traders buy scheduled food from peasants for resale purposes. The latter trading practice was illegal before 1986. In practice, it is difficult to make a distinction between the two forms of trade, which insulates marketeers from official detection.

Secondly, there is the 'shuttle' food market. This involves some members of the family ferrying one to three bags of grain by bus or lorry to the nearby town which promises a higher price than the one at the traditional food market. When returning from town, peasants take the opportunity to buy other consumer goods which are not available in the village, or if available are expensive. Other participants in this market are town dwellers who buy from producers in cash or kind and carry food away with them during their up-country travels.

Thirdly, there is the 'inter-regional' food market. This usually involves bulk shipment of food commodities from one region to another by unlicensed traders for resale purposes. Some traders in this market are habitual in the sense that they have specialized in this trade; some, however, are 'occasional' in the sense that they happen to be transporting other goods inland and rather than returning empty they return with grain. Although it has been difficult to establish the exact volume involved in the inter-regional trade in food commodities, the direction of food transfers is quite clear. Our survey data, coupled with information generated by the Market Information Services (within MDB), seem to indicate that generally food grains flow from surplus to deficit regions (see Figure 3.1, page 150). In the case of maize, the surplus regions are mainly Arusha, Iringa, Mbeya, Rukwa and Ruvuma. Arusha region normally supplies Tanga, Dodoma, Dar, Mwanza and Mara regions. Rukwa supplies the north-western regions. Tabora supplies Kigoma. Mbeya and Iringa supply Dar, Morogoro and Dodoma. Ruvuma feeds Lindi and Mtwara. In the case of rice and paddy, Ruvuma supplies Mtwara and Lindi. Mbeya, Morogoro and Coast supply Dar. Mbeya also supplies Rukwa, while Mwanza and Tabora supply Kagera, Kigoma and Mara.

Closely connected to the inter-regional food market is the 'urban' or 'soko' open market. The urban open market, like the traditional food market, has been in existence for quite a long time. In large towns such as Dar es Salaam, Arusha, Tanga and Mwanza there are several open market places. Generally, the urban open food market mainly involves trade between urban residents. They buy bags of grain from inter-regional food truckers, national distributors, or from NMC for retailing in open urban markets. Food commodities may be bought in processed or unprocessed form, and may be sold in either form. Generally the volume of trade handled by urban food markets has grown year after year. In Dar es Salaam, for example, it is estimated that the volume of trade has been growing at an annual average of between 25 and 30 per cent for the period 1970–80 – a higher rate than the city's population growth-rate.[14]

Lastly there is the 'export market' where crops are smuggled out of the country. Cross-border transactions involving food crops are common along the Tanzania/Kenya border (involving Arusha, Kilimanjaro and Mara regions); and the borders with Burundi (Kigoma region) and Uganda (Kagera region). Food crops are normally exchanged against industrial consumer goods. Cross-border transactions are not a new phenomenon, however. What is new about this trade is its dramatic increase, both in volume and in its growth beyond the traditional exchange of goods. The political boundaries dividing Tanzania from her neighbours were drawn up by the former colonial powers. These borders were arbitrarily drawn without regard to tribal or ethnic affiliation. The Tanzania/Kenya/Uganda borders, for example, artificially separate people who share a common language and culture. In some cases (e.g. the Haya along the border with Uganda and the Masai along the Kenyan border) members of the same family live on both sides of the border. As a result such border populations tend to ignore rules of international trade in their trading transactions. Interviews with a sample of traders at

Namanga (along the Tanzania/Kenya border) and at Kyaka (along the Tanzania/Uganda border) revealed, however, that cross-border trade is no longer confined to people living near these borders. In the area around Namanga 75 per cent of the traders had no tribal or ethnic affiliations with the neighbouring Kenyan tribes. 45 per cent of these came from regions outside Arusha. In Kyaka area 32 per cent of the traders were in no way related to people living near the border.

Perhaps a good example of the existence of a large second economy food market is that shown by Tanga, Kilimanjaro and Morogoro regions. Table 3.3 (page 151) shows that in 1976-7 NMC purchases of maize grain from the three regions amounted to 36,100 metric tons and accounted for 28.3 per cent of NMC's total purchases from 20 regions. Tanga alone contributed 20,800 tonnes (about 16.3 per cent of the Corporation regional purchases). However, five years later NMC's procurement of maize grain had dropped from 36,100 to 956 tonnes, accounting for just 1.2 per cent of NMC's regional purchases. The 1986-7 figures show that the share of the three regions in NMC total maize grain purchases stagnated at the 1980-1 level. Data from the World Bank's agricultural sector report for Tanzania further reveal that, whereas, in 1974-5, 91.1 per cent of Tanga City's food needs were met by sales from NMC, this percentage had dropped by 24.4 per cent in 1979-80.[15]

There is no evidence to indicate that the decline in official procurement of maize grain from Tanga, Kilimanjaro and Morogoro was associated with a fall in per capita maize production. In fact, per capita maize production in the three regions remains among the best in the country.[16] It seems most probable then that the fall in official procurement reflects increases in second economy food market sales especially after the introduction of a pan-territorial pricing policy. In effect, pan-territorial pricing penalized regions with least transport costs and subsidized regions with high transport costs. Peasants in low-cost transport regions experienced a *de facto* fall in producer prices. This may explain why peasants in Tanga and Kilimanjaro (with their large urban demand and border with Kenya) and Morogoro (with easy access to a sizeable Dar es Salaam city market) had to resort to selling grains in the second economy food market where prices were more than twice the official producer prices. Peasants in remote, high-cost transport regions like Iringa, Rukwa and Ruvuma, however, experienced a *de facto* rise in the prices they received under a pan-territorial pricing policy, and so had an incentive to increase production and sales to the official marketing agents. In 1986-7 the four Southern Highland regions of Iringa, Mbeya, Rukwa and Ruvuma accounted for an estimated 42 per cent of estimated total maize production in the country, and 63 per cent of NMC total regional purchases. Rukwa and Ruvuma which provided a mere 2-3 per cent of total official maize purchases in the early 1970s presently account for over 30 per cent of NMC purchases.

3.1.3   The Magnitude of the Second Economy in the Food Crop Sub-sector

Estimates of the relative magnitude of the second economy in the food crop sub-sector are made difficult by the absence of production and subsistence consumption figures. There are virtually no figures on actual crop production because crop-cutting surveys have not been carried out. Only estimates are available, and these lack reliable information on post-harvest losses and inter-season carry-over stocks. Year-to-year production fluctuations which reflect changes in weather and Government policy make estimates of crop production even more unreliable. Apart from the 1968–9 and 1976–7 household budget surveys, no consistent time series data exist on on-farm consumption. Official estimates of food crops sales show only the volume of crops marketed through official channels and therefore exclude crop sales to private legal and illegal channels. Data on food crop production and consumption are even more limited for food crops other than maize, rice and wheat. Our focus in this section will be on maize and rice where data problems are less severe.

A useful indicator of the magnitude of the second economy in the food crop sub-sector is the unexplained residual which remains after subtracting consumption on-farm and official market surplus from estimated total production. Available estimates suggest that the residual factor is large. For example, Temu[17] estimates that between 1964 and 1974 about 70 per cent of total maize produced was consumed on-farm, 10 per cent was sold through official marketing channels and the remaining 20 per cent was sold through legal and illegal private market outlets. This shows that for each 100 kg of marketable maize surplus, about 67 per cent was sold outside the official marketing channel. Estimates by Keeler et al.[18] suggest that, on average, NMC supply of food in urban areas was sufficient to meet between 70 and 80 per cent of urban food needs. The balance of between 20 and 30 per cent was met from second economy markets and own urban farming sources.

The proportion of maize marketed through second economy food markets has varied every year depending on weather conditions and the level of official producer prices. Odegaard's study[19] suggests that 80–85 per cent of maize production is consumed on-farm, leaving a marketable surplus of between 15 and 20 per cent. Odegaard finds that in a normal year about 70 per cent of marketed maize surplus is channelled through second economy food markets. However, when harvest is bad as in 1974–5, the proportion of maize sold outside official channels may rise to well over 90 per cent while in years of bumper harvest, as in 1977–8, it may fall below 50 per cent. In another survey Bevan et al.[20] found that only 18 per cent of crop sales were made outside the official market.

More consistent estimates of the distribution of production between on-farm consumption, official sales to NMC and other outlets have been provided by the MDB, which uses crop production estimates provided by Kilimo's Early Warning and Crop Monitoring Project in the Ministry of Agriculture. Estimates on subsistence consumption and marketed production are based on the 1976–7 household budget survey and the ongoing Kilimo research. These estimates, although useful, do not adequately take into account post-harvest losses and inter-year carry-over stocks.

According to MDB estimates, an average of 80 per cent of maize production and 50 per cent of paddy production are consumed on the farm. Of the 20 per cent marketed surplus only 5 per cent of total production is sold through official marketing agents, while the remaining 15 per cent (or 75 per cent of marketed surplus) is sold in the second economy food market. However, in years with abundant supplies (for example 1985–6), MDB estimates that the share of marketed maize production in total production rises from 20 to 25 per cent. About 64 per cent of marketed maize surplus (or 16 per cent of total production) is therefore sold in the second economy market.

Table 3.4 (page 151), which is based on estimates from MDB, provides information on the proportions of maize and rice going to both official and second economy food markets (SEFOMA). It is evident from Table 3.4 that the second economy food markets have handled a significant proportion of maize and rice. On average, between 1971–2 and 1986–7 these SEFOMA have handled about two-thirds of marketed maize surplus and over four-fifths of marketed rice annually. Official purchases fell sharply between 1981 and 1985, reflecting a combination of bad weather, increased inefficiencies in the official marketing system and diminished incentives to producers. While official purchases of maize increased in 1985–6, official NMC purchases of rice continued to fall.

In addition to data available at the macro level, we have carried out detailed investigations seeking to establish levels of production, consumption and disposal of marketed food surplus among a sample of 50 peasant households in each of the three major food-producing regions. Table 3.5 (page 153) summarizes the information thus gathered in terms of mean weighted proportions. This information was collected during 1984–5. Although the overall regional average for the proportion of maize and rice sold through parallel food markets is consistently slightly lower than the national average (Table 3.4), these figures provide added evidence of the existence of second economy food markets. As the MDB has observed, 'The parallel market for grain is important because it is the means by which the majority of food grains are bought and sold in Tanzania.'[21]

3.1.4 Second Economy Food Market Prices

Our survey data, those generated by MDB's Market Information Services and Odegaard's estimates[22] consistently reveal that although prices in the second economy food markets vary from one region to another and from one place to another within the same region, they have always been higher than officially set prices. Comparing official and parallel market prices for 13 Lake region villages in 1979–80 and 1980–81, and for 13 districts in 1980, Keeler et al.[23] found that parallel market prices were usually two to four times higher than official producer prices. Time-series data on changes in producer prices of maize and rice are only available from 1982. However, the limited evidence available does confirm that prior to the 1984–5 marketing season both producer and consumer prices for foods handled by NMC were substantially higher on second economy markets than on official markets.

Figures 3.2 and 3.3 (page 152) summarize the recent developments in the average official and unofficial (second economy) producer prices for maize and paddy. Second economy market prices for maize reached peak levels in early 1984 with an average farm-gate price of T.Shs 13 (four times higher than the prevailing official producer price). Since then open market prices have been declining. Second economy market prices for paddy fell in mid-1985 but have shown a rising trend since then. The average second economy farm-gate price of rice during 1985–6 was about 3.5 times higher than the official price paid by NMC. These figures mask important regional variations, however. Our survey during September–December 1985 showed that second economy prices for maize were T.Shs 6.50 per kg in Moshi, T.Shs 11.00 in Musoma and T.Shs 4.00 per kg in Mbeya. The average second economy price per kilogram of rice was T.Shs 19.85 during 1985–6. Our survey results showed that corresponding prices were T.Shs 14 in Moshi, T.Shs 15 in Mbeya and T.Shs 25 per kg in Musoma.

Table 3.6 (page 153) gives the evolution of consumer prices for maize grain and rice for the period 1970–1 – 1986–7. It shows that generally second economy market prices have until recently been much higher than official prices. The higher prices partly reflect the forces of supply and demand, partly the higher transport and distribution costs which informal traders have to pay, partly the higher unofficial producer prices, and partly increasing risk and uncertainty which second economy transactions entail. The problem of excess demand is real and has been exacerbated partly by high rates of population growth with falling per capita food production.[24] In part, excess demand for grains is attributed to increased demand for locally brewed beer, which appears to be largely a function of drastic shortfalls in modern beer production and the subsequent steep rise in its price.

Recent developments, particularly after 1986, have not only resulted in ample supplies of grains but also, in the case of maize, in second economy prices which were on average below official levels. NMC's purchases of maize, the major staple, rose by almost 2.5 times between 1984 and 1987 - i.e. from 71 to 173 thousand metric tons (Table 3.2). According to MDB in 1986-7 official purchases of maize and rice were above target. By March 1987 NMC's maize stocks had reached a record level of about 200,000 tons. This was partly made possible by substantial increases in estimated production of maize which rose by almost 1.5 times between 1983 and 1987. Increased supply of maize is also corroborated by consumer price movements in the second economy food markets. In the 1986-7 season, for example, the average price of food grain in the parallel market was only T.Shs 10.35 per kg - just 85 per cent of the official price (the unofficial price in 1984 was 2.1 times the official level). However, at the time of writing (1988), the parallel market prices for rice are still well above official price levels, increases in production largely reflecting absolute shortfalls in this most preferred staple crop.

Increases in production and official sales of maize and rice are the result of a combination of positive factors. Weather remained favourable for the period 1984-8. The impact of substantial increases in producer prices, although not decisive, cannot be ignored. Estimates by MDB show that they resulted in a corresponding increase of about 111 per cent in the daily return to labour between 1984 and 1987. A more flexible approach, which recognizes the role of private traders in the retailing of food staples, has also had a positive effect in reducing the dispersion of second economy market prices, thus facilitating increased food flows in both rural and urban areas. Government measures to reform the food crop marketing system (for example, by re-establishing co-operatives) have yet to bear the intended fruits. Both co-operative unions and NMC continue to incur high marketing costs which are translated into higher consumer prices. Inefficiency in food distribution is increasingly becoming a major source of inflationary pressures through both the resultant higher consumer prices and the increased credit requirement by NMC, co-operative unions and other marketing boards.

What the preceding analysis has shown is that in Tanzania emphasis on the importance of incentives as a factor in stimulating agricultural performance is not misplaced. With increased urbanization, and the growing demand for cash, the commercial market for food crops has grown. Food production is no longer viewed simply as a means of sustenance but also as a source of cash income for the majority of peasants. But when inflation has eroded the real value of farmers' official earnings from the sale of crops, and where procurement and payment are excessively delayed by the ineffectiveness of the public marketing institution, one cannot expect a farmer, being a rational producer, to continue participating in the official economy; at least not where alternative marketing channels exist. In such circumstances a necessary condition for increased output and improved sales through official channels is a realistic producer pricing system and the restoration of a flow of incentive goods and inputs into rural markets.

These short-term measures should not be allowed to distract attention from other structural constraints to agricultural growth. Reliance on rain-fed agriculture has meant increased vulnerability to drought. The backward technology of hoe-farming and the underdeveloped research infrastructure suggest only a limited chance for access to the Green Revolution technology of the Asian style. Above all, improved food production and distribution presuppose extensive infrastructural development in transport and communications, storage and processing capacity. Corrective measures are urgently needed in this area, particularly when Tanzania has moved from a food deficit to a food surplus situation. They are also needed because the deterioration of infrastructures, especially roads and capital equipment, has contributed significantly to increases in marketing costs incurred by official marketing agencies, and led to increases in marketing margins. This of course has tended to neutralize the positive effects of increased producer prices.

At the institutional level there is need to alter the composition of units. There are two important areas where restructuring of the food marketing system is necessary. First, the market agents need to be strengthened, and secondly the marketing chain needs to be streamlined. NMC has neither the administrative nor the financial capacity to monopolize the procurement, processing and distribution of food grains. Therefore Government's restoration of co-operative unions (in 1982) with the primary responsibility for crop procurement, storage and delivery to marketing centres should be viewed as a positive step towards rationalizing crop marketing arrangements. Since 1988 Government has gone even further. Co-operative unions have been allowed to be involved in inter-regional trade in maize and other drought cereals, a function which has so far been monopolized by the NMC and RTCs. This is deemed necessary because both NMC and RTCs have been dummies in performing this function. They have often failed to cope with the volume of commodities allocated to them, mainly because of lack of funds. As a result consumers in rural areas have experienced artificial shortages, a factor which has fuelled the growth of second economy transactions. Allowing co-operative unions to be involved in inter-regional trade is crucial, particularly in food deficit regions or during temporary grain shortfalls, for this would permit the co-operative union in a deficit region to procure grains from another co-operative union in a surplus region, or from the NMC if grain is imported by the latter.

Yet the responsibilities of procuring produce from growers and distributing food in the region will be formidable at least for the early years of the co-operatives' establishment. Thus during the interim period of infancy it will be advisable for the Government to explicitly allow licensed private traders to distribute food from co-operatives in surplus regions to deficit regions. In fact during 1986–7 private traders were the cheapest source of staples. Co-operatives could be encouraged to establish recognized agents to perform this function. Although Government indicated as early as 1987 that private traders could take part in the distribution of grains, no legal licensing procedures have been instituted – a situation which creates uncertainty among participants and hence raises the price to the consumer in order to hedge against any possible penalty.

Since June 1988 the role of NMC has been limited to the control of trade in rice and wheat, commercial buying and selling of limited quantities of maize, cassava, millet, beans and sorghum, and milling on a commercial basis. NMC is also responsible for maintaining the Strategic Grain Reserve whose purpose is to ensure adequate grain reserves for emergency situations and deficit areas. The decontrol of maize and other minor grains would mean the number of times these commodities were handled in the marketing chain from the farmer to the consumer would be reduced from about seven to four or less, because NMC and RTCs would be bypassed in the process. It also means that NMC would have to close down some of its regional offices. In turn this would reduce food marketing costs and help to keep consumer prices within reasonable limits.

The decision for Government to continue to set producer prices for all food crops and to act as a buyer and seller of last resort can be defended on the grounds that it is required to stabilize prices received by farmers especially during periods of bumper harvests. Producer prices for food crops should also continue to be set centrally because they are an important tool for agricultural policy which has wider macro-economic implications. However, in the light of past experience it is highly questionable whether Government would effectively enforce consumer prices for maize grain and rice which it also continues to set. It would be advisable to leave the consumer prices for maize grain and rice to be determined by the co-operative unions in their respective regions.

Overall the volume of the second economy in the food crop sub-sector appears to have been significant, particularly during the 1980s. In view of the scant information available about incomes derived from second economy markets very little can be said about its impact on the livelihood of peasants. Studies by Ellis[25] and Jamal[26] suggest that real cash incomes of smallholders fell almost continuously throughout the 1970s and early 1980s as receipts from official crop sales failed to keep pace with inflation, and that the rural–urban terms of trade turned against the farmer. Both estimates, however, fail to take into consideration subsistence consumption and incomes from second economy market crop sales. Indeed, the latter may have been substantial, in view of the increased channels and higher prices than those prevailing in the official market. Thus the farmers' total real incomes must certainly have been underestimated.

In fact a recent ILO study[27] which takes into consideration subsistence consumption for both farmers and urban workers argues that the rural–urban gap is narrowing. The study divides farmer and worker incomes into food and non-food items. For wage-earners, prices are assumed to affect the entire food and non-food consumption basket; while for farmers, prices affect mainly non-food items since they produce and consume their own food. On this basis it is estimated that real incomes of farmers increased by 9 per cent while those of wage-earners dropped by 50 per cent between 1973 and 1980. As a result the wage-earner–farmer gap was reduced from 3.81 in 1973–5 to 1.96 in 1980. And in 1980 urban workers' average standard of living was only 20 per cent higher than that of the rural household. This study, however, does not take into consideration the fact, which will be proven shortly, that most urban consumers have been purchasing both food and non-food items at the relatively higher unofficial prices; that also a proportion of their food consumption is derived from own-urban farms, and that the majority of urban workers supplement their formal wage earnings by other informal incomes. It might also be argued that, compared to the past, farmers have generally been worse off because their cash incomes buy much less than before, and that they are increasingly obtaining their non-food items at relatively higher second economy market prices. Thus unless we know the values of incomes derived from and expenditures spent on second economy transactions, we can only speculate about the rural–urban income gap.

We may conclude this section by observing that, although the second economy food markets destabilized the state by depriving it of the larger volume of food grains harvested, they may also be seen as having had a stabilizing effect on the total quantity of food produced. Higher second economy food prices provided incentives for increased food production, helping to reduce the gap between overall food supply and the greatly increasing food demand arising from rapid population growth, high rate of urbanization, and changes in urban diets which have been shifting away from coarse grain staples (sorghum and millets) to the more preferred staples of maize, rice and wheat. Perhaps this partly explains why during 1978-81 Tanzania was, according to FAO (1984) statistics, one of only 11 countries in which food production per capita rose, and when later, in 1982-4, it fell, the decline was slower than in the majority of countries.[28] Moreover, the existence of a sizeable second economy sector was one of the reasons which prompted the Government to embark on the recent reform seeking to rationalize agricultural pricing and marketing.

3.2 The Consumer Goods Market

This section examines two important ways in which the second economy has manifested itself in the production and distribution of industrial products - namely, gaps in supply and demand for industrial goods, and discrepancies between official and unofficial prices for basic industrial commodities. We shall also attempt to identify key policy weaknesses that could have contributed to the growth of second economy activity.

3.2.1 Control Mechanisms in Industry and Trade

There are several ways in which the Tanzanian Government has intervened to regulate the production and distribution of industrial products. These include direct controls through state ownership, allocation of foreign exchange, tariffs, industrial licensing, price controls and confinement policy. This section will examine briefly the nature and impacts of four of these regulatory policies - state ownership, price controls, industrial licensing and confinement policy. Tariff and foreign exchange policies will be discussed in the next section.

(i) Ownership and control

In response to the Arusha Declaration, the subsequent First and Second Five Year Plans placed strong emphasis on the development of public sector industries. Initially, this was achieved through nationalization of the existing major industrial enterprises. Later it increasingly took two forms: expansion of newly acquired firms and the establishment of new industrial units with full or majority ownership by the state. As early as 1965 the National Development Corporation (NDC) was established as a holding company, primarily to supervise the activities of other parastatal industrial units. But the size and complexity of industrial activities has increased tremendously since then. In 1986 for example, industrial parastatals accounted for around 47 per cent of production value-added and 48 per cent of employment in the manufacturing sector. In trade, parastatals accounted for about 53 per cent of the sector's total employment. For medium- and large-scale industries parastatals account for virtually all the production in iron and steel, cement, beer, fertilizer, refined sugar, and tobacco. In textiles the public sector accounts for 83 per cent of total output. Parastatals also account for more than two-thirds of the production in food and food products, tanneries and leather, paper, glass, rubber and basic metals.

In view of the growing size and complexity of industrial activities in the public sector it became necessary to rationalize the supervision of these activities along sectoral lines. Thus of the 54 parastatals affiliated with the Ministry of Industries and Trade, NDC supervises only 22, while others fall under the supervision of nine other holding companies. But since most of the parastatal enterprises are monopolies in their lines of operation, it also became necessary for the Government to establish a comprehensive price control system in order to limit the potential monopoly power of parastatals (and hence to protect consumers). In addition, a system of trade confinement, whereby most domestic and foreign wholesale trade operations were restricted to a few trading parastatal agencies, was established in order to prevent the emergence of private profiteering especially during situations of acute shortfalls in consumer products.

(ii) Price control

In Tanzania price control dates back to the colonial period. The post-war acute commodity shortages of 1918–20 and 1945–50 resulted in increased hoarding of consumer goods products, forcing the colonial administration to regulate commodity distribution and impose price ceilings on most consumer goods. Special Price Control Ordinances were issued in 1920 and 1951, and hoarding of products and selling above official price ceilings were declared illegal and punishable if detected. By 1951 there were about 32 classes of goods which were price-controlled, including foodstuffs, cigarettes, imported tinned milk, baby foods and motor tyres. After independence a Price Control Ordinance was passed in 1965 with three orders for fixing maximum prices for rice, wheat flour and bread. Initial signs of inflationary build-up began to emerge during 1965–7, and in 1967 Government issued the Wages, Incomes and Prices Policy which expressed the need to restrain wages, incomes and prices in order to avert further inflationary pressures. The Permanent Labour Tribunal was formed in 1967 to put into force restraining measures on increases in wages. The National Price Control Advisory Board was established in the same year to regulate consumer prices. It drew representation from consumers, trade unions, retailers, wholesalers, ministries and the Government's newly-formed State Trading

Company. The Board advised the Price Controller who was the Principal Secretary to the Ministry of Industries and Trade.

Prior to 1973 the only items under price control were rice, wheat flour, sembe, bread, khanga, grey sheeting, beer, matches, sugar, beans, jute bags and sisal bags. Up to this time the controlled prices were effectively maintained and price differences between official and unofficial prices were extremely rare. But as already pointed out, the 1973–4 drought and the 1973 oil shock resulted in excess demand which could not be sufficiently covered by imports. This exerted strong upward pressure on the prices of both controlled and uncontrolled products. The National Price Control Advisory Board, which could only provide an advisory role, was deemed to be ineffective as the difference between official and unofficial prices widened. As price rises were even higher for uncontrolled products, Government had to extend control over such products. The crisis nature of the situation, and the increasing number of controlled products caused the Government to establish the National Price Commission (NPC) in 1973. According to J.F.K. Mongi, the National Price Commissioner, the important functions of the NPC are:

(i) to determine reasonable price structures on a national basis and to provide for their orderly variation when necessary;

(ii) to ensure that prices of goods and services in Tanganyika are compatible with and conform to the principles of socialism and the political and social aspirations of the people.[29]

Initially (in 1973) the number of products under price control was 1,000. By 1978 there were 3,000. Since then the number of products and individual items under price control has declined, to 235 items (226 locally manufactured and 9 imported) in 1984, and in the 1988–9 budget, to 12 commodities. Thus up to 1985 most consumer goods (such as salt, milk, sugar, beer, soft drinks, cooking oil, radios and soap) and a significant number of intermediate inputs (for example, fertilizers, hoes, farm implements and major construction materials) were subject to price control. Although the prices of maize, rice and wheat are set by the Cabinet, the NPC has the responsibility of ensuring their supervision.

For locally manufactured products the NPC uses a cost-plus method when fixing their maximum prices. Price reviews are carried out at least once annually. After production costs have been taken into account the NPC allows a 30 per cent pre-tax rate of return on assets. Profit margins are set depending on the turnover rate. For fast-moving products they are generally lower (and average between 5 and 15 per cent for wholesale prices) than for low-turnover products (which average between 10 and 20 per cent). For most domestic products a retail margin of between 10 and 20 per cent is allowed. Imported goods are controlled by percentage margins. Importers present the cost structure, add the approved margin and take the suggested retail price for the product to the NPC for approval. For essential items controlled at national level prices are set pan-territorially. However, within regions the Regional Advisory Committees are also empowered to set prices for items which are not price controlled centrally, but which they consider essential for the region.

(iii) The confinement system

In trade, the Arusha Declaration (1967) nationalized the export–import firms and set up the State Trading Company (STC) to cater for the export–import business. Internal wholesale trade was nationalized in 1971, and STC assumed additional tasks of distributing goods into the regions. Thus by 1971, the inexperienced STC had assumed responsibilities initially carried by about 400 private importers, 400 private wholesalers and some 4,000 sub-wholesalers.[30] In 1973 STC was decentralized and reorganized into six parastatal importing companies and 18 (later 20) regional trading companies (RTCs), under the new Board of Internal Trade (BIT) management system. With the dissolution of the co-operatives in 1976, some of their functions (for example, the distribution and retailing of essential commodities in regions and districts) were passed to the already overburdened BIT. In the same year a directive on 'Operation Maduka' was passed which sought to phase out all private shops, and directed that all essential commodities would be sold in specially designated village (co-operative) shops.

Thus up to 1984, under the system of confinement the wholesale, and in some cases the retail, trade for essential domestic and imported commodities was confined to certain parastatal organizations. Producing industries – private and public – had to sell specified goods to specially designated national and regional trading companies, and were required to purchase certain inputs from (or place their purchase orders through) specific parastatal trading firms. At the national level the Ministry of Trade (through BIT) and the Bank of Tanzania (BOT) supervised the administration of this trade. BIT decided how much of the supplies should go to the regions and how much to urban centres. Once in the regions the RTCs took over BIT's role.

(iv) Effectiveness of price control and the confinement system

In principle both price control and the confinement system in Tanzania combine the objectives of ensuring overall price stability with the pursuit of equity (i.e. by protecting the average consumer against unnecessary price hikes and all forms of monopoly rents; by making sure that the consumer pays the official price, and during commodity shortfalls ensuring effective rationing). To what extent have the two policy controls been effective in achieving these broad objectives?

Two major factors have undermined the effectiveness of price control and the confinement system in Tanzania. One is the economic crisis, which can be treated as exogenous. The other is administrative capacity, which is purely an internal problem. Let us start by pointing out that in 1973 the rationale for price control was valid, and it is still valid today. There are genuine and good reasons for this. First of all the prevalence of monopolies in production (beer, cement, cigarettes, roofing sheets, etc.), services and distribution is a potential breeding ground for monopoly rents. Moreover, given the limited size of the market, and because the growth of these state monopolies has been sanctioned by the state, they are bound to remain in operation for a while. An intelligent application of price control is needed not only to limit monopoly rents, but also (and particularly where demand and supply are elastic) to force monopolies to increase output levels and/or to reduce cost of production at the administered price level. The existence of non-competitive markets would moreover tend, at least in theory, to permit more effective regulation of prices. This is because in a non-competitive market the producer can allocate output at the ceiling, in contrast to a competitive environment where the Government has to perform the impossible task of allocating output and enforcing the ceiling price. It is also easier to police a few producers than many.

In practice, the success of a price control programme depends not only on how markets are organized, but also on the characteristics of the supply schedule. Both theory and indeed the Tanzanian experience have shown that irrespective of the type of market, prices of products cannot be set and maintained by decree against the pressure of supply and demand without negative side effects. Such side effects as observed in Tanzania have been second economy sales, loss of quality, redefinition of products and reduction in output. This happens because when price control is set at a level below the clearing rate excess demand results. And since in Tanzania foreign exchange shortages have meant that the shortfall in demand could not be covered by imports, potential rents have been created as the unsatisfied market becomes willing to pay above the controlled price. Trade has taken place in the second economy where pressures of supply and demand and the increased risk of detection have dictated a higher price than one set administratively.

Shortages in industrial intermediate inputs and consumer goods in Tanzania have been real – both at the production level and at the consuming end. While capacity creation has continued to expand, capacity underutilization has been rising, suggesting that the newly created capacity has not been translated into additional output.[31] Table 3.7 (page 154) shows that since the mid-1970s the structure of Tanzania's imports has shifted from intermediate goods (essential for sustaining existing capacity utilization levels) to capital goods (for the expansion of capacity). By 1987 installed capacity in the intermediate and capital goods industries had reached two-thirds of total industrial capacity. This massive expansion in industrial capacity is consistent with the long-term industrial strategy (1975–1995) which places strong emphasis on building basic industries with strong sectoral linkages. While installed capacity in the intermediate and capital goods sectors accounts for two-thirds of industrial capacity, the two sectors accounted for only 50 per cent of total industrial value added (in 1987), suggesting the existence of gross inefficiency in the utilization of economic resources by the two sectors.

Taking a sample of 10 industries where comparable data on capacity utilization levels have been consistently available, and comparing average rates for 1976 and 1987, a significant drop in the levels of utilized capacity is discernible. Capacity utilization dropped from about half in 1976 to a third in 1987 (Table 3.8, page 154). Although these average figures mask important variations between specific industries, the declining trend in capacity utilization is generally typical for each of the industries examined. In a significant way, declines in capacity utilization explain the absolute declines in output shown in Table 1.1 (page 139). For example, in 1987 the production of fertilizers was 37 per cent of the 1980 production level. Similarly, textiles were 79 per cent; cigarettes 55 per cent; rolled steel 55 per cent and dry cells 33 per cent of the 1980 production levels. Much of the observed excess capacity is supply constrained – prompted largely by lack of raw materials, power failures, intermittent water supply, lack of spares, and so on.

Extremely low levels of utilized capacity, coupled with a reduction in the imports of consumer goods (Table 3.7), have resulted in absolute real shortages in the domestic market for consumer goods. The magnitude of the problem is vividly depicted in Table 3.9 (page 154), which presents the proportion of demand for cement, cooking oil and sugar not satisfied by the official allocation in each region. Due to critical shortages prevailing at the time it would not be unreasonable to assume that regional demand estimates were inflated in order to induce higher allocation considerations by BIT. But even if this upward bias were to be allowed for, the magnitude of excess demand would remain abnormally high.

Evidence on consumer goods shortages was also corroborated by responses from a sample of consumers selected randomly from both rural and urban households. Consumers were asked to estimate the percentage of times they visited official and unofficial retailing market places for a specific item and managed to find that item available.

Table 3.10 (page 155) summarizes their responses. It is evident that on most occasions the items intended for purchase were not available in both official and unofficial retailing market places. It seems that the chances of obtaining goods in second economy markets were higher than those in the official market. In both markets, however, the degree of uncertainty about product availability was high. Bevan and others have found that this uncertainty is reflected in the very small quantities of goods purchased (compared to normal average purchases) in both the official and unofficial markets, and by the wide variations in the quantities bought at different purchases.[32] Table 3.10 also reveals that consumer goods shortages were relatively more critical in rural areas than in urban areas. This partly reflects difficulties involved in transporting goods to rural areas, resulting from worsening road conditions and ineffective capital equipment (lorries which lacked spares and fuel). It also reflects the conscious move by BIT to try to improve the supply of basic goods to the urban population which is potentially more politically sensitive.

With such a large and extended disequilibrium, it is obvious that enforcement of price control which attempted to keep prices below market clearing levels would exert strong upward pressure on prices, thus encouraging second economy activity. This is what happened in Tanzania. As in the case of food grains, second economy market prices have always been much higher than official market prices (Tables 3.11 and 3.12, pages 155 and 156).

As indicated earlier, pan-territorial pricing had also been extended to the pricing of consumer goods. In principle this policy was intended to minimize the inter-regional differences in real incomes by implicitly subsidizing the regions which were far from producing centres. But in the absence of formal rationing, excess demand pressures tended to create incentives for the distributors to limit sales to areas close to the producing centres. Table 3.11 gives the average prices for selected consumer goods in four towns in Tanzania during September 1984. It shows that in most towns second economy prices were between 100 and 400 per cent higher than those announced by the NPC. Differences between official and unofficial prices were much wider for regions (like Kagera) far from Dar es Salaam, indicating access problems but also weakness in setting uniform prices nation-wide without a careful assessment of transportation costs.

The confinement system, strongly enforced after 1978, was seen by the Government as a form of commodity rationing intended to rationalize the allocation of commodities in the face of worsening commodity shortfalls. Allocation committees were set up at ministerial, regional, district and village levels. Their members were senior Government and Party officials, who were supposed to design and supervise criteria to guide NMC, BIT and RTCs in the allocation of essential commodities. The distribution of essential commodities became in essence a political question with NMC, BIT and the RTCs implementing the politically determined allocation criteria.

In principle one would expect that when prices are set and enforced by decree below the market clearing rate, the emerging rents and the subsequent second economy market deals could be avoided by a strict rationing system which would allocate commodities on criteria other than that of purchasing power. In Tanzania neither the systems of price control nor rationing worked out as planned. It has been pointed out that there were persistent second economy market deals and growing uncertainty among consumers about the availability of supplies. This requires an explanation, particularly when the market structure was in theory conducive to effective price control. The markets were strictly speaking not competitive, and given supply constraints on capacity utilization supply was inelastic, and demand pressures were unduly high.

(v) Factors undermining the effectiveness of Government controls

For a price control programme and a rationing system to work effectively at least three interrelated conditions have to be fulfilled: (a) effective policing, (b) strong public support (i.e. producers, distributors and consumers), and (c) small rents (i.e. the difference between market clearing and controlled prices). Effective policing is required to detect defaulters and to advise on the necessary corrective measures. This requires sufficient staff of capable and honest administrative capacity, which the NPC currently lacks. It is forced to rely on unprofessional price inspectors appointed by regional commissioners in the respective regions. Co-operation of the producers is required for several reasons. The producer or manufacturer has to submit promptly genuine information on costs and support this with relevant statements. Co-operation from producers is also required because they have alternatives by which they can frustrate or undermine price regulation. For example producers can tactfully inflate costs or over-invoice, make quality alterations in the product itself or switch to the production of uncontrolled product substitutes. In a regime where both input and output prices are administered by decree and allocation is effected through rationing, one way in which a producer can increase revenue from a given volume of sale is by inflating costs. Moreover in a situation of severe foreign exchange shortage, and where foreign exchange is administratively rationed, inflated costs act as a bargaining chip for the allocation of a higher quota of foreign exchange. Under the cost-plus pricing method, higher costs would imply a higher price for the product.

Inflated costs are no longer a major worry for the NPC because its 15 years' experience has taught it how to handle such anomalies. The Commission has established both historical and standard cost-input formulae for the major products it deals with. The formulae specify the physical quantities of raw materials and labour required in the production of a given volume or quantity of output. In most cases prices for key raw materials are controlled and hence known by the NPC. Wages are regulated by Government. The Commission has also worked out standard formulae for dealing with overheads.

The major worry for the NPC as far as producers are concerned is with changes in product quality and product specification, and/or switching production to new products in order to circumvent price control. For example in 1977 when the NPC set a price for a toothpaste known as Alfi-Dent, produced by Alfi Company based in Arusha, the firm was not happy about the price. It immediately stopped producing Alfi-Dent and switched to the production of a new product called Blendax. As a new product, Blendax was not price-controlled and for some time the manufacturer sold the product at the market clearing price. In 1984 we selected a random sample of 60 toilet paper rolls from three boxes containing 155 toilet paper rolls each, and which were bought from three different shops. The Tanzania Bureau of Standards (TBS) requirements stipulated that each toilet paper roll should have 200 clearly demarcated pieces. Counting them, we found that only 7 rolls had 150–170 pieces. The rest (53) had less than 150 pieces. In surveys conducted in Arusha and Dar es Salaam, on the informal sector, Bagachwa[33] found that many small manufacturers of ready-made garments had switched from ready-made garment manufacturing (which was price-controlled) to custom-made tailoring which was not price-controlled, and hence profitable from the private point of view.

Significant cost savings can be achieved when a product is not well packaged or labelled according to officially stipulated norms. We report in Table 3.13 (page 157) our findings on how some producers have tried to undermine price control regulation by selling products at the official price but saving on costs of packaging and labelling. For the three sampled products, beer, white bread and laundry soap, most of the packaging and labelling requirements stipulated by the TBS were not fulfilled. Another important form of price control evasion is made when a producer sells his products directly to consumers, bypassing the state marketing agencies. Collusion between the consumer and producer takes place particularly when the gap between supply and demand is very wide.

On product distribution, the NPC would in principle have expected maximum co-operation because most of the importers and distributors are state agencies. But this need not be and in fact has not been the case. Price control evasion has penetrated deep even within the official allocation mechanism. Some public service and parastatal officials have used this situation of shortages to enhance their own material interests. First, they have created loopholes within the rationing system by classifying customers according to the criteria which best suit their needs. Certain customers or retailers can get special permits or coupons (*vibali*) to obtain essential commodities directly from the trading parastatals (for example, NMC, NDL or RTCs). Permits are issued at the discretion of the Allocation Committee or somebody acting on its behalf. They can be obtained through personal or political influence; or through any form of corruption. Officials with power over allocation use it for private gain – to obtain illicit cash or implicit cash. In the latter case an official of NMC might give an official of the National Bank of Commerce a permit to obtain essential food from an NMC distribution depot, expecting that whenever he, the NMC official, visited the bank, he would be given priority of service. This sort of malpractice happens at all stages in the distribution system, from wholesale to retail levels, involving individual households.

Bevan and others[34] have described the system of allocating supplies within the regions in Tanzania as amounting in practice to a lottery. Villages were often not informed (by RTCs) in time to collect their quota, and so often lost their allocation because, given the short notice, they could not obtain the necessary cash, or organize transport to pick up their quota. Failure to pick up their quota meant that RTCs could sell the supplies to private traders at the controlled price, but would be guaranteed *asante* – a tip. Bevan *et al*.[35] have also demonstrated that the severity of consumer goods shortages has contributed to declines in sales of crops.

It became clear that there was a conspicuous discrepancy between the intended outcome of the price control programme and the real economic outcome. The collusion between parastatal officials and private consumers is one of the many examples of how the private sector has managed to escape from state controls such as taxes, often with the connivance and help of the state apparatus which was intended to stop such behaviour. It is also one of the many objectionable examples of state sector economic assets being used to enhance private gains contrary to the intended social purpose. Indeed it became quite common for people to buy their own rights: some form of payment had to be made for access to what was normally considered a free public service. Undoubtedly such behaviour, coupled with a widening gap between official and unofficial prices, which most consumers had to pay, was bound to lead to distrust in the parastatal system and to general public disillusion and demoralization. This was clearly reflected in the widespread reference to the country's only governing Party (Chama cha Mapinduzi – CCM) as *Chama cha Majambazi* – a party of gangsters, apparently reflecting some sort of rough justice, or *Chama cha Makulaji*, a party for misappropriation of funds. Registration numbers for vehicles belonging to parastatals in Tanzania start with SU. This came to be interpreted as *Suka Ule*, meaning 'one has to corrupt' in order to survive – apparently referring to the illicit rents reaped by parastatal officials. The fact that public officials succumb to corruption largely explains why the second economy, although visibly conspicuous, has been tolerated by public authorities.

This leads us to the third aspect which is essential if the price control and rationing programmes are to be effectively enforced: the disequilibrium should be small enough to be manageable. When the gap between the market clearing rate and the controlled price is very large the implied potential rent becomes large, creating a strong incentive for the producer, distributor and consumer to bypass the official channel. In such circumstances even the consumer, who, according to J.F.K. Mongi, the Price Commissioner, is the most reliable price inspector, fails to co-operate. Galbraith explains why this is so with a large disequilibrium:

> The given supply can be sold at higher prices – it can be sold because buyers, however unhappily, would prefer to pay the higher price than to accept their alternative opportunity which is to do without. The sellers, it can readily be assumed, prefer the higher price to the lower one. Thus if the price increase is arrested by authority, the action runs not only against the interest of sellers, but also against the interest of those buyers who are not able to satisfy all or substantially all of their wants, at the fixed price.[36]

In Tanzania there were other reasons for the customer to collude with the trader, particularly at the retail level. Even where supplies were available at the official prices, additional implicit costs were involved before such supplies could be obtained. At the retail level, Government had advised that essential goods be allocated through queuing. But at the depth of the crisis, the queues became very long and it look several hours to obtain the intended supplies. When they were obtained they were normally very much less than the amount requested. This meant that workers had to direct all their energies to searching and queuing for the scarce commodities. Naturally people had to trade off the inconvenience of queuing and the small quantities involved against obtaining more goods by paying a higher price through the second economy window. An important by-product of the queuing system was the emergence of a group of marketeers – the 'queuing boys'. These were the unemployed or under-employed persons who could afford to wait for any time in the queue and bought the commodity at the official price, reselling it at a higher unofficial price to those who could not afford to queue. It was also not uncommon for retailers selling essential commodities at official prices to sell these supplies with strings. Customers wishing to buy commodities at the official price were forced to buy other slow-moving items as a package. In most cases customers did not take away the slow-moving items, but they had to pay for them. This was another subtle form of price evasion, in which the officially designated shops for selling official supplies (*kaya*) reaped rent.

(vi) Industrial licensing

Under the Industrial Licensing and Regulation Act all manufacturing firms have to be licensed. The unit in charge of enforcing the Act is the Industrial Licensing Board, within the Ministry of Industries and Trade. The Board has well established criteria to guide its decisions. They include such aspects as the viability of the project, kind of ownership, kind of activity and the whole range of economy-wide implications of the proposed project.

The official requirements for obtaining an industrial licence (as detailed in the Prelude) make a lot of sense. But the many steps involved lead to subjectiveness in judgement on the part of the officials concerned, and are hence a potential breeding ground for corrupt practices. We have interviewed a number of private operators with industrial licences about their views on the present industrial licensing procedures. The general observation is that small-scale operators are likely to suffer most because they not only tend to lack the required technical information, but also do not have the lobbying strength. The time taken may vary from a few months to years, depending on how quickly one can provide the necessary information and how one can persuade officials to ignore unnecessary details.

3.2.2 Were the Controls Justifiable?

On the whole the price control and confinement programmes have been associated with increasing second economy activities, poor services and ineffectiveness in making scarce consumer goods available at the official price, in both urban and rural areas. Could such failures constitute a case against price control and Government intervention in the marketing of food and consumer goods? Before an attempt is made to answer this question it is instructive to examine briefly some of the underlying causes of these policy failures.

As pointed out in Chapter 1, the years 1978–86 have been a period of unprecedented economic retrenchment for Tanzania. According to C. D. Msuya, the Minister for Finance,[37] the manifestations of the economy in distress were clearly visible: sharp declines in living standards; a deterioration in the nation's physical infrastructure; recurring dislocations in oil supplies, and the critical shortage of inputs into productive and service sectors.

Growth and high inflation rates have eroded the real incomes of both rural and urban dwellers. According to ILO estimates,[38] rural incomes have declined by 13.5 per cent while non-agricultural wage incomes have fallen by 65 per cent in real terms between 1979 and 1984. The National Consumer Price Index (NCPI), which measures the living costs of all families in urban areas in the mainland, is the most widely used official measure of inflation. Domestic inflation rose from less than 10 per cent per annum in the early 1970s to an average of about 15 per cent in the late 1970s and to over 30 per cent in the mid-1980s (Table 1.1). The impact of this on the real incomes of the minimum wage earners is shown in Table 3.14 (page 157). This table shows that it was increasingly becoming practically impossible for minimum wage earners relying solely on wage incomes to feed their families, even if they had access to official supplies of food from NMC, NDL or RTC. For example, while in 1973 one day's minimum wage could buy either 10 kg of maize or 4.8 kg of rice, in 1985 it could buy only either 2 kg of maize or 1.9 kg of rice at the existing official prices. In practice, however, since most purchases were made in the second economy food market, this meant that a day's minimum wage could earn only 1.3 kg of maize flour or only 0.8 kg of rice in 1985. (An average family in Tanzania has six persons.)

Real wage declines have been faster in the top and middle salary groups than in the minimum wage groups. Whereas in 1984 minimum real wages were just 41 per cent of their 1969 level, those for medium and upper group salary were respectively 20.7 and 11 per cent of their 1969 levels.[39] Since prices have been increasing faster than growth in nominal wages the purchasing power of the income groups has been eroded.

The situation has been exacerbated, particularly in the middle and higher salary groups, by the higher tax rates (averaging 15 per cent and 28 per cent of monthly incomes for the T.Shs 2,000 and T.Shs. 5,000 salary earners respectively between 1974 and 1985). Falling real incomes, to the point where wage earners can no longer provide the basis for minimum subsistence, have acted as a disincentive to formal employment. For some civil servants and parastatal workers this resulted, as we observed, in shorter hours at their workplaces and the use of the rest of the day for other productive or informal activities to supplement formal income. But also it has had the negative impact of encouraging corrupt practices such as theft of public assets, selling of free public services, bribes, diversion of public resources for personal use, and so on. For the peasants it has meant the selling of their produce directly to consumers, bypassing the state trading agencies.

Yet the pervasiveness of second economy activities does not totally argue against price controls. What it calls for is an intelligent application of controls in which the circumstances of each market are carefully considered. Similarly, the ineffectiveness of the confinement system does not argue against state intervention in the marketing of strategic food and consumer goods. Rather it suggests first the need for tailoring the mandate of the public sector to match its administrative, technical and financial capacities. Secondly, it calls for flexibility in the system and recognition of the role of the private sector in providing support whenever necessary. Lastly, it reminds policy makers that state enterprises should not be allowed to use their monopoly power to insulate themselves against the costs arising from their inefficient operations.

As pointed out earlier the need for price control arose when the market allocation mechanism failed to satisfy the aspirations of Tanzanian society. To date these aspirations, which combine objectives of growth with equity, have not changed significantly.

The foreign exchange constraint translated into input supply bottlenecks for most firms in Tanzania which are import-dependent. In the short run capacity utilization could not be increased to planned levels, meaning that supply of essential goods was fixed in the short term. The supply curve for most firms was nearly vertical. Theoretically this meant that no increase in price, however large, would have increased the supply of goods produced. Now suppose that Government had not introduced price control. Prices would then have been allowed to rise until quantity demanded and quantity supplied were equal. At the depth of the crisis, it is questionable whether demand would have been brought in line with supply. First, almost every essential commodity was in short supply, so people had a lot of cash because there was virtually nothing to buy. In a sense their money income could be assumed to have risen. Moreover, if it happened that an essential commodity became available, consumers tended to buy an unusually large amount at any given price, fearing that it might be a long time before they would obtain the next supplies. The movement was not along the demand curve, but a shift of the demand curve to the right, and in such a situation if Government does not intervene, a shift of the demand curve threatens to produce a price spiral indefinitely.

There are three strong arguments for price control in this case. First, the indeterminate price would create uncertainty among consumers. Secondly, allowing such indefinite rises in price levels would depress the real wages of the consumers. Lastly, only the rich in urban areas would get access to essential commodities. In Tanzania, equity considerations meant that these aspects were neither socially nor politically acceptable; socially because of the inequity involved, and politically because a politician sounds more convincing blaming the few greedy, unscrupulous marketeers who sell commodities above official prices, than attributing these problems to supply constraints. In fact when the subsidies on *sembe* (maize meal) and fertilizer were lifted in 1983, there were mild complaints because consumers were used to paying much higher prices in the second economy market.

We therefore take the view that price control and the confinement system were socially and politically necessary programmes. It remains to suggest how these programmes could have been made more effective. First there is a problem of scale. At its peak in 1978, with a staff of about 20 officials and not having even a mini-computer, the NPC set prices for 3,000 items and was supposed to ensure their enforcement. Certainly these tasks were beyond the NPC's capacity and capabilities. Additionally, such a blanket application of price control did not allow the NPC enough time to study in detail the peculiar market characteristics and circumstances of each product. The process of decontrolling some of the less essential products currently in hand is not a reversal of policy but a rationalization of the policy, something that deserves utmost support.

Price controls can be made more effective when accompanied by formal rationing. But effective rationing presupposes that Government purchases the entire supply of the major commodities and then allocates them on its own criteria. Effective rationing, in other words, presupposes some form of Government intervention. However, the NMC, BIT and RTCs were set up hurriedly, and almost all price-controlled items had to be rationed and distributed by these parastatal enterprises, which were also technically, administratively and financially ill-equipped, as well as lacking in transport. Given the capacity of the BIT at the time, it was premature to assign to it the functions of managing the export–import trade, and wholesale and retail trade in the villages. What was required was selective rationing and distribution involving a few essential commodities, and as in the case of food crops, the less essential commodities should have been left to the private traders. Even in a socialist economy, no person in his right mind would want to see the procurement, payment and distribution of supplies from and to the producers and consumers excessively delayed by the ineffectiveness of a public marketing institution. Neither can we tolerate parastatal managers who receive a significant proportion of their income from activities other than the proper fulfilment of their managerial functions. Thus parastatal marketing institutions have to be efficiently and effectively managed to survive. This is not necessarily an argument for privatization, but for the streamlining and rationalization of parastatal firms to match existing capacity. In turn, this recognizes the need to reward managers for their successes, to punish them for their failures and to restrain parastatals from using their monopoly positions to insulate themselves from bearing the costs which are attributable to their inefficiencies.

Subsidies could be used to avoid official price increases, while encouraging marginal producers to increase output. Until 1983 Government maintained a 55 per cent explicit subsidy on *sembe* (maize flour) sold by NMC and on fertilizers. Theoretically, subsidies ought to be limited to marginal output, but in practice this is difficult. In the case of fertilizers it was inequitable because the bulk of fertilizers were used by large farmers. Moreover, some of the factors determining expansion of output were exogenous to the firm (for example, foreign exchange availability). In fact, in both maize and fertilizers the use of subsidies became perverse not only because of the rising Government deficit, but also because they were continued even when output was falling. In effect, it amounted to subsidizing inefficiency.

The long-run solution however, to offsetting pressure for price increases is to increase the supply of commodities. Increased supplies would alleviate shortages, raise real standards of living, increase incentives among agricultural producers and even make it possible to lift the burden of rationing. In particular, a long-term solution lies in encouraging greater utilization of industrial capacity. This would have to involve a deliberate shift in emphasis from the importation of capital goods to intermediate goods. It also presupposes a healthy balance of payments position and hence improved capacity to import. Current Government policy which allows traders to use their own privately generated foreign exchange to import intermediate and consumer goods could be defended during the interim period as necessary for providing psychological satisfaction to consumers and incentives to rural producers. It cannot, however, stabilize prices because most of these supplies are bought with foreign exchange which is valued at second economy and not at the official exchange rate. To the extent that the gap between the official and unofficial foreign exchange rates remains high, imported goods under the 'own imports' scheme would still be consumed exclusively by the well-to-do.

3.3 The Second Economy in the External Trade Sector

This section analyses certain aspects of second economy transactions in Tanzania's external trade sector and their repercussions on the domestic economy. Particular attention is paid to four main manifestations of the second economy in the foreign trade sector: illegal exports and imports, over- and under-invoicing, black market exchange rates and own-funded imports. An attempt is also made to discuss some of the factors that may explain particular developments in external trade transactions.

3.3.1 Exchange Rate Management

The three important policy instruments which have significantly influenced the nature, magnitude and direction of foreign trade transactions are exchange rate management, the administrative system of foreign exchange allocation, and tariffs. Generally foreign trade policy from the early 1970s to the early 1980s was dominated by quantitative controls introduced to deal with the growing excess demand for foreign exchange. Between 1966 (when the Tanzanian shilling was introduced) and January 1979 the exchange rate policy pursued was essentially one of nominal exchange rate rigidity characteristic of a fixed exchange rate regime. In 1979 the Tanzanian shilling (T.Sh) was devalued by 10 per cent, its peg to the SDR was discontinued and a new peg to the basket of currencies of Tanzania's major trading partners was introduced. In March 1982 the T.Sh was again devalued by about 10 per cent. This was followed by another devaluation of 20 per cent in June 1983, and a further 20 per cent devaluation a year later. The T.Sh, which stood at T.Shs 17 to the US dollar at the beginning of 1986, was left to slide to T.Shs 25 to the dollar before being devalued to T.Shs 40. Since March 1986, the T.Sh has been depreciating further through a crawling peg, and had dropped to T.Shs 95 to the dollar by June 1988.

Since 1977, Tanzania's domestic inflation rate has generally been slightly higher than world inflation and much higher than in the industrialized countries which are Tanzania's major trading partners (Table 3.15, page 158), suggesting that the real exchange of the shilling has been appreciating relative to other major currencies.

Another important indication of the appreciation of the T.Sh is the thriving parallel (second economy) market for foreign exchange. Although the buying and selling of foreign currency is restricted to the Bank of Tanzania (BOT), the National Bank of Commerce (NBC) and a few other authorized dealers such as tourist hotels, unauthorized exchange involving foreign currencies is widespread and relatively open. There are no official data series on second economy exchange rates, but ruling rates are common knowledge. The main locations for second economy deals in foreign exchange include tourist hotels, international ports and airports and border towns. Second economy exchange rates vary from one place to another and over time. They also depend on the foreign currency concerned (US dollars and British pounds sterling are preferred, except at the Tanzania–Kenya border where the Kenyan shilling is traded at a premium) and the size of bills (a $US100 bill has a higher quotation than a $US10 bill).

Table 3.16 (page 158) sets parallel market foreign exchange rates against the official (nominal) exchange rate. It shows that the differences between official and unofficial exchange rates are enormous. The second economy foreign exchange rate was 2.6 times the official rate in 1980, but the gap widened until it peaked in 1985, with the second economy exchange rate at 5.7 times the official rate. Substantial adjustments,in the official exchange rate undertaken since June 1986 have resulted in a significant devaluation of the real exchange rate, and have been associated with a reduction in the gap between the official and second economy exchange rates. Nevertheless the gap remains large, suggesting that in a situation of large and prolonged disequilibrium exchange rate adjustment cannot on its own eliminate the extended disequilibrium.

3.3.2 Foreign Exchange Control

The persistence of balance of payments disequilibria and the widening gap between official and parallel market exchange rates are clear indications of the growing excess demands for foreign exchange. Instead of relying on deflationary monetary and fiscal policies (expenditure reducing policies) and/or exchange rate flexibility (expenditure switching policies), Tanzania has until recently consistently resisted the use of these market instruments and increasingly relied on rationing through the administrative allocation of foreign exchange in dealing with excess demand.

The Government, through the Bank of Tanzania and the People's Bank of Zanzibar, maintains full control of foreign exchange. Control over exchange operations is exercised through the issue of import and export licences. Import licences are allocated on a firm-by-firm basis, taking into consideration such factors as potential linkage generation, basic consumer requirements and export orientation. In practice allocation is significantly influenced by the political, economic and lobbying strength of the applicant, the need to support fiscal revenue earners (brewing and cigarette-making firms have had high priority), and the crisis nature of the economy. In principle all manufacturing exports are subject to licensing. However, manufacturing exports are not in effect subject to restrictions. Before 1984 the procedures for obtaining both export and import licences were extremely cumbersome, involving the filling in of several documents and numerous consultations and interviews. By 1987 the excessive bureaucratic procedures had been streamlined, and in fact one could obtain an export licence on the spot. Strictly speaking prior to 1984, Tanzania was typically mentioned as an exchange control regime. The T.Sh was made totally inconvertible (officially). Local residents were required to surrender all foreign exchange earnings to Government authorized dealers. Any residents wishing to make foreign exchange transactions had to apply to the Bank of Tanzania.

For social, economic and/or political reasons, a few categories of imports are prohibited from entering the country. These include all goods from South Africa, seditious literature, imports of Tanzanian currency, gold coins, pornography and narcotics. There are also goods that are classified as 'restricted', which can only be imported under a special permission guaranteed by specially designated Government authority. These include drugs, foreign currency, foodstuffs, plants and animals, arms and ammunition, computers, telex machines and motor vehicles of less than 1 ton capacity.

3.3.3   Tariff Policy

The emphasis placed on import licensing and other physical prohibitions as a means of centralizing the allocation of foreign exchange to protect domestic industry has, to a significant extent, diluted the potential role of tariffs as a mechanism for allocating resources. The main consideration when setting tariffs seems to have been Government revenue generation. Others included the protection of domestic industries and restraining the consumption of luxury goods. Typically high duty rates (60 per cent and over) are levied on goods with a low elasticity of demand (for example, consumer goods and luxuries), and low duty rates (between 20 and 30 per cent) are applied to most intermediate and capital goods which also have a high elasticity of demand. Goods imported by Government and diplomats are exempt from duty.

Before 1983 goods categorized as luxuries were charged customs duties at rates averaging between 200 and 500 per cent. These included refrigerators, all types of musical instruments, sound recorders and reproducers, television and video recorders, saloon cars, radios and the like. Since 1984, however, these rates have been lowered to an average of about 120 per cent and less. Even so a study commissioned by the Ministry of Finance, Economic Affairs and Economic Planning found that in 1986 goods with tariff rates of 100 per cent and above had very low collection rates (averaging 10 per cent), and for some items the import value was unexpectedly low, falling to zero in several items. The study attributes these results to under-reporting and/or tariff evasion because of prohibitive rates. It also found that although these goods were regarded as luxuries they enjoyed generous discretionary exemptions (from duty) resulting in a weighted average revenue loss of T.Shs 285 million.[40]

3.3.4   Volume of Unrecorded Exports and Imports

Growing differentials between domestic and international prices, disparity in currency values, the non-convertibility of the T.Sh together with acute shortages of essential goods, the excessive demand for foreign exchange, import prohibitions and controls and high import duties have created incentives for importing and exporting unregistered goods, under- and over-invoicing of imports. As already pointed out, illegal transborder trade has been rampant along the Tanzanian borders, with major trading centres along the Tanzania/Kenya border at Tarime, Suna, Namanga and LungaLunga; Kigagati on the Tanzania/ Uganda border; Mosi and Tunduma on the Tanzania/Zambia border; Chamba, Mwamba and Namiranga on the Tanzania/Mozambique border.

Most of the transactions involving smuggled goods do not pass through these well-known border markets. Rather there are several hidden smugglers' routes which in fact outnumber official border posts. Smuggled goods may be transported by caravan, or by boats across rivers and lakes, by head or by mules across uncontrolled territory generally at night. They may also go through officially controlled posts through collusion with border-post officials. Transborder trade is no longer confined to the traditional exchange of goods and services between residents sharing a common border with the primary purpose of meeting shortfalls in subsistence consumption. It now embraces products and commodities intended largely for resale in urban and rural areas quite far from the border, and sometimes for re-export. Besides barter exchange transborder trade is effected through the exchange of national currencies at parallel market rates. International convertible currencies play a very minor role.

The spectrum of products involved in transborder trade before liberalization is very wide. Imports of consumer goods (in short supply domestically and hence in high demand) rank high in terms of frequency of transactions. The main ones are cooking oil, sugar, salt, toilet and laundry soap, toothpaste, matches, shoes, ready-made clothes, vehicle spare parts, beer, whisky and cigarettes. The major exporters of these goods are Kenya and Zambia. Tanzanian residents pay in maize, wheat, beans, goats and sheep. The second category of goods smuggled across the border and through other international ports (generally Dar es Salaam and Tanga) includes those goods which are officially classified as restricted and which involve substantial capital outlay and relatively sophisticated organizational arrangements – for instance cardamom, coffee, cotton, cattle, gold, hides and skins, ivory and precious stones. Most of these are traded primarily for export or re-export. Trade in these commodities is normally carried out with convertible foreign currencies, which include in this case the Kenyan currency. The third category of smuggled goods involves luxury goods which either are in short supply in Tanzania or bear high import duties. These include whisky, vehicles and vehicle spare parts, electronic equipment, television sets, radios and video cassette recorders.

Smuggling along the Tanzania/Kenya border sometimes involves the movement of herds of cattle, sheep, goats or camels across borders. At times this is achieved by force, as when armed bandits cross the border and steal cattle at night. It may also be smoothly carried out as when the nomadic Masai pastoralists cross official borders and sell their animals at will, or sometimes unaware that they are indulging in illegal transactions.

The volume of unregistered exports and imports is visibly enormous and, as one customs official put it, many traders have made fortunes out of this business. In the absence of official estimates or records that is probably all that can be said. We have observed the occurrence of widespread unregistered border sales and purchases and open trade deals in foreign currencies at various places. Unfortunately such spot checks mask important evolutionary trends and do not say much about the volume involved.

In the circumstances we have found it instructive to use the value of goods seized by customs authorities in order to provide some rough indications of the volume of unrecorded trade. Goods seized by customs are normally those which have been illegally imported or exported or have otherwise contravened the Customs Management Act by misreporting of value, weight, volume, quantity or description. Unfortunately, figures for only 1985 and 1986 could be traced in the files. Tables 3.17 and 3.18 (pages 158 and 159) show the volume of goods impounded by the Tanzania Customs for those years. It can be seen that most illegal exports are agricultural produce, livestock, foreign currencies, agricultural foodstuffs, carvings and trophies, hides and skins. Illegal imports are very diversified and, if currency is excluded, consumer goods, especially luxuries (cosmetics, motor vehicles, radio cassettes, television and video recorders), dominate. The absence of intermediate and capital goods is not unexpected given that these generally carry very low tariff rates and most capital goods are totally exempt from duty. In 1986, for example, figures from Tanzania Customs reveal that total customs duty exemptions amounted to T.Shs 3.9 billion out of which T.Shs 2 billion (51.3 per cent) was attributed to capital goods and T.Shs 1 billion (25.6 per cent) to intermediate capital goods.

In 1986 exports worth T.Shs 1.7 million were seized by Tanzania Customs as compared to T.Shs 5.5 million in 1985. These figures represented 0.02 per cent and 0.09 per cent of the total value of registered exports in the respective years. Impounded imports were valued at T.Shs 18.9 million in 1986 and T.Shs 42.8 million in 1985. In relation to total imports these represented 0.05 per cent and 0.25 per cent of the value of official imports in 1986 and 1985 respectively. Such statistics are useful as a pointer to the volume of illegal trade if they are related to the probability of seizure for illegal imports and exports. According to Tanzania Customs officials' experience, the probability of seizure for illegal goods would, at the most optimistic estimate, be around 10 per cent, and at the most pessimistic about 1 per cent. On average, therefore, we may assume that only 5 per cent of illegally traded goods would be seized. Table 3.19 (page 160) shows estimates of unrecorded exports and imports, based on the assumption that only 5 per cent of illegal imports and exports are seized.

According to these estimates, illegal exports as a proportion of recorded exports have fallen from about 1.8 per cent in 1985 to about 0.31 per cent in 1986. At the same time unrecorded imports as a proportion of recorded imports have declined from 5 per cent in 1985 to 0.15 per cent in 1986. This does not necessarily imply a real decline in second economy activities. Partly, the figures may reflect the fact that customs officials became lax in 1986, particularly with the full implementation of the 'own imports' programme. Partly they may also suggest that some items like televisions and video recorders which used not to be allowed to be imported have since then been allowed. The limited available information on seized ivory trophies does not seem to corroborate the declining tendency in second economy activities (Table 3.20, page 160). The number and value of ivory tusks seized by customs and other Government authorities declined from $US337,000 in 1982 to $US44,000 in 1986, but shot up to $US13.5 million in 1988. Similarly, illegal trade in cardamom has been rising.

In 1974 official purchases of cardamom amounted to 760 tons. At that time the world market price of cardamom was $US3.54 or T.Shs 25.28 per kg while the nominal domestic producer price was T.Shs 17 (67 per cent of the world market price). While world market prices continued to rise, domestic real producer prices consistently declined. As a result official purchases have consistently declined since 1974. The only period which recorded a slight rise in official purchases was in 1984, probably resulting from the transient effects of the Government campaign against 'racketeers and economic saboteurs'. The decline in official purchases was not due to a decline in production, but rather to an increase in producer sales to non-official traders – i.e. to the second economy, due to the buoyant world market situation.

Using a conservative scenario, it is estimated that production in 1974 could not have been below the official sales figure of 760 tonnes, and may well have been within the 800 tonnes range. Taking into account the general decline in agricultural production within the country, but also taking note of the buoyant world market situation, it is estimated that overall production could not have below 700 tonnes per annum in 1986. This figure is indeed much lower than that indicated by the Marketing Development Bureau[41] which also estimates that 'a large portion of the crop (up to 90 per cent) is marketed outside the official marketing system'. Despite the relatively high production, the low official purchases, coupled with the diversion of official purchases to the underground economy carried out through pilfering at Gapex godowns, have ensured that cardamom is predominantly a second economy-dominated commodity. Table 3.21 (page 161) presents estimates of illegal exports of cardamom for the years 1984–6. These figures indicate that while unofficial sales accounted for about 40 per cent of cardamom production in 1984, by 1986 second economy sales had risen to 80 per cent.

Some money figures on illegal foreign currency holding impounded during the crackdown exercise in April 1983 are also available from legal case proceedings. The Ministry of Home Affairs recorded T.Shs 33,835,041 (equivalent to $US1,990,297); $US23,148; pounds sterling 27,527; deutschmarks 11,900; Arabian puba 1,020; Indian rupees 3,112; Kenyan Shs 9,095; Somalian Shs 27,975; and other insignificant foreign money.

3.3.5   Over- and Under-invoicing of Imports and Exports

Comparing partner country trade data is instructive in revealing the volume of unrecorded trade. Exports from one partner country to another correspond to imports of the recipient partner. Since imports are normally valued at cost, insurance and freight (CIF) and exports at free-on-board (FOB), the value of exports in the exporting country should be equal to the value of imports in the importing partner, less CIF value. Such trade data would be easily comparable if trading partners classified their goods in the same way. Differences in this case may arise due to either over- or under-invoicing of exports or imports.

Over-invoicing of imports (i.e. the declaration of higher values for imports than the actual ones) is intended to take out foreign exchange from the import recipient country. Thus a Tanzanian importer would overstate the value of the import shipment when applying for foreign exchange from the Bank of Tanzania. The difference between the actual and inflated costs of the shipment could then be paid to the Tanzanian importer in an overseas account. Over-invoicing of imports is one form of capital flight and may be effected through three main forms: (i) inflating the invoice price of an item to be imported; (ii) importing goods of less quality than those specified in the invoice, and (iii) actually importing a lower volume or quantity of goods than that shown on the invoice.

Under-invoicing of imports is the declaration of lower values than the actual ones for imported items, and is generally intended to evade or reduce the amount of customs duty payable on the product. For example, if the duty is 100 per cent and the imported item is under-invoiced by 30 per cent, the importer actually pays 70 per cent. For a Tanzanian importer who does not own an overseas account, the additional foreign exchange has to be purchased from the second economy. This means that in order for under-invoicing to be profitable, the rate of duty should be higher than the second economy exchange rate premium. Thus under effective foreign exchange control, high tariffs would tend to encourage tax evasion through under-invoicing. Conversely, where there is scarcity of foreign exchange, low duties on imports would tend to encourage over-invoicing of imports.

In order to investigate the existence of over- or under-invoicing of imports in Tanzania, it was necessary to obtain and compare statistics of imports into Tanzania as recorded by Tanzania Customs and those recorded by the countries of import supply. It proved difficult to obtain records of statistics from various countries which supply Tanzania's imports. The only available statistics refer to Britain for the years 1985 and 1986. Imports from Britain normally constitute about 12 to 13 per cent of Tanzania's total imports. Thus British trade with Tanzania is sufficiently large to allow conclusions to be made and generalized from Tanzania's total trade. Tanzania's trade with Britain was therefore closely examined in order to determine the existence or non-existence of the practice of over- and under-invoicing of imports.

As a starting point, we examine the import statistics as recorded by Tanzania Customs and the UK Department of Trade and Industry. Both Tanzania and the UK classify their goods according to the Standard International Trade Classification (SITC). Since Tanzania Customs records imports at CIF while Britain records her export on FOB, to obtain comparability the British data in pounds sterling is converted into Tanzanian equivalent data by first adding to it a 15 per cent factor to take account of the freight and insurance elements, and then converting the resulting figures into Tanzanian shillings at the average annual mean exchange rate for British pounds sterling.

The results of these conversions are summarized in Table 3.22 (page 162) in which it is shown that Tanzanian imports data were under-recorded by T.Shs 430.5 million in 1985 and over-recorded by T.Shs 297.7 million in 1986 when compared to British data. This suggests that Tanzanian imports from Britain were under-invoiced by 18.7 per cent in 1985 and over-invoiced by 8.1 per cent in 1986. Generalizing from the above calculations it is possible to estimate the extent of under-invoicing for total recorded imports (at 18 per cent) to be equivalent to T.Shs 3,049 million (about $US177 million) in 1985 and the extent of over-invoicing of total imports in 1986 at 8 per cent, equivalent to T.Shs 2,471 million (about $US65 million).

Under-invoicing in 1985 can partly be attributed to the existence of high duty rates on a substantial number of imports which encouraged importers to seek to minimize the amount of duty. Partly, there was also a strong incentive to misstate the precise nature of the goods because of the existing controls and ban on certain categories of imports. In 1986, however, the list of commodities to be imported under own-funds imports was expanded, customs duty rates were reduced on a number of commodities, and the export retention measures were introduced. Moreover, since importers and exporters could now safely operate overseas accounts, it became much easier to deposit the difference between the inflated price (paid for with foreign exchange obtained from the Bank of Tanzania) and the real cost. Certainly this was a much safer method of obtaining illegal foreign exchange than by buying it in the second economy market or keeping these funds frozen in local currency when the T.Sh was depreciating very fast.

Bevan et al.[42] have estimated the amount of money sent outside Tanzania through over-invoicing of imports alone between 1976 and 1979 as amounting to T.Shs 2,015 million (about $US400 million at the 1975 exchange rate). The value of over-invoicing is estimated to have risen from T.Shs 106.5 million in 1976 to T.Shs 789.7 million in 1978, with the larger magnitude of the latter year relfecting the aftermath of the coffee boom and the subsequent liberalization of imports. The study projects that if the outflow of foreign exchange during 1982–5 continued at its 1981 level of equivalent to about T.Shs 766.2 million, then by 1986 the amount of illegal holdings would have been more than $US800 million.

Under-invoicing of exports is the declaration of lower values for exports and is intended to generate illegal foreign exchange and keep it outside the country. Part of the full export value is not surrendered to local official exchange authorities but deposited in exporters' overseas private accounts by trading partners. This balance in foreign exchange may then be used to acquire illegal imports or sold in the second economy. The incentive to under-invoice exports is much stronger where higher *ad valorem* taxes on exports are in force. In this case under-invoicing is also a form of tax evasion and results in loss of Government revenue.

Over-invoicing of exports, however, is the declaration of higher values for exports than the actual ones and is intended to facilitate the inflow into the country of foreign exchange illegally held abroad. Over-invoicing of exports is most likely to take place where Government provides export subsidies to promote export sales.

As with imports, investigation of the extent of under- and over-invoicing of exports is carried out by using the statistics of Tanzanian exports to Britain as reported by Tanzania Customs and the UK Department of Trade and Industry. Tanzanian export trade with Britain is quite substantial and accounted for 15 per cent and 12 per cent of total imports in 1985 and 1986 data respectively. Figures for these years were the ones readily available. To ensure comparability between Tanzanian data and British data, British statistics in pounds sterling have been transformed to Tanzanian equivalent data by first deducting 15 per cent to eliminate the insurance and freight elements and then converting the resulting figures into Tanzania shillings at the average annual mean exchange rate for British pounds sterling. The results show that for 1985 and 1986, Tanzanian exports to Britain were under-invoiced. In 1985 under-invoicing was slight – less than 1 per cent, but in 1986 it was quite substantial, amounting to 17.1 per cent, equivalent to T.Shs 279.7 million (Table 3.22). If we assume this extent of under-invoicing applied to all types of exports, the amount of money involved translates to T.Shs 1,875 million (about $US49 million)

The incentive to under-invoice exports in 1986 was provided partly by the high premium in the second economy market for foreign exchange (a dollar was being exchanged at 5.2 times more shillings than in the official economy – Table 3.17). Under-invoicing also became relatively easy as Government allowed private operators to export more diversified non-traditional agricultural and manufactured goods whose world prices were not commonly known.

Overall, there is sufficient evidence to indicate that a substantial amount of foreign reserves is generated outside the official external sector. Based on the above calculations, second economy trade balance – the difference between unrecorded exports and imports – was (–) $US40.6 million in 1985 and (+) $US113.7 million in 1986. Part of the illegal reserves is legalized by under-invoicing of imports and part of it is kept in foreign accounts and remains as Tanzania's unofficial assets abroad. Such assets are taken out through over-invoicing of imports and under-invoicing of exports. These estimates of course underestimate the actual magnitude of illegal reserves. They do not, for example, include illegal foreign exchange generated and used in the services sector, for example in tourism, street banking, medical and education.[43]

4

The Impact of Liberalization Measures

4.1 The Impact of Interest Rates on Capital Flight

Comparison of interest rates in Tanzania and the international money market is made in Table 4.1 (page 162) in order to indicate the relative attractiveness of the domestic and international money markets for investors from Tanzania. The picture which emerges from this table is that domestic interest rates in Tanzania have been quite low in nominal terms throughout the 1980s up to 1986, as well as being negative in real terms.

Interest rates in the international money markets, as represented by the London Interbank Offer Rate on US dollar deposits for 12 months (columns 3 and 4 in Table 4.1) have generally been significantly higher than Tanzanian money market rates both in nominal and real terms. They indicate that it is clearly more profitable for Tanzanian investors to hold deposits in the international money markets than in Tanzanian financial institutions.

Nevertheless, a more concise result is obtained by examining the profitability of investments abroad in terms of Tanzanian shillings for officially approved investments (for example in officially sanctioned foreign exchange accounts) and for illegal (i.e. non-authorized) investments (for instance in illegally-held foreign accounts) (columns 5 and 6 in Table 4.1). It is shown that while the profitability of international money markets has been consistently higher than Tanzanian money markets at least up to 1985 for officially approved investments, and up to 1984 for illegally held investments, there is a movement towards making the Tanzanian money market more profitable than the international one, as illustrated by the figures for 1986. This is shown by comparing

109

columns 5 and 6 with column 2 in Table 4.1. Certainly, following the introduction of the new economic policy represented by the 'Economic Recovery Programme', domestic interest rates have been regularly adjusted to much higher levels.

Column 6 of Table 4.1 shows clearly, however, that the real interest rates applicable to illegal foreign exchange deposits from Tanzania in the international money market have been consistently negative since 1981, implying that interest rates in the international money markets cannot be the cause of capital flight from Tanzania. There are clearly other factors or reasons for it. Before 1986 strict controls on the remittance of foreign exchange by both domestic and foreign investors played a part in providing incentives for capital flight. Even after the partial liberalization of imports and the introduction of the export-to-import scheme, controls on the remittance of foreign exchange remained in force. There was, however, an added incentive for capital flight, namely the retention scheme which enabled private importers to import goods into Tanzania which, because of the prevailing excess demand for such goods, could be sold at extremely high prices. In addition there are those Tanzanian residents who simply accumulate illegal foreign reserves as an insurance for smooth flight in case of turbulence in the country.

4.2. The Impact of Liberalizing External Trade

The tightening of the foreign exchange constraint in the early 1980s was initially accompanied by severe import restrictions. However, as industrial capacity utilization fell sharply and imports became less and less, even the most essential goods disappeared from shops. Government's first pragmatic move was to allow residents to import commercial vehicles in order to ease commuter bottlenecks. Under the 1983–4 budget a provision was made permitting Tanzanian residents to import goods using foreign exchange acquired from their relatives, friends and associates living abroad or through their own savings. In addition to 'own- funded' imports, an 'export-to-import' scheme, which initially allowed exporters of traditional exports (i.e. coffee, cotton, tea, sisal, cashew nuts, tobacco, pyrethrum and diamonds) to retain 10 per cent of their export proceeds, was extended to non-traditional exports.

Since 1986 the export retention scheme has been extended to three categories of exports: category A covers about 25 traditional agricultural exports which are handled by the marketing boards; category B covers non-traditional industrial products, while category C covers non-traditional products and services. Exporters in categories B and C operate under the cover of a blanket incentive which permits them to retain 50 per cent of their foreign exchange earnings to enable them to purchase production inputs and spare parts. Exporters under category A are covered by individual commodity agreements which allow retention of variable percentages of export earnings (about 10 per cent in general).

The number of items permitted under 'own-funds' imports has increased substantially since 1983–4 and currently includes consumer goods, building materials, transport equipment, electrical goods and basic inputs for manufacturing. Items under own-funds licences are not subject to price control or confinement.

Following the introduction of the policy of partial import liberalization in 1984 a very significant share of imports is now financed through the 'own-funded' arrangements, as shown in Table 4.2 (page 163). It will also be noted from Table 4.3 (page 164) that while total licences issued had declined during 1982–3 compared with earlier years, due to the decline of foreign aid funds and the Bank of Tanzania's own free resources, the introduction of import liberalization resulted in an increase of almost 92 per cent in the number of import licences issued over the space of one year. Indeed, import licences issued under the 'own-funded' basis during 1984–5 were about equal to or slightly greater than the total value of exports during 1985 and 1986. At the same time, licences issued on the 'own-funded' basis have risen very significantly, constituting 26.6 per cent of total import licences issued during the first year of the programme in 1984–5 and about 42.3 per cent during 1985–6. On the basis of calendar years, import licences issued on the 'no payment' basis rose from 17.5 per cent of total import licences issued in 1984 to 33.9 per cent and 37.0 per cent in 1985 and 1986 respectively. 'Own-funded' imports also increased from 4.7 per cent of total imports to 22.6 per cent and 26.6 per cent in 1985 and 1986 respectively.

The 'export-to-import' scheme has also resulted in a spectacular increase in the number of registered exporters of both traditional and non-traditional exports. Registered exporters rose from 104 in 1980 to 1,787 in 1986 (17 times). Since traditional exports are still confined to a few parastatal trading firms, the increase in the number of registered exporters overwhelmingly reflects increases in the number of exporters of non-traditional exports. Between September 1986 and May 1987 the value of non-traditional exports attributed to the 'retention' scheme was $US4 million. The retained foreign exchange could in principle be used for the purchase of inputs, spare parts or to cover the cost of foreign services. In 1988, imports financed from retained foreign exchange amounted to $US7.8 million.

The overall impact of the 'own-funds' import programme has yet to be established. In terms of Government revenue generation the impact has been positively spectacular. Revenue from customs duty and sales tax levied on own-funded imports rose from T.Shs 77.4 million in 1984 to T.Shs 1,078.2 million in 1986 (i.e. 14 times). The latter figure was about 40 per cent of the total revenue generated from duty levied on total imports.

Casual observation would also tend to indicate that the programme has resulted in import availability of essential consumer goods in most shops particularly in urban areas. Although some of these goods are luxuries and have been an important target for public criticism, it is also true that a significant part of the goods imported under the 'own-funded' imports programme have been vital intermediate inputs and capital goods. In 1984, for example, intermediate and capital goods accounted for three-quarters of total 'own-funds' imports. Important items in the capital goods category included machinery and equipment (about 39 per cent), spares, accessories and building materials (about 17 per cent). In 1986 the share of consumer goods in 'own-funded' imports increased slightly to 33 per cent while the rest (67 per cent) was composed largely of capital goods (35 per cent) and intermediate inputs.

Already some local firms (particularly in the textile sector) producing similar goods are complaining about increased competition from the influx of imported goods. On the one hand this is a welcome development as it has resulted in some price reductions in certain items and quality improvements in others. On the other hand, imported consumer goods and industrial inputs are still priced well above the average market for consumers and the average firm. For firms, this is indicated by the absence of significant improvements in capacity utilization.[1] Our survey during September–December 1986 revealed that most of these goods and inputs were being sold at between 4 and 7 times their import prices valued at the official exchange rate. However, some consumers are not surprised by these high prices because they used to pay probably just the same high prices to obtain similar goods in the second economy market before liberalization. The relative advantage of liberalization is the high probability of being able to obtain goods in the desired quantities. Indeed it could plausibly be argued that the inflationary impact of devaluation was not as high as might have been expected because of the increased supply of food and consumer goods made possible by a succession of good harvests, the 'own imports' scheme and donor import support.

An interesting aspect of 'own-funded' imports is the manner in which the imports are financed. While it must be true that 'own-funded' imports have been financed through foreign exchange resources obtained from relatives, friends and associates, it must also be a fact that some have been financed through own savings maintained in accounts abroad. Thus, to some extent the volume of 'own-funded' imports indicates the extent of foreign exchange resources held abroad (illegally) by Tanzanian residents. It is one of the manifestations of the second economy.[2] In turn this suggests that a significant proportion of foreign payments for Tanzanian exports and services bypass the official foreign exchange system. This reinforces our earlier findings about increasing levels of illegal imports and exports and other more subtle foreign exchange outflow mechanisms through over- and under-invoicing.

Another interesting aspect of 'own-funded' imports relates to the implicit realized exchange rate for these imports. As indicated earlier they were being sold at 4 to 7 times their CIF prices. This roughly corresponds to an implicit realized exchange rate of between T.Shs 90 and 120 to the US dollar. The average official exchange rate for 1986 was T.Shs 35 to $US1. Once again this lends further support to the existence of parallel exchange rates in Tanzania.

In a way therefore, the complaint by local firms that the competition from 'own-funded' imports is unfair, because some traders evade proper duty and sales tax payment, is valid. For even if importers of 'own-funded' imports paid the official duties, in so far as these duties are levied at the official exchange rate while imports are sold at the parallel exchange rate, then importers are *de facto* paying import duties far below the scheduled rates, i.e. in relation to realized exchange rates.

4.3 The Dilemma of Liberalization

Liberalization measures were introduced in stages during the years 1982-3 to 1984-5 under the general theme of Structural Adjustment Programme. The discussions with the IMF about an agreed reform programme had broken down in 1981 because several of the conditions attached were not acceptable. The country had been a fully-fledged member of the IMF for many years and had benefited substantially from low interest loans. The Government was faced with the problem of how far it could go with scrapping controls while maintaining overall control and without giving up major policy objectives. For many years the international lending institutions had disapproved of Tanzania's policies as being radical and wished the economy to be exposed to the more direct impact of market decisions. It was argued that the policies followed until the late 1970s had impeded growth and that institutional controls had distorted the development of the economy. The desperate shortages of foreign exchange had led to drastic cuts in imports which badly affected agricultural exports and led to a vicious circle of contraction. The problems were greatly compounded by these events: the drought of 1973-4; the break-up of the East African Community in 1979; the cost of the Uganda war in 1979; the two major oil price increases of 1974 and 1979; and the slump in primary commodity prices.

All these factors gravely weakened Tanzania's negotiating position because reserves for financing imports had become virtually exhausted and beggars cannot be choosers. The desperate situation was exacerbated by the fact that failure to come to an agreement with the IMF might have stemmed the flow of aid from traditional and other donors, although Tanzania's grants and aid receipts increased significantly during the period when her interventionist policies were increased. It is interesting, therefore, to speculate why the Structural Adjustment Programme was adopted when it was as a first step towards liberalization.

Bates[3] has argued that this question can be answered in socio-political terms on the grounds that the interventionist policies had favoured a small elite with political power. A large growth in the public employment sector, involving some element of political patronage; the operation of price policies by the export marketing boards, and an overvalued currency with tight import controls were instruments of economic and political power of the ruling groups. These policies enabled favoured groups to accumulate assets which they were reluctant to surrender or see undermined by policies of liberalization. The argument runs that it was the interventionist policies which had created power positions that the leadership was unwilling to surrender or to share with newcomers. This argument is less relevant for Tanzania because in the first place liberalization policies would obviously lead to far greater opportunities for the accumulation of assets. No one has suggested that the top leadership was motivated by the desire to accumulate assets. To provide potential supporters with positions of influence is a recognized device for consolidating political power, but this is not an adequate explanation for a political switch. Bates's argument would not be of relevance to Tanzania if the economic controls were seen in their widest sense to include undermining the rise of political rivals through economic strength.

In examining the same question, of why Tanzania veered towards liberalization when it did, Hodd[4] arrives at a different set of explanations. In the first place he thinks it likely that the ruling elite had more to gain from a more rapid growth of GDP than from the continuation of existing policies. In the second place he felt that the acquisition of assets had gone as far as could be expected, and that improving the circumstances of the wider community would safeguard the status quo. In the third place he is convinced that the World Bank and the IMF have over the years been successful in persuading potential aid donors and commercial lenders that market oriented policy reforms are essential.

While all these explanations may be relevant for other countries they certainly do not explain adequately why Tanzania began to liberalize. Tanzania's traditional donors did not give up on her, despite the IMF argument that lending should depend on prior agreement. Simpler explanations were probably more important. First was that, encouraged by long periods of conservative governments in the USA, Germany and

Britain, which favour market decisions, the IMF was able to pressurize Tanzania with more intensity. Sir Geoffrey Howe, Britain's former Foreign Secretary, has recently confirmed:

> that only by agreeing terms with the 'international financial institutions' would African countries find willing donors in Europe and the US. 'There is ever wider recognition that peace and reconciliation, political stability and the discipline of economic liberalism are the key to national recovery.'[5]

A second simpler explanation is that the Government's efforts to revive the economy through the SAP and NESP required immediate availability of resources and the vulnerability and sheer size of the economic crisis were enough to cause alarm. The third simpler explanation, and probably by far the most important of them all, is the timing of liberalization just two years before the impending retirement of Nyerere from the Presidency, and the conclusive evidence that all three Presidential candidates saw liberalization as the immediate option. While the late Premier Sokoine liberalized the importation of pick-ups, Salim Ahmed Salim liberalized the importation of *mitumba* (second-hand clothing) at a rally in the south of Tanzania. Well before all this the then President of Zanzibar, President Mwinyi, was quoted as hailing economic improvements for Zanzibar following the country's import liberalization. It is only sensible to argue that Nyerere preferred a smooth transfer of power while bankruptcy was staved off.

In the circumstances gradual acceptance of liberalization seemed to be the lesser evil, for it left the Government with some flexibility of timing although without much choice. The liberalization programme started in quite a small way, for complete liberalization would have involved the abandonment of all major control institutions created since independence. It would also have entailed a high cost in social and political terms which the Government was not prepared to risk. A beginning was made with partial liberalization of imports.

How successful have the liberalization measures been? It has to be admitted that they conceal a large amount of window dressing in the sense that many negative effects have been ignored. In practice, there is a long list of difficulties with liberalization as a prelude to privatization adding to the already harsh economic and political problems. The difficulties of implementation are pointed out as being immense; the lack of managerial skills and abilities; lack of market mechanisms in a poor country; the likelihood of new monopolies and the development of uneven economic growth where regional and ethnicity balances may not be priorities to the private investor whose objectives are basically big profit margins. Then there are the problems of lack of incentives to invest in a country whose economic policies are rather unstable due to regular shifts of policies. Will grants, loans and/or aid flow easily with privatization, and where does a country get all the necessary funds to pay for the interim period while the system is being overhauled? Will the external shocks – such as the oil and manufactured goods crisis, the persistent problem of low commodity prices which create trade imbalances – cease simply because a country has switched to market decisions? And what of inflation and price increases brought about by massive devaluation? As Premier Warioba expressed to a visiting US Under-Secretary of State for Economic Affairs:

> the measures being taken to rehabilitate the economy are hard hitting to peasants. The peasants were seriously affected by the increase in the price of agricultural inputs and consumer goods.[6]

In an almost similar tone, the *Tanzanian Economic Trends* cautions the Government against a policy of high interest rates:

> High nominal interest rates act as an added burden to the crop marketing system, increasing the need for credit expansion. In the Tanzanian institutional context it is to be doubted whether high nominal interest rates, largely applied to intra-parastatal transactions, serve much useful purpose and it could even be argued that they reinforce inflationary pressures. The time should come when the effort is made to squeeze inflation out of the system rather than attempting to adjust to inflationary conditions through exchange rate movements and high nominal interest rates.[7]

To cap it all, since Tanzania still lacks a powerful indigenous entrepreneurial class with a strong capital base, privatization will necessarily favour foreign investors whose investment decisions are determined to fit margins regardless of social and political implications, such as uneven development. But Tanzania has no choice in dealing with the hard lending terms of the Fund (IMF) and present Western governments in favour of market decisions. *Africa Analysis* writes about this:

> A commission appointed by President Reagan had meanwhile called for an acceleration of these efforts (privatisation campaign). In a report in March, the high level advisory panel urge US aid and multilateral agencies like the World Bank to make their grants and loans directly contingent on recipient's willingness to carry out privatisation schemes.[8]

There have been many reports of increased cattle and elephant rustling and a greater volume of smuggling. There is no evidence that the manufacturing sector has gained competitiveness. If money overseas pays for additional imports it generates extra customs duty and relieves budgetary pressures. Liberalization has permitted the lowering of taxes and the cutting of subsidies which eases the Government's problems. Those who favour liberalization ˙argue on grounds of what the programme has been able to achieve so far, and those against the programme insist it helps only the rich; they see liberalization as a highway to privatization in Tanzania. Opinions on liberalization are divided among the Tanzanian policy-makers.

Yet another set of views comes from the four groups which we interviewed: rural households, urban workers, traders and transporters. Opinions on liberalization were measured by the 'yes' and 'no' type of response, where 'no' represented dislike for liberalization. There were two very clear messages from all four groups tested. While liberalization was considered useful, the question of price reduction scored even higher percentages.

The four groups showed similar patterns with regard to responses within the sub-categories of each sector. For example those who considered themselves businessmen gave a high positive rating for liberalization in all four groups, and those in trades scored lowest. As Table 4.4 (page 165) shows, lower ratings were from the rural households. Professionals in the rural areas were almost equally divided: 51 per cent being in favour, 49 per cent against.

On the whole Table 4.4 shows that workers ranked liberalization more highly than the other three groups, probably because they were badly hit by shortages. The transporters' group showing of 50 per cent in favour can be explained by the fact that some of their needs – fuel, oil and tyres for example – were still available through official sources. The traders' high preference for liberalization – 76 per cent – may be explained by the possibility of large profit margins and employment which they foresaw.

The indifference of rural households to liberalization is of great interest. Their reaction may be based on the high prices charged for commodities, which are usually higher than those of the Price Commission and even higher than prices charged in urban free markets. Or it may be that in 1985 the rural areas were still starved of commodities due to transportation difficulties. Also, liberalization may be rejected in rural areas for ideological reasons. But in Tanzania power is balanced in favour of urban dwellers, as evidenced by the Government subsidies for staples.

5

Dynamics of the Second Economy

5.1 Participation in the Second Economy

The magnitude and different manifestations of participation in the second economy are relevant for a number of reasons, two of which are key ones. On the one hand participation explains the degree of pervasiveness to which second economy activities manifest themselves in a society. Pervasiveness thus measures the extent to which these second economy activities are integrated. On the other hand, an analysis of participation, ranging from individual participants and the goods they trade in down to the manner and means by which such activities are carried out, sheds light on the structural and organizational nature of such activities. A study of goods traded in seeks to identify sources and markets.

5.1.1 Organization

A good number of second economy analysts have stressed the importance of organization as a major element that allows illegal activity to take hold and challenge the primary economy. Both the 1983 crackdown and the 1985-6 survey data seem to suggest a lack of any significant systematic structures of organization in the system.

Two main explanations for the absence of organization seem plausible. First, there appears to be no one strong supportive base for *Ulanguzi* in Tanzania. Green[1] identifies transportation as the supporting base for *Magendo* in Uganda, suggesting that a large volume of *Magendo* depends on organized means of transportation. His proposition is unquestionably logical, since a large part of the second economy involves the movement of goods. For instance, coffee, which fetches high incomes under *Magendo* in Uganda, being a bulky commodity, requires organized transport if it is to be traded in any volume.

Tanzania is different. In the first place, private firms have little stake in water, rail or air transport, and although over 50 per cent of the country's vehicles are in private hands unavailability of spares, fuel and oil and non-preferential allocation have hampered the movement of quantities of goods by private trucks over long distances. This helps us to understand why, apart from maize and rice, the second economy is confined to items with high unit transport value like cardamom, cloves and gemstones, and livestock, which provide their own transport.

Secondly, the centres of trade in Tanzania – the regional cities – are quite distant from each other, and movement from one point to another entails thousands of kilometres over bad roads. For example, of the 33,722 kilometres of road in the country, only 2,625 kilometres, or roughly 8 per cent, are hard surfaced. 14.5 per cent are gravel roads, while the rest are dirt roads, sometimes accessible during the dry season only.[2] Thus transportation difficulties have been a deterrent to the spread of second economy activities in Tanzania.

Another characteristic of the second economy in Tanzania, which probably also influences the level of organization, is the absence of any single commodity that can be traded in volume regularly. Most Tanzanian goods that would be attractive to the second economy trade are publicly controlled through co-operatives, crop authorities or state trading corporations. Besides, primary co-operatives at the village level were not dismantled. To deflect large quantities of goods from these public corporations would be very conspicuous and could not continue for long unless everyone conspired in their disappearance. There have been very few cases of bales of coffee disappearing between the producing areas and the ports. Smuggling of raw cotton or sisal has been even less common.

With public control of major cash crops, the absence of an active large-scale private transport base on account of irregular supplies of fuel, oil and spares and bad roads, as well as the long distances to markets, most of the second economy has remained substantially a less integrated operation. Thus it is not surprising that the initial study of the economic sabotage activities, especially those revealed by the crackdown operation of 1983, suggested no systematic organization or linkages domestically. The external linkages simply reflect family ties emerging from the very transient nature of most Tanzanian traders. The earlier study concluded that the marketeering activities occur spontaneously, serving as a safety valve to permit sheer survival under hard economic circumstances.

Indeed some form of organization is inevitable for quantities of goods smuggled in and for access to markets beyond the borders of Tanzania in such commodities as ivory, gemstones (including gold) and those other tradable commodities with high unit transport value. The difference is that such organizations are not strong enough to threaten state legitimacy. They do not, for example, have with them armed support services and they do not, as the 1983 crackdown revealed, rely on political and economic power centres.

5.1.2. Pervasiveness: by Types of Crime

In order to determine the degree to which buying and selling in parallel markets has penetrated society, the concept we refer to as pervasiveness of second economy practices, cross-sectional data were gathered for eight rural area households and for three districts in Dar es Salaam, representing three different economic strata for workers. Questions on the ways and means of obtaining household needs were put to both groups. The intention was to understand how Tanzanians live amidst dire shortages of basic commodities for daily life. In addition another two groups, traders and transporters, were requested to respond to questions on how they obtain their commodities for sale. Other specific questions pertinent to these groups were asked, and replies are discussed under the relevant sub-headings below.

When responses from these four groups of participants were compared with the bulk of the information gathered during the 1983-4 economic sabotage crackdown operation, there was no change of pattern to the four major manifestations of participation:[3] geographical participation; participation according to major economic activities; participation by employment patterns, and participation by ethnicity, broken down to household level. We shall return to the data on rural households, on urban workers, on traders, and on transporters, but it is important to describe first the participation patterns revealed above by the 1983 crackdown.

(a) Geographical participation in the second economy presented an interesting pattern. For instance, the Mbeya and Mara regions had the biggest share of cases involving illegal possession of arms and ammunition. For Mara there was also a high incidence of cases involving unlawful possession of army property, ranging from clothing and gunnery to food supplies pilfered from army stores.

Regions which are endowed with minerals, especially gold and diamonds, but also almandine, garnet, loilite, amethyst, quartz and obsidian, had a high incidence of cases involving the unlawful possession of minerals. Such regions include Mbeya, Shinyanga and Tabora. We noted, however, that as you move away from these regions cases decreased, but the likelihood of the buyer having a fake piece of gold or diamond increases. The Tribunal record revealed that in Arusha, Dar es Salaam, and a few other towns, several cases of possession of fake minerals were dealt with.

For regions which are situated near Government game reserves and national parks a high incidence of poaching and trafficking in

Government trophies was observed. The regions with most cases were Morogoro, Iringa, Arusha and Mara.

(b) Illegal foreign exchange dealing was prevalent in Dar es Salaam more than elsewhere. This can be explained by the fact that Dar es Salaam is the largest port of entry and also the centre of the tourist trade in the country. Other favourite tourist centres like Arusha also had a high incidence of cases involving illegal dealing in and possession of foreign currency. In this connection it is pertinent to mention one notable phenomenon: most of the foreign currency acquired was simply accumulated in the person's home. It appears that the persons involved were not buying foreign currency for immediate use but simply as an insurance for smooth flight in case of turbulence in the country. It is reasonable to think that in the border regions of Mbeya or Mara currency from neighbouring countries was being acquired for immediate use in the purchase of goods from across the border. In Dar es Salaam and Arusha, however, the illegally held English pounds, US dollars, deutschmarks and Swiss francs appear to have been simply stockpiled for smuggling out of the country.

Like hoarding, the possession of local currency in inordinate amounts was an offence which extended over the whole country. The records show that many people were found with hundreds of thousands of Tanzanian shillings in their homes, some even moving about with it in their vehicles and in their briefcase offices which had mushroomed at that time. Evidence of possession of money in large quantities, a practice well spread over the whole country, more than supports the demand for a currency approach for measuring the size of the second economy, as mentioned earlier. Additionally, it is felt that due to the highly unpredictable market situation, traders and others in search of essential commodities had to keep their assets liquid and available to take advantage of opportunities as they arose. Therefore, the large amounts of cash uncovered in the course of the crackdown were not actually 'hoarded'. The money was circulating, but it was not doing so through the banks. No wonder, therefore, that cash outside the banking system increased fourfold from T.Shs 2.4 billion in 1977 to T.Shs 9.4 billion in 1984 (Table 2.3, page 143).

As for the offence of hoarding essential commodities (these include sugar, rice, cooking oil, clothing, soap and other toiletries, motor vehicle spares, etc.) or illegal trading in those commodities, regions with a better supply of these goods (relative to other regions) demonstrated the highest incidence. Although hoarding was among the most common offences discovered in every region, its intensity in some regions was notable. These included Dar es Salaam, Shinyanga, Mwanza, Arusha, Mbeya and Kigoma, which are basically supply centres for other regions; and regions such as Kagera, Tanga, Arusha, Kigoma, Mara, Lindi,

Ruvuma and Mbeya, which are farthest from the principal supply centre – Dar es Salaam. For example, in Mbeya and Mara, more than forty cases of illegal possession of hospital medicine were prosecuted before the Tribunal, and this suggests a high prevalence of illegal medical practice in those regions. For the other commodities there was also a very high degree of illegal trading in these regions. Large quantities of gasolene, bottled beer, clothing (especially *khanga* and *vitenge*), machine and motor vehicle parts were the most important goods impounded during the crackdown.

(*c*) Particular employment opportunities and personal circumstances also explain the involvement of certain ethnic groups in illegal foreign exchange dealings. The dominant involvement of Asians in the unlawful acquisition of foreign currency was probably the result of the turbulent history of Asian settlement in East Africa, a history which has seen them expelled from Uganda at short notice. They had, therefore, good reason for being apprehensive about the permanence of their stay in Tanzania. However, a limited number of indigenous Tanzanians were also arrested for involvement in the unlawful acquisition of foreign currency. These were individuals who, in one way or another, were connected with the tourist trade. Some were associated with tourist hotels, others operated tour companies which gave them easy access to foreigners entering Tanzania. The rates of foreign exchange offered on the black market at the time were invariably at least five times the official rate.

As for involvement in hoarding and illegal trading of basic household goods, the persons concerned were mostly indigenous Tanzanians, many of whom were trading without licences. In the three years preceding the crackdown operation, the number of people giving up office employment to engage in illegal trading grew. Many prospered because of their access to Government supply institutions through other corruptible employees who remained in their former offices.

Records did not show that any public company or other state institution was brought before the Tribunal to face criminal proceedings for economic sabotage. Officers of Government institutions who were arrested for sabotage activities were called to answer the charges as private individuals, although it is arguable that some of the actions with which they were charged had been done while they acted in an official capacity.

(*d*) With regard to the identity of those engaged in the second economy, evidence was that internal marketeering and profiteering had been primarily carried out between businessmen (and self-made businessmen of the briefcase company variety) and the quasi-state corporations. This is inevitable, given that a large proportion of trade and manufacturing is in the hands of the parastatals and parastatals have a monopoly over the distribution of domestic appliances, grain, other foodstuffs, and regulated household goods. During the crackdown in April 1983, the largest proportion of those arrested were businessmen and pseudo businessmen. By mid-April, out of 3,150 arrested (which rose to 4,216 around the end of April), 2,872 were classified as businessmen.

The arrests of businessmen were followed in frequency by the arrests of public employees engaged in the manufacture and distribution of essential goods, while fewer arrests were reported for persons in unlawful possession of foreign exchange or firearms and ammunition, or for persons engaged in the traffic of Government trophies or minerals, or for Government or Party employees suspected of having accumulated unexplained wealth.

The crackdown also revealed other dimensions of participation in *Ulanguzi*. First, it would appear that the persons engaging in economic sabotage activities were overwhelmingly Tanzanians, since no significant foreign element was uncovered. Even where a few non-nationals were netted for economic sabotage, the record revealed that their sphere of operation was local. These were mostly persons from neighbouring countries who had filtered into the country without going through the necessary procedures which would make them lawful immigrants. They also included a small group of people of Asian extraction who had lived in Tanzania for a long time without completing the citizenship procedures to become nationals.

Another notable feature of *Ulanguzi* revealed by the crackdown was that the involvement of particular social or ethnic groups in economic sabotage activities paralleled the participation of these groups in the general Tanzanian economy. For example, the motor vehicle industry, which in Tanzania includes the sale of vehicles and supply of parts and spares, is dominated by traders of Asian origin. Not surprisingly, the majority of those arrested for hoarding motor vehicle spares were Asian traders.

5.1.3 Pervasiveness: by Livelihood

A second measure for pervasiveness of the second economy sector was determined by analysing data on individual livelihood, itemized by the different additional informal economic activities in which people engaged in addition to their principal occupations – by patterns of ownership of those secondary/informal activities, by comparing incomes derived from the secondary activities (usually unlicensed and untaxed) to the incomes derived from the primary activities, and by looking at the source of basic commodities/supplies for the four groups of people interviewed. They were: rural households, urban workers, traders and transporters. The primary occupation was regarded as the principal occupation or main job which a particular individual was publicly known to be doing.

5.1.3.1 Traders

The sample revealed eight common occupations among the traders, ranging from shopkeeping (49 per cent) to butchering (about 2 per cent), which seem to represent a vivid picture of the urban-type economic activities. Hawkering scored 19 per cent as the third ranking among the common occupations. Shops, hawkers and bar/restaurants accounted for 83.5 per cent of all traders and they also accounted for 86 per cent of all the employment in the primary occupation category. The garage and petrol station industry was found to be the industry with the highest number of employees per establishment (on average 6 workers/employees per unit). Hawkers generally operated singly, i.e. virtually no hiring at all (Table 5.1, page 166).

Additional data are also presented in Table 5.1. For example, the ratio of male to female employment is 2:1, while that of adults to children is 19:1. Within the activities there is a marked difference, in that while bar/restaurant employment is 3:2 in favour of males, in butchering males account for over 85 per cent of total employment. Family employment accounts for a third of total employment, explaining the usual extended family pattern. Individual and family ownership accounts for 86 per cent of the primary occupation trade. Individual ownership is concentrated in the tailoring, shoe-dealing and hawking trades. Companies predominate in garages. The least common type of ownership is the co-operative.

Agriculture and trade account for 87 per cent of all secondary occupation activities, and agriculture is the most important single activity (see Table 5.2, page 167). Retail shopkeepers were commonly engaged mostly in agricultural work and hawking; carpenters double-jobbed in shopkeeping and in agriculture; and hawkers and butchers double-jobbed as workers. Employment in the secondary occupation favours males and there is a low rate of child participation. All the employees in the retail shops were males. Bar/restaurants employed more females than males. Generally the employment of children was found in the secondary activity except in hawking, although the level does not reach that in the primary occupation where 4 per cent of the workforce were children. Family employment is reduced very little in the secondary activities, by only 3.5 per cent to 27.5 per cent of total employment, suggesting that employment patterns are similar to those observed for primary activities. Again, individual and family ownership is the largest, accounting for 82 per cent of all the secondary kinds of activities, well ahead of co-operative ownership which accounts for a mere 3 per cent, similar to the primary occupation activities (Table 5.3, page 168).

Most traders (64 per cent)in the primary and secondary occupations do not purchase their commodities from public trading institutions. Butchers in both the primary and the secondary sectors do not derive their commodities for sale from the official sector (Table 5.4, page 168), which was expected, and garage/petrol owners purchase about two-thirds of their commodities from the public sector. Perhaps the remaining third is the oil lubricant purchased in the parallel market, which would tend to account for the regular disappearance of oil lubricant at petrol stations in the mid-1980s. Retail shop owners obtained their materials/commodities from 43 per cent official and 57 per cent other sources, and the percentages for hawker, bar/restaurant, and tailoring are 29 per cent and 71 per cent, 30 per cent and 70 per cent, 33 per cent and 67 per cent respectively. In short, two-thirds of their requirements are derived from unofficial and other sources, meaning that for every single commodity available to the trader from public institutions, there were two more from non-public institution sources. These figures must be interpreted with caution because obtaining a commodity or a given raw material from a source other than public institutions could simply mean ease of access to the other source and not necessarily an indication of non-availability from public institutions.

Income figures are higher in primary than in secondary activities (Table 5.1). Most traders (72 per cent) engaged in a secondary activity derived the bulk of their income from primary activities. This means that 28 per cent of all traders get most of their incomes from secondary activities. However, incomes from the secondary activities measured against time spent (allowing for leisure, etc.) seem to be higher than incomes from primary activities. Traders on average spend two hours in their primary activity to earn the equivalent of one hour in the secondary activity.

5.1.3.2 Workers

Workers were interviewed for similar purposes as the traders: to discover the extent of their participation in the secondary economic activity, as shown by kind of extra engagement in addition to their regular employment, and by gender participation. The indicators for participation would also show where they bought their household requirements and what incomes were derived from their involvement in the secondary activities. A total of 347 were interviewed in three distinct areas of Dar es Salaam, including Manzese (the most densely populated squatter area and notable for unrecorded economic activities), Ilala (which is representative of residential areas at the lower end of the middle incomes), and Mwenge (a typical middle income workers' residential area). The interviews identified (in descending numbers) teachers, accountants, secretaries, cleaners, managers, agriculturalists, engineers, doctors, community workers, drivers, economists, security guards, Party officers, shopkeepers, carpenters, lawyers and 8 others. The main workers' primary and secondary occupations are presented in Table 5.5 (page 169).

Table 5.6 (page 170) shows that workers' participation in the secondary activities was 54 per cent of the total number of workers, a little higher than for traders. Of those workers who engaged in the secondary activities, 133 out of 189 household heads, or 70 per cent, were engaged in farm-related activities, which include livestock – a point also noted by Belshaw[4] for Uganda: 'In Bunyole at least, civil servants are now farmers first, of necessity', and Gargan:[5] 'Tanzania Economics: First, a Cow'.

Another activity attractive to workers as their secondary activity was trade. This association suggests that surplus yields from farming are sold. Agriculturists in the worker trades seem to be consistent in that a high percentage of those in agriculture as their primary sector were also engaged in agriculture for their secondary activities, and accounted for 56 per cent of the total compared to 41 per cent of teachers and 39 per cent of doctors. Interestingly enough the 50 per cent of all the Party officers engaged in the secondary activity are all in trade. All the economists indicated that they were engaged in secondary activities, 80 per cent of them in farming. Managers not identified by nature of trade or by ownership were 50 per cent in farming and 42 per cent in trade as their secondary activities.

As with the traders' participation in secondary activities, workers showed no tendency to take advantage of transfer of experience. Only 11.5 per cent of workers participated in the second layer (third job), and this is only 21 per cent of the workers who had a secondary activity. Farming (agriculture and livestock) accounted for nearly 70 per cent of all employment in the undeclared sector (Table 5.6). Six out of seventeen primary occupation categories did not involve themselves in the second layer of the secondary activity; these were secretaries, drivers, Party officers, shopkeepers, carpenters and lawyers.

Workers were also asked to indicate where they obtained their daily basic needs/commodities – whether official source, unofficial market (non-public) or 'other', which includes own (home-grown food) source and gifts. Commodities were divided into three groups: price-controlled maize, rice, sugar and wheat; non-price-controlled other foodstuffs; and kerosene and other commodities (like soap and cooking oil). Of all those who responded, 37 per cent said the main source of their supplies was the market (unofficial); 26 per cent said public institutions, while for 29.2 per cent their main source was 'other'. The percentages for staples and other foods are higher in the other category: 25 per cent and 42 per cent respectively, compared to only 15 per cent for other commodities (Table 5.4). These results are not surprising considering that the workers' predominant secondary activity was agriculture. A second possible reason for the high percentages under 'other' source may be receipts of foodstuff from up-country. There are many Tanzanian workers with up-country family ties. In fact the present workforce in urban areas of mainland Tanzania have a first home where family members and the majority of distant relatives live, and the contact is usually kept up through visits and exchange of gifts – money and city commodities flowing to the countryside in exchange for food and services, for example a week's labour in the worker's up-country shamba.

The higher percentage of kerosene procurement in the 'other' column is hard to explain. Probably kerosene/petroleum is siphoned from public vehicles for cash or in exchange for goods and/or services. Possibly kerosene or even some foodstuffs may be bought from public institutions in bulk and dumped back on the open market, which was not an unusual occurrence.

Income earned was almost evenly split between primary and secondary activities: 53 per cent and 47 per cent respectively. Only the accountants and doctors (among the traditional professions) and the security guards reported secondary activities to be the most important source of income: 70 per cent of accountants, 54.5 per cent of doctors and 62.5 per cent of security guards. This divergent trend may have been a reflection of the low salary scales offered to these professionals. Doctors and accountants may have been engaged in intensive farming activities, especially considering the lucrative incomes derived from pigs and poultry. Moreover, all the doctors engaged in secondary activities were in agriculture and not in private practices (probably because of barriers), and only 16 per cent of the accountants who were engaged in secondary activities were in trade (probably doing accountancy privately), the rest were in agriculture: cropping and livestock. The surprising finding was the number of Party officers whose incomes were evenly divided between primary and secondary activities (secondary activities being trade).

5.1.3.3 Rural households

In total 385 household heads of eight regions were interviewed to ascertain sources of their incomes, expenditure and participation in the second economy, both directly and indirectly. In general, the specific questions put to rural household heads were slightly different from those of the other three groups. The objective here was to determine total production of both cash and food crops and to reveal proportions of the produce sold to official as well as to unofficial markets. Secondly, the interviews sought to discover the sources of household basic needs and to see if double or multiple jobbing was a common practice. Monetary figures on incomes and expenditures were used for the micro-economic approach to the measurement of the size of the second economy reported in Chapter 2.

Table 5.7 (page 171) reveals the expected high percentage (78 per cent) of the rural household heads reporting farming as their primary activity. A closer analysis of the data clearly shows that, although a few peasants are engaged in other activities, the majority of the remaining 20 per cent of heads of households are professional or non-farm workers. These other professionals include teachers, doctors and carpenters, just to mention a few.

There was a heavy representation in farming by spouses engaged in primary activity. Of the 80 per cent of the household heads whose primary occupation was farming, 88 per cent had spouses engaged in non-wage employment occupations. In other words, there are few females engaged in paid employment in the eight regions covered by the survey. The picture changes in urban areas where a much larger proportion is engaged in the cash economy. This is further demonstrated by the high frequency of household basic needs buying which involves males twice as frequently except for charcoal and cooking oil where women do most of the buying. Thus by implication the purchasing power of Tanzanian rural women is much smaller than that of their counterparts in the urban areas. 43 per cent of all household heads engage in some secondary activity (i.e. 164 household heads), agriculture being the most important, and more so when livestock, fisheries and poultry are added to farming.

Farmers declared most income to have come from their secondary non-farm activity, and this group accounted for 47 per cent of all those who have a secondary activity. Trade was found to be the single largest category, involving 34 per cent of all the farmers engaged in any secondary activity (Table 5.5: note that this table has separate columns for 'Business' and 'Trade', whereas in the text 'Trade' has been inserted for 'Business').

If we ignore the heavy weight of farmers in the sample, we see that 67 other households admitted to being involved in the secondary economy. Of these, 60 households, or 87 per cent of the total, were involved in farming proper, whereas 95.5 per cent were involved in the widest definition of agriculture. Farmers themselves disclosed their secondary income source as being the most important. The remaining non-agricultural households declared that their primary occupation was in the main their major income source (Table 5.7). These two findings further support the contention that poor producer prices for agricultural produce have, until recently, often led farmers to engage in other activities to supplement their household incomes. Villages within reach of towns usually supply charcoal, firewood and non-staple foods like milk, eggs and goats to town dwellers, and for some people such activities may bring more income than does their farm.

The predominant income findings were not surprising in that 39 per cent of the eight regions' respondents who had a secondary occupation indicated that their primary occupation brought them their higher income, while 52 per cent said their secondary activities were more significant, as shown in Table 5.7. This 52 per cent represents 22 per cent of the households earning most in the secondary activities. Low income earning from typical farming activities seems to support a long-held conviction that non-farm income accounts for 30 to 40 per cent of the household incomes in some regions, and that in real terms incomes are lower there since inflation is higher outside towns.

Table 5.8 (page 172) shows the dominance of the household head male income as shown by the percentage of the replies to the question of who earns more. The percentages are: 70 per cent, 15 per cent and 15 per cent for heads, spouses, and for both categories respectively. However, there is little involvement of children in the secondary activities. Children selling commodities represent only 2.5 per cent and 21.5 per cent for buying commodities from non-public sources.

In general, rural households reported that they derived their basic needs largely from the unofficial market, by 85 per cent compared to 30 per cent when other sources are excluded and when a third source 'other' is included. For the rural household and workers alone the sourcing of basic needs is lowest for official sources, and in almost equal proportions for 'other' and private sources. Of all the commodities in the sample, only sugar was obtainable in both public and non-public enterprises in almost equal proportions for the Mbeya region.

5.1.3.4 Transporters

Transporters were surveyed in Kigoma, Arusha, Moshi and Musoma, subdivided by operators of taxi, bus, lorry, lorry and bus, and any other. The key questions were designed to obtain information on availability of spares, petroleum products and tyres and on fares charged and real costs.

In general, Table 5.9 (page 173) shows that taxis were the most common type of service, with almost 33 per cent of all transporters involved. Buses and taxis taken together accounted for nearly 60 per cent of the total figure. There were differences within each region. Kigoma had the most transport by lorry, taxi and bus, at 20 per cent each, as against Arusha which had 37 per cent of its transporters in the taxi business. Moshi had 70 per cent of all its transporters in buses and taxis, while Musoma had 80 per cent of its transporters in lorries and taxis. While these differences reflect transportation requirements in the regions, we hasten to caution that the figures could have been influenced by sampling.

Individual ownership was by far the most important form of ownership, accounting for 56 per cent of all the transport businesses.

Individual ownership is particularly prevalent in Musoma (75 per cent). Family ownership was found to account for 25 per cent and was most marked in the 'bus and lorry' category, two-thirds of all the firms were family-owned companies and accounted for 18 per cent of all transporters. However, family ownership was not common in taxi and 'any other' categories. Co-operative ownership did not feature at all.

Product acquisition in the transportation sector is by and large from public institutions. Overall 80 per cent of all fuel is purchased from official outlets. Arusha, Moshi and Musoma acquired 95 per cent of their requirements from official sources. Kigoma stands in marked contrast, where only 30 per cent of all transporters obtained their product from official outlets. At the same time, Kigoma was the only region that showed its transporters to rely for their requirements about equally on public and private sources. When all products are put together, transporters buy 18 per cent in the unofficial market. These percentages are no surprise since at one time there was a serious shortage of tyres and spares, and allocation of fuel and oil favoured public transportation even though by and large petroleum products would not enter the parallel market.

The buying of tyres in Arusha and Moshi was pretty evenly shared between official and other sources, while Kigoma obtained 80 per cent and Musoma obtained 100 per cent of their tyres from official sources. This is surprising, given that the tyre factory is located in Arusha. Tyre purchasing was 68 per cent official for all regions combined.

It seems transporters are not as dependent on public sources in the procurement of tyres as they are in fuel, 68 per cent and 80 per cent respectively. Again, Kigoma shows marked differences in the buying of its transportation requirements, being almost entirely dependent on official sources for tyres and buying fuel in the official sector exclusively. Probably privately owned boats cross to neighbouring countries and come back with petroleum products.

Family members do not seem to be heavily engaged in this sector and they account for only 11 per cent. Employment in lorry and bus enterprises is 31 per cent female. No females were recorded under taxi operation, which is surprising considering that private ownership accounts for over 80 per cent of all transport firms.

The broad indications are that the second economy activities tend to be similar for all the tested groups and that they correspond quite closely to the existing formal economic activities, led by agriculture. Urban/rural differences are not so marked in terms of the main secondary activities by the household heads, traders and urban workers (professions and those in various trades). The other common occurrence is that those who are in a given primary profession engage in completely different informal secondary activities, i.e. lack of specialization. Further evidence shows that rural households are less reliant on official sources for basic needs than urban workers.

Major income sources are from the primary activities for the traders, and less so for the workers, but from the secondary activities for the rural household heads engaged in agriculture. Secondary activity for the rural households accounts for 30 per cent of employment, and 20 per cent of them earn most of their income from the secondary activities. Farmers' participation in secondary activities is very low. In the worker group, although 45 per cent of them do not have a secondary activity, the remaining 55 per cent create 52 per cent of total employment. This means secondary activity employment is larger than that of the primary activity by 10 per cent as Table 5.7 shows.

Table 5.10 (page 174) clearly shows that individual ownership for the primary and secondary economic activities is highest among traders, workers, rural households, and hauliers. Company and co-operative ownership is minimal among the traders and zero for hauliers. Participation through selling and buying is done by adults alone as child involvement amounts to only about 4 per cent (Table 5.11b, page 174). Gender participation reflects the normal picture of male domination in the rural areas. In the urban areas, particularly Dar es Salaam, most purchasing is done by females for all the three categories of commodities, and the proportions are virtually the same (Table 5.11c, page 175). Our earlier data, collected in 1983–4, presented in Table 5.12 (page 176), however, suggested that more males engaged in selling than females, particularly non-food products for all the areas: Dar es Salaam, Dodoma and Tanga, except for Tanga where females sold more beans and maize than males. This is consistent with our earlier observation, and that of Tripp,[6] that the economic crisis and subsequent rise of the informal sector have given a new importance to the economic role of the disadvantaged groups, especially women.

Overall, the preceding evidence has clearly demonstrated that, in the first place, most urban wage earner households derive a larger proportion of their earnings from participation in side-line, informal sector activities than from their main employment. This finding emphasizes the extremely low levels of formal earnings (mainly wages), and reflects the underlying high rate of profitability of the informal sector. Informal sector activities are profitable partly because they do not pay taxes and other social charges, and partly because they are technically efficient. Their reliance on, and productive use of, domestic material, tools equipment and artisanal skills make them less vulnerable to external shocks such as foreign exchange shortages, lack of imported inputs and spares.

In the second place the findings reinforce our earlier observation that since the official economy was supply constrained, Government controls on prices, marketing and distribution of commodities, goods and services was made less effective by the widespread existence of second economy transactions. Lastly, the growth of informal sector activities has given an added impetus to the expanding economic role of women, especially in the urban household economy.

Whether or not the growth of the legitimate informal sector in the 1980s is sustainable in the the long run remains an open question, but there is no doubt that during the interim period of economic recovery the informal sector will continue to play an important role in sustaining the livelihoods of most households, especially in urban areas.

In the longer term, the development of the legitimate informal sector will be crucially dependent on three closely interrelated factors: Government policy, the speed of economic recovery, and market constraint. Recently there has been implicit recognition of the informal sector by some Government officials. So far, however, Government has not issued any explicit policy about the status or promotion of the informal sector. Certainly the Party Leadership Code is still in force. Government promotion policy and support are necessary especially in the provision of credit (capital being a major constraint in the informal sector) which is tailored to meet the needs of small-scale artisanal operators who lack sufficient collateral; and provision of basic infrastructure and a conducive working environment (for example, providing sites and stopping harassment by public officials).

The scale and magnitude of informal sector activity is likely to decline if Government can manage to reduce inflation, offer real positive prices to producers, increase supply of goods produced in the formal sector, rationalize marketing and distribution arrangements, and pay wages and salaries that are consistent with cost of living conditions. For example, there is evidence indicating that the recent process of liberalizing food and consumer goods markets has almost brought prices of goods traded in these markets to near equilibrium levels, thereby reducing the rental incomes of second economy traders.[7] With rental incomes reduced, the incentive to involve in marketeering is likely to be minimal.

It has also been observed that although import liberalization has given impetus to some of the informal economy activities by providing them with raw materials, tools and spare parts it has resulted in plant closures in the less competitive informal activities such as soap making and tie-and-dye cloth making.[8] The availability of cheap imported shoes has had a detrimental effect on the traditional sandal (*kubazi*)-making industry which used to thrive during the pre-import liberalization period.

Finally, future expansion of informal sector activities will be determined by market constraint. If rural–urban migration remains unchecked, and a growing number of wage earning households enters into the informal sector out of necessity, there is a danger that the number of street sellers and artisans would increase faster than the turnover of sales, resulting in lower earnings.[9]

5.2 Summary and Conclusions

The main purpose of this study has been to try to answer the question of how Tanzanians live in a country where official indicators of economic performance, evidenced in Chapter 1, paint a gloomy picture. Chapter 1 set out to prove that the second economy is part and parcel of the official economy, which is really part of the integrated world economy. It was pointed out that the Tanzanian economy has drifted into distress as a result of imposing external events and conditions which were largely responsible for the protective internal economic policies introduced in response, namely: nationalization and indigenization of the economy; the controls discussed in Chapters 2 and 3, and a seeming retreat from the country's long-term objectives.

The manifestations of an ailing economy persist in the form of declining output; shortages of foreign exchange; balance of payments problems; a rising debt burden; high birth rates as a safety valve for the recurring high infant mortality rates due to low living standards, and a shortage of effective health measure; corruption and the persistence of a second economy whose participants are those able to see the risks of further falling living standards and a breakdown of welfare economics, to mention only a few.

We have estimated the size of the second economy using both macro and micro approaches, both of which show that the second economy has grown as the official economy entered distress, and that it has now reached some 30 per cent of official GDP. Our study points to a gradual movement from credit to a cash economy – much use of legal tender. Despite the difficulties of these approaches, one factor remains true and that is that much of the stock of large denomination currency notes disappeared from the banking system, the reason being insecurity and preparedness to buy whatever was available as quickly as possible, usually at extremely high unofficial prices.

The other hypotheses which we set out to test were dealt with by sector-by-sector analysis. Previous policies in agriculture, trade and industry were found to have been equally to blame, in that they too were responsible for breeding second economy activities. The controls popularly referred to as interventions, introduced to support the newly established institutions, and as a mechanism for an equitable production and distribution system, stifled economic activity.

Poor producer prices, deteriorating infrastructure and a number of administrative and marketing problems associated with some crop authorities and parastatals caused even the unsophisticated producers to avoid official channels. Real incomes went down as inflation soared and the lack of consumer goods drove the majority of people to second economy sources. Smuggling in and out of the country increased, as did the need for hard currency, primarily to permit the importation of manufactured goods in order to secure high profits, and, in the case of some hard currencies, to act as security in overseas banks.

Government response to all this was to increase the level of controls, prohibitions and taxes, but the very institutions empowered to police others were also found to be participating in the second economy activities. Although the second economy is largely controlled by secrecy, so that it is difficult to place much confidence in figures, participation levels are high enough to conclude that the majority of Tanzanians are involved in second economy activities in one way or another, and that previous Government strategies to solve the problem have not been very effective. The arrest of economic saboteurs temporarily slowed down the pace and may have deterred new entrants, but did not go anywhere close to controlling these illegal activities. Pervasiveness is now deep-rooted and even those who would otherwise not want to get involved find themselves participating through sheer necessity.

We have accepted the hypothesis that the second economy emerged to reach the present levels as a result of (a) the economic crisis, made worse by the poor terms of trade (pressures on balance of payments on account of poor commodity prices and oil crises), droughts, war with Uganda and mismanagement of the economy within Tanzania; (b) inefficient Government regulations which have generated costly barriers and stifled formal economic activity; (c) Government's failure to institute adequate legal and institutional control mechanisms which would back up and supervise the implementation of its own interventionist programme, and (d) failure of the agricultural sector to adequately support the rapidly growing population.

This study found that the motive behind second economy activities was non-political, owing to the absence of organizational channels or political ideology. Most people who were engaged in the second economy activities were either businessmen in search of profits or ordinary people – workers and peasants – out to survive. Such second economy activities are not a political threat, at least not at present, but they certainly pose an economic challenge to the official establishment. State legitimacy is threatened in the sense that the challenge to the official economy makes official policies and distributive channels ineffective by diverting the flow of goods and services and by creating its own rent levels.

This being the case the official national accounts data in Tanzania do not describe fully the economic reality of the country. For example, official data capture only 20–30 per cent of the market in food staples. Data on prices for most consumer goods explain less than 50 per cent of the actual prices paid. Obviously, any policy analysis based on official statistics is bound to be misleading. The present analysis has generated useful insights which could serve as guides to policy formulation. The second economy in Tanzania should largely be seen as a less confrontational response to the political and economic realities in the country. The second economy operator has to bypass licensing, marketing and production regulations not only because they are expensive in terms of fees and labour-time, but also because it happens to be the only way to meet his basic needs. In this particular case, the second economy has become inevitable because the formal economy has failed to fulfil its obligations. Indeed where the formal economy has been effective in fulfilling its function (for instance, the distribution of tea, which was readily available in almost every retail store), the second economy has been practically non-existent.

In this context, and for the sake of policy analysis, it is instructive to distinguish two broad types of second economy activities which have different policy implications. On one hand there are those worthwhile productive activities initiated with honest (legal) objectives either to make ends meet (for example, when urban wage earners engage in farming activities, or a housewife is involved in part-time selling of buns on the streets) or to raise additional income over and above subsistence consumption (as in the case of an unlicensed small-scale furniture maker). Such activities need not only to be treated with benign neglect, but, as President Mwinyi has emphasized, they need some official encouragement. To avoid the cluster and congestion usually associated with such activities as street vending, Government, through city councils, could make available a number of conveniently located plots for such activities. Instead of specifying minimum social and health standards, which are sometimes even beyond the capacity of operators in the formal sector, Government should concentrate on educating operators and the general public on the virtues of meeting such standards. Government support may also be needed in such cases. Of course we must recognize Government's legitimate needs for revenue. Thus for the medium-sized informal sector operators, such as small-scale bakeries, custom milling units and small garage operators, Government could make tax collection more effective by cutting the cumbersome bureaucratic procedures required to obtain a licence.

The second category of second economy activities is that in which operators are in business primarily to reap rents – for example commodity racketeering, speculation in foreign exchange, and over-invoicing. Clearly this category of activities has illegal objectives and denies Government its legitimate revenue. It suggests the need for policy reform. There are two important considerations here: policy and institutional reforms. First, as already pointed out, the growth of the second economy has been fuelled by acute shortages of goods and basic services occasioned by the prolonged macro-economic disequilibrium. Policy reforms currently initiated by the Government under the Economic Recovery Programme (1987–9), and intended to restore the macro-economic balance (as discussed in detail in Chapter 1), should be given support.

We must not overdo the cuts in spending on public infrastructure, health, education and wages. Low wages will lower workers' morale, increase the incidence of corruption and lower productivity. Even the peasant economy requires some knowledge of agriculture, and health is necessary for long life expectancy and a low mortality rate, which might influence rates of population growth. Tanzania is a vast country and cannot afford to ignore her roads, railways and ports because the cash crops depend on good transport. As we have seen, transport difficulties in Tanzania breed a second economy in rural areas as peasants seek to clear their accumulating crops by selling privately.

There has been a marked shift towards the principle of market determined exchange rate, but the speed of exchange rate adjustment has been rather rapid with occasional shock devaluations. Fatigue is already setting in, and the Tanzanian shilling seems to have reached a level of devaluation beyond which the Government might fail to explain its justification to its otherwise peaceful citizens. This is so especially since inflation continues to run at over 30 per cent annually, eroding away the little nominal increases in producer prices and wages. The policy of raising interest rates to positive levels (in real terms) is increasingly being questioned. There are no signs that the higher nominal interest rates have stimulated domestic savings or deterred capital flight. Instead, they have imposed an extra burden on the crop marketing system, necessitating increased need for credit and hence reinforcing inflationary pressures.

Private traders can provide a challenge to state-owned monopolistic practices and co-operatives in buying and selling. The 'purpose' is man, and if man can get the commodity through the benefit of competition a further stride would have been made towards the long-term objectives of Tanzanian society.

In broad terms, in agriculture producers must be paid realistic prices for their produce, and this must be done promptly. They must get the requisite inputs in time and must have incentive goods at their disposal. The importance of a producer price reform cannot be over-emphasized. Richardson and Ahmed[10] have reported that in Tanzania the farmers' share of the export price of coffee was only 40–50 per cent in 1984, compared to 90 per cent in Kenya. While it is difficult to separate the effects of weather conditions from those of price, it is a fact that coffee production in Tanzania has stagnated over the past decade while coffee deliveries in Kenya are reported to have grown by 7 per cent per annum during the 1979-84 period when producer coffee price in Tanzania was low. It is therefore not surprising that Tanzania's coffee found its way to Kenyan markets illegally. However, producer prices were increased between 1985 and 1988. Coffee prices in Tanzania have risen by more than three times, cardamom by 2.5 times, cotton by 1.7 times, maize by 1.7 times and paddy by 2.2 times. Hopefully higher producer prices were intended to encourage official sales, although the fact is that despite increased price incentives by 1987 there has been no recovery yet in the volume and dollar value of recorded agricultural exports, except for cotton. This suggests that as well as price reforms there is a need to emphasize structural reforms – to strengthen rural infrastructure, roads, extension services, agricultural processing and research – to effect technological change and move away from hoe and rain-fed agriculture. It also suggests that, for these reforms to be successful, a favourable international arrangement for Tanzania's exports would be necessary. (For example, in 1987 coffee prices in the world markets fell by 38 per cent in dollar terms while unit prices of tea and tobacco fell.) In turn this calls for the need to strengthen regional markets such as the SADCC and the PTA (in spite of their existing problems).

In industry it may take time for the intended benefits of the current policy reform to be realized, because of the long gestation period. The long-term solution to improve capacity utilization and raise output rests in increased allocations of foreign exchange for importing spares and raw materials. Given that most of the industrial production units are foreign exchange intensive and inefficient, devaluation will in the short run hurt domestic industry. This is because most industries will fail to compete head on with imports, and imported material inputs and equipment will become increasingly expensive with continuous devaluation. Availability of foreign exchange will depend not only on the rate of recovery of exports, but also on an improvement in the terms of trade, appropriate external economic assistance and debt relief.

The other important policy reform relates to the intensity, magnitude and costs of Government intervention. If the public sector is to survive both the impact of the economic crises and the pressures of privatization, it needs to be streamlined and rationalized. This entails reducing its functions to match its administrative, technical and financial capacities. It will also involve amalgamating some units to avoid duplication of responsibilities. Efforts should be made to restore a sense of production and administrative discipline. In particular, public institutions should not be allowed to use their monopoly positions to insulate themselves from bearing the cost of their inefficiencies. Parastatal managers have to be accountable for the performance of their enterprises. They must be rewarded if they perform well and punished if they do not. Government must also ensure that the public sector does not crowd out or stifle private sector initiative. Indeed as the range of public tasks narrows, so a degree of acceptance of the supportive role of the private sector becomes necessary. The Government should be able if necessary to separate the two issues which are often confused – ownership and management. The goal should be for the Government to work with simpler systems and fewer controls to improve the system of enforcement.

The forces of wholesale privatization need to be resisted, however. There are formidable social, political and economic difficulties associated with divestiture: for instance, problems concerning possible lay-offs of labour and evaluating the fair value of the assets. But more important is the danger that in the absence of a strong indigenous entrepreneurial class with a substantial capital base, the beneficiaries of privatization would be the multinational corporations.

There is no panacea which will resolve Tanzania's problems overnight. However, sustained economic recovery is a prerequisite to the reduction in the volume of illegitimate economic activity. In the Tanzanian context, sustained economic stability will depend not only on the provision of market incentives to producers,[11] but also on the implementation of far-reaching structural reforms such as the provision of rural infrastructure, improved agricultural processing, rural extension services and developing farming systems that are less dependent on the vagaries of weather. It will also depend on an extended period of good weather, and improved international terms of trade.

Tables and Figures

Appendix I

Table 1.1 *Major economic trends of the Tanzanian economy*

	1970–6	1977	1978	1979	1980	1981	1982	1983	1984	1985	1986	1987	1988
Real GDP Growth Rate (Percentages, 1976 prices)													
Overall GDP	5.1	0.9	1.1	1.9	2.5	1.8	1.8	1.2	1.3	1.4	1.6	3.9	4.1
Agriculture	4.5	1.2	-0.3	0.1	1.0	1.0	1.1	0.8	0.6	0.9	1.1	4.4	4.5
Manufacturing	6.7	-6.1	-1.5	0.1	1.2	-3.3	-3.3	-4.1	-3.2	-3.3	-3.7	4.2	5.4
Public Administration	13.2	11.0	12.0	12.7	11.8	10.8	10.3	9.6	8.7	8.2	8.7	7.9	3.1
Real GDP per capita	1.5	2.4	-1.9	0.6	0.9	-4.3	-1.1	-5.7	-0.2	-0.1	-0.3	1.1	1.3
Inflation (Percentage change in NCPI, 1977 = 100)	11.1	11.6	19.8	13.3	36.0	22.7	32.6	19.2	44.0	29.2	33.2	22.9	28.2
Government Finance													
Total Revenue (T.Shs millions)		6,129	6,082	6,812	7,757	8,872	10,960	14,193	17,957	20,832	31,387	47,730	70,212
Current Expenditure (T.Shs millions)		4,702	5,563	8,229	9,229	10,136	13,214	18,182	21,337	27,402	40,390	61,765	90,272
Development Expenditure (T.Shs millions)		3,606	2,411	4,741	5,184	4,795	5,185	5,736	5,391	5,817	15,090	15,091	28,400
Overall Budget (T.Shs millions)		-2,179	-1,892	-6,158	-6,656	-6,059	-7,439	-9,725	-8,771	-12,387	-24,093	-29,126	-46,135
Overall Budget deficit as percentage of GDP		8.5	6.6	19.1	17.8	13.8	14.1	15.5	11.2	11.5	16.8	15.7	17.6
External Balance and Trade													
Trade Account ($US millions)		-234	-668	-618	-713	-607	-697	-435	-486	-714	-670	-745	-813

Table 1.1 *cont'd*

	1970–6	1977	1978	1979	1980	1981	1982	1983	1984	1985	1986	1987	1988
Current Account Balance ($US millions)		– 49	– 436	– 350	– 565	– 407	– 539	– 308	– 369	– 415	– 312	– 286	+ 284
Overall Balance ($US millions)		137	– 319	– 50	– 178	– 102	– 109	– 138	– 159	– 395	– 384	– 341	
Barter Terms of Trade (1980 = 100)		143	123	106	100	88	88	91	94	90	101		
Purchasing Power of Exports (1980 = 100)		186	149	129	100	119	92	79	83	63	77		
Exports as percentage of GDP		17.4	12.8	13.3	11.2	9.9	6.6	6.4	6.5	5.2	7.9	11.9	14.5
Imports as percentage of GDP		6.5	30.1	27.8	26.7	20.8	16.0	13.1	16.6	15.2	24.0	37.6	46.2
Exchange Rate T.Sh/$US (June)	7.50	7.50	7.68	8.25	8.19	9.31	9.32	12.24	17.17	17.73	44.43	63.50	97.2

Sources: URT *Economic Survey* (various years); National Accounts of Tanzania (1986); Bank of Tanzania; Ministry of Trade and Industries; UNCTAD: *Handbook of International Trade and Development Statistics.*

Table 1.2 *Exchange rate of T. shilling against selected currencies*

		Exchange Rate[a]			Percentage Change, 1 year		
		US dollar	Pound sterling	Deutsch-mark	US dollar	Pound sterling	Deutsch-mark
1979	June	8.24	17.93	4.48			
	December	8.22	18.34	4.77			
1980	June	8.19	19.28	4.66			
	December	8.18	19.54	4.17	– 0.5	6.5	– 13
1981	June	8.31	16.21	3.47			
	December	8.32	15.95	3.70	1.8	– 18.4	– 11.3
1982	June	9.32	16.71	3.99			
	December	9.52	15.51	4.02	14.4	2.7	8.6
1983	June	12.24	18.70	4.81			
	December	12.46	18.09	4.58	30.9	16.6	13.9
1984	June	17.17	23.23	6.17			
	December	18.11	21.11	5.78	45.3	16.7	26.2
1985	June	17.73	22.45	5.74			
	December	16.50	23.59	6.59	– 8.8	11.7	14.0
1986	June	40.43	61.83	18.34			
	December	51.41	75.52	26.45	212.6	220.1	301.4
1987	June	63.48	101.58	34.71			
	December	83.72	155.51	52.49	62.8	105.9	98.4
1988	June	98.10	179.50	57.00			
	December	119.00	220.0	–	42.0	41.0	–

Note: a) End of quarter.

Source: Bank of Tanzania.

Table 1.3 *Ginning and transportation of cotton 1986/7–1987/8 (30 June to March)*

	1986–7 (tons)	1987–8 (tons)
1) Seed-cotton purchased from peasants	193,315	235,560
2) Seed-cotton transported to ginneries	187,640	142,102
3) Purchased seed-cotton still in buying posts/godowns	5,674	93,458
4) Ginned cotton	62,045	39,301
5) Ginned cotton transported to Dar es Salaam	58,063.4	21,084.7
6) Ginned cotton stranded in ginnery godowns	811.8	3,933.7
7) Ginned cotton stranded at railheads	1,915.0	14,266.8

Source: *Tanzanian Economic Trends*, Vol. 1, no. 1, 1988: Table vii, p. 40.

Table 1.4 *Effectiveness of major policy instruments in Tanzania, 1980–1987*

	1980	1981	1982	1983	1984	1985	1986	1987
Producer price as % of world price								
Coffee (mild Arabica)	37.7	59.6	53.0	70.9	61.1	52.4	34.2	28.7
Cotton (AR)	23.6	16.1	27.6	32.6	28.8	27.6	35.6	38.2
Change in exchange rate T.Shs/US dollar								
Nominal	–	–1.8	–14.4	–30.9	–45.3	–8.8	–212.6	–62.8
Real Effective[1]	–	6.7	8.5	8.3	14.2	39.3	–189.0	–55.8
Government expenditure in 1980 constant prices								
Recurrent	100	89.5	88	102	83	83	92	123
Development	100	75	62	57	37	31	61	53
Revenue as % of GDP	20.7	20.2	20.8	22.7	22.9	19.3	21.9	24.1
Budget deficit as % of GDP	17.8	13.8	14.1	15.5	11.2	11.5	16.8	15.7
Index of weighted agricultural export volume (1980 = 100)	100	143	119	97	100	81	85	89
Growth in money supply (nominal %)								
Actual	–	13.5	21.2	13.6	20.2	11.6	28.0	21.9
Target	–	–	–	19.6	19.1	13.0	10.0	10.0
Commercial interest rates (NBC, savings)								
Nominal	5.0	5.0	5.10	5.50	5.50	7.50	10.0	24.0
Real[2]	5.0	–16.4	–18.2	–16.9	–22.5	–19.4	–16.9	–8.0

Notes: 1. Nominal exchange rate deflated by difference between national and US rate of consumer price inflation.
2. Deflated by inflation rate (National Consumer Price Index 1980 = 100).

Sources: Marketing Development Bureau; Bank of Tanzania; Table 1.1; International Monetary Fund, *International Financial Statistics*, January 1988.

Table 2.1   *Informal sector units by year of establishment*

	Arusha		Dar es Salaam	
Period of Establishment	Number of units	Percentage	Number of units	Percentage
1950–9	2	2.1	0	0
1960–9	3	3.1	1	0.7
1970–9	18	18.5	26	18.2
1980–7	74	76.3	116	81.1
Total	97	100.0	143	100.0

Source: M.S.D. Bagachwa and B.J. Ndulu, 'The Urban Informal Sector in Tanzania', Dar es Salaam, Mimeo, 1988, Table 11, p. 33.

Table 2.2   *Corruption cases 1980–1983*

	1980	1981	1982	1983
Number of cases	149	161	111	132
Persons arrested	174	183	126	167
Persons convicted	26	28	6	3
Persons acquitted	58	31	9	–
Pending cases	90	124	111	164

Source: Ministry of Home Affairs (Anti-Corruption Squad).

Table 2.3   *Evolution of money supply, 1967–1986, at current prices (In T.Shs million)*

	Currency in circulation[a] (C)	Demand deposits (D)	Narrow money (M_1)	Time and savings deposits (T)	Total deposits (D + T)	Broad money (M_2)	Currency velocity[b]
1967	511.7	680.4	1,192.1	347.6	1,028.6	1,539.7	13.2
1968	528.6	685.3	1,213.9	285.0	970.3	1,498.9	13.6
1969	605.0	867.4	1,472.4	407.1	1,274.5	1,879.5	12.3
1970	818.4	860.5	1,678.9	540.7	2,219.6	2,219.6	10.0
1971	986.4	1,072.0	2,058.4	566.0	1,638.0	2,624.4	10.0
1972	1,201.1	1,125.7	2,326.8	762.9	1,888.6	3,089.7	8.4
1973	1,198.6	1,576.1	2,774.7	878.3	2,454.4	3,653.0	9.6

Table 2.3   *cont'd*

	Currency in cir-culation[a] (C)	Demand deposits (D)	Narrow money (M$_1$)	Time and savings deposits (T)	Total deposits (D + T)	Broad money (M$_2$)	Currency velocity[b]
1974	1,517.3	1,939.0	3,456.3	1,005.7	2,944.7	4,462.0	9.8
1975	1,755.8	2,528.0	4,283.8	1,268.9	3,796.9	5,552.7	9.7
1976	2,071.3	3,260.5	5,331.8	1,615.0	4,875.5	6,946.8	10.5
1977	2,379.7	4,003.1	6,382.8	1,963.9	5,967.0	8,346.7	10.8
1978	2,915.2	3,911.1	6,826.9	2,569.4	6,481.1	9,396.3	9.8
1979	4,055.4	4,380.0	8,435.4	3,371.2	7,751.2	11,806.6	8.0
1980	5,245.5	5,380.0	10,625.5	4,173.9	9,553.9	14,799.4	7.1
1981	5,992.2	5,855.0	11,847.2	4,952.7	10,807.7	16,799.9	7.3
1982	7,178.3	6,907.5	14,085.8	6,277.2	13,144.7	20,363.0	7.3
1983	7,794.2	7,733.9	15,528.1	7,598.0	15,331.9	23,126.1	7.8
1984	9,389.2	9,439.4	18,828.6	8,981.1	18,420.5	27,809.7	8.1
1985	10,680.2	10,185.5	20,865.7	10,163.2	20,348.7	31,028.9	9.3
1986	13,679.2	12,566.0	26,245.2	13,467.8	26,033.8	39,713.0	9.6

Notes: a) Refers to currency in circulation outside banks.
            b) GDP/currency ratio.

Sources: Bank of Tanzania.

Table 2.4   *Estimated size of the second economy in Tanzania*

Year	Official GDP at factor cost (T.Shs million)	Second economy GDP (T.Shs million)	Second economy GDP as percentage of official GDP
1975	16,988	1,116.9	6.6
1976	22,620	644.0	2.8
1977	26,105	*	–
1978	28,430	2,779.9	9.8
1979	32,452	6,842.0	21.1
1980	38,667	9,262.3	24.2
1981	45,193	12,308.3	27.2
1982	54,845	15,483.5	28.2
1983	60,702	13,354.4	22.0
1984	74,608	18,989.0	25.4
1985	97,767	28,211.6	28.8
1986	131,346	41,187.2	31.4

Note: * Second economy assumed to be negligible.

Source: Computed from Table 2.3 and Appendix II, Table B1.

Figure 2.1 *Per capita currency in circulation in current prices, 1967–1986 (in T. Shs)*

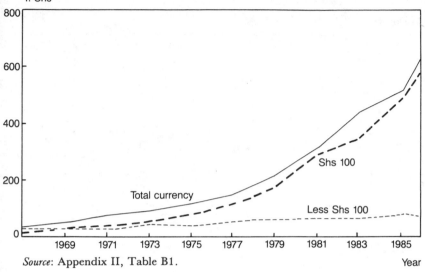

Source: Appendix II, Table B1.

Figure 2.2 *Share of total currency in circulation by denomination (in percentage)*

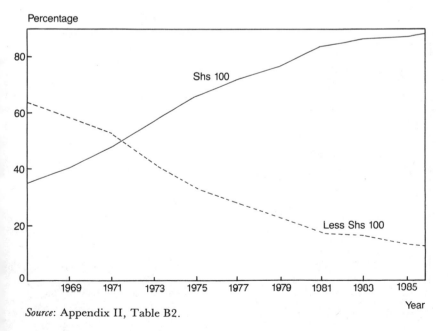

Source: Appendix II, Table B2.

Figure 2.3 *Ratio of currency in circulation to demand deposits and to money, 1967–1986 (in percentage)*

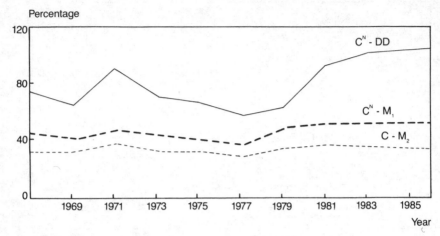

Source: Appendix II, Table B1.

Figure 2.4 *Per capita currency in circulation in 1970 prices, 1967–1986 (in TZ.Shs)*

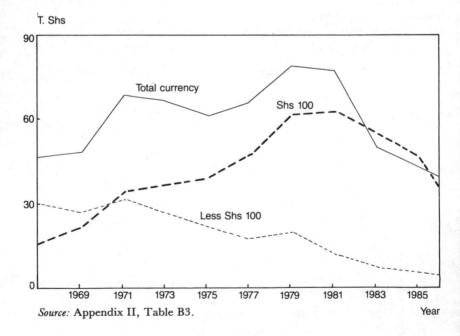

Source: Appendix II, Table B3.

Table 2.5   *The size of the second economy in various countries*[a]

Country	Year	Second economy as percentage of official GNP	Author
Australia	1978–9	10.0	Tucker (1982)[b]
Canada	1976	14.0	Mirus and Smith (1982)[c]
Ghana	1978	7.4	May (1985)[d]
	1979	11.5	May (1985)
	1980	24.5	May (1985)
	1982	32.4	May (1985)
Tanzania	1978	9.8	Authors
	1979	21.1	Authors
	1980	24.2	Authors
	1982	28.2	Authors
	1986	31.4	Authors
United Kingdom	1979	7.5	Diln'ot and Morris (1982)[e]
	1979	7.2	Diln'ot and Morris (1982)
USA	1976	13–14	Gutmann (1979)[f]
	1976	8–11.7	Tanzi (1982)[g]
	1979	13.0	Molefsky (1982)[h]
	1980	14.3	Molefsky (1982)

Notes:
a) Arrived at by using the monetary approach.
b) M. Tucker, 'The Underground Economy in Australia', in V. Tanzi (ed.), *The Underground Economy in the United States and Abroad*, Toronto: Lexington Books, 1982, pp. 315–22.
c) R. Mirus and R. Smith, 'Canada's Irregular Economy', in ibid., pp. 273–83.
d) E. May, 'Exchange Controls and Parallel Market Economies in Sub-Saharan Africa: Focus on Ghana', *World Bank Staff Working Papers*, no. 711, Washington DC: World Bank, 1985.
e) A. Diln'ot and C.N. Morris, 'What Do We Know About the Black Economy in the United Kingdom?' in V. Tanzi, *The Underground Economy in the United States and Abroad*, pp. 163–79.
f) Peter M. Gutmann, 'The Subterranean Economy', *Financial Analysts Journal*, Vol. 34, November–December 1977, pp. 24–7.
g) V. Tanzi, *The Underground Economy in the United States and Abroad*.
h) B. Molefsky, 'America's Underground Economy', in ibid., pp. 47–67.

Table 2.6   *Household income–expenditure estimates*

Income/expenditure category	Urban	Rural
Income	(Shs)	
Self-employment income	4,572,904	10,344,843
Wages and salaries	12,847,405	3,183,028
Interest, dividends and profits	1,306,516	477,454
Rents and royalties	1,524,268	795,757
Pensions, annuities, estates and trusts	653,258	793,878
Capital gains	435,505	190,981
Others	435,505	525,199
Total income sources (600 households)	21,775,361	15,915,140
Average household income	36,292	26,525
Estimated income for all households	21,666,485,190	89,734,075,000
Expenditure		
Food, beverages and tobacco	19,638,979	16,578,293
Clothing and footwear	4,284,846	2,703,528
Rent, fuel, water and power	4,998,987	2,295,449
Medical care, education and communication	2,142,423	714,139
Household assets (furniture, equipment, etc.)	2,499,494	892,674
Recreation and entertainment	1,428,282	1,810,854
Miscellaneous goods and services	714,141	510,099
Total expenditure (600 households)	35,697,152	24,790,897
Average expenditure per household	59,495	41,318
Estimated expenditure for all households	35,518,664,250	139,778,794,000

Source: Survey data.

Table 3.1 *Index of real producer prices for agricultural commodities, 1975–6 – 1987–9*

Year (1986–7 = 100)	Predominant food staples[a]	Drought food staples[b]	Perennial export crops[c]	Annual export crops[d]	All crops
1975–6	135	142	80	134	112
1976–7	132	159	110	124	121
1977–8	138	165	146	124	137
1978–9	119	148	112	111	114
1979–80	105	116	89	108	100
1980–1	88	92	78	93	86
1981–2	96	77	67	87	81
1982–3	83	82	68	85	78
1983–4	87	87	79	84	83
1984–5	106	99	80	85	88
1985–6	110	110	76	102	93
1986–7	100	100	100	100	100
1987–8	107	100	107	94	102

Notes: a) Includes maize, paddy, wheat and beans.
b) Includes cassava and sorghum/millet.
c) Includes coffee, cashew nuts, tea, pyrethrum, cocoa and cardamom.
d) Includes cotton and tobacco.

Weighting factor for composite groups was total value of purchases for the seasons 1984–5, 1985–6 and 1986–7.

Source: Marketing Development Bureau.

Table 3.2 *NMC purchases of main staples, 1975–6 – 1988–9 (000 mt)*

	Maize	Rice	Wheat
1975–6	91.1	12.0	24.5
1976–7	127.5	14.6	27.1
1977–8	213.2	35.1	35.3
1978–9	220.4	34.0	28.8
1979–80	161.6	30.2	26.7
1980–1	104.6	13.5	27.9
1981–2	89.4	15.0	23.1
1982–3	86.0	20.9	31.2
1983–4	71.0	22.0	28.3
1984–5	90.0	12.2	33.2
1985–6	178.5	15.9	50.3
1986–7	173.0	11.0	34.0
1987–8	229.0	43.0	43.0
1988–9	110.0	45.0	44.0

Note: a) Estimates.   *Source:* Marketing Development Bureau.

Figure 3.1 *Inter-regional second economy food market network in Tanzania (1986)*

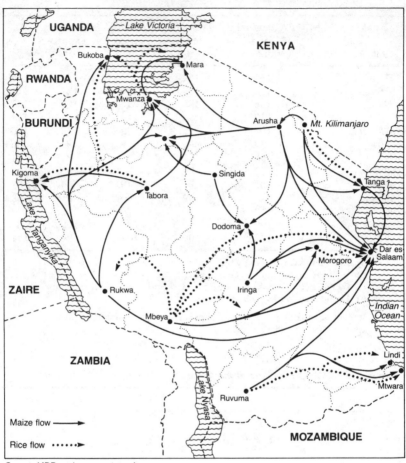

Source: MDB, various reports and own survey.

Source: MDB, various reports and own survey.

Table 3.3   *NMC purchases of maize grain from surplus regions*

	1976–7		1980–1		1986–7	
	Tons	Percentage of total	Tons	Percentage of total	Tons	Percentage of total
Present surplus regions						
Iringa	14,700	(11.5)	21,754	(26.3)	38,006	(21.3)
Mbeya	5,500	(4.3)	5,351	(6.5)	15,987	(9.0)
Rukwa	11,800	(9.2)	17,818	(21.5)	29,338	(16.4)
Ruvuma	10,000	(7.8)	14,082	(17.0)	29,116	(16.3)
Former surplus regions						
Kilimanjaro	6,100	(4.8)	134	(0.16)	769	(0.43)
Morogoro	9,200	(7.2)	733	(0.88)	776	(0.43)
Tanga	20,800	(16.3)	89	(0.12)	625	(0.35)
Tabora	3,500	(2.7)	2,381	(2.9)	1,428	(0.80)

Sources: National Milling Corporation and Marketing Development Bureau.

Table 3.4   *Disposition of marketed surplus for maize and rice, 1971–1987 (in percentages)*

	Maize share of marketed surplus sold to		Rice share of marketed surplus sold to	
	Official markets	SEFOMA[a]	Official markets	SEFOMA
1971–2	23.6	76.4	52.2	47.8
1972–3	54.5	45.5	44.3	55.7
1973–4	38.8	61.2	33	67.0
1974–5	6.0	94.0	11.2	88.8
1975–6	25.1	74.9	7.5	92.5
1976–7	30.7	69.3	9.3	90.7
1977–8	58.2	41.8	18.1	81.9
1979–80	51.2	48.8	25.9	74.1
1980–1	33.5	66.5	20.8	79.2
1981–2	21.6	78.4	13.5	86.5
1982–3	20.8	79.7	9.4	90.6
1983–4	14.6	85.4	11.9	88.1
1984–5	17.4	82.6	12.4	87.6
1985–6	34.7	65.3	5.7	94.3
1986–7	36.0	64.0	7.0	93.0

Note: a) SEFOMA: Second economy food markets.

Source: Computed from MDB reports (various years).

Figure 3.2 *Maize producer prices*

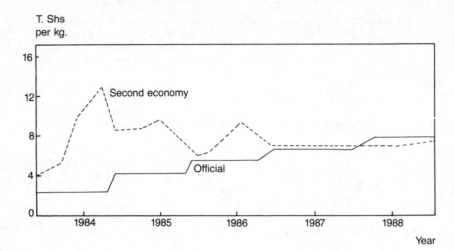

Source: Appendix III, Table C1.

Figure 3.3 *Paddy producer prices*

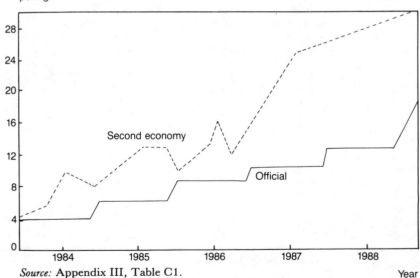

Source: Appendix III, Table C1.

Table 3.5   *Distribution of production between consumption and sales to various markets in selected regions (in percentages)*

	Output	Subsistence consumption	Marketable Official	Marketable SEFOMA	SEFOMA sales as percentage of total market surplus
Maize					
Arusha	100	68.0	8.0	24.0	75.0
Mbeya	100	71.0	11.0	18.0	62.1
Ruvuma	100	73.0	10.0	17.0	63.0
Average	100	70.7	9.7	19.7	66.7
Paddy					
Arusha	100	60.0	7.0	33.0	82.5
Mbeya	100	48.0	12.0	40.0	77.0
Ruvuma	100	53.0	12.0	35.0	74.5
Average	100	53.7	10.3	36.0	78.0

Source: Survey data.

Table 3.6   *Consumer prices for maize and rice, 1972–1988 (T.Shs per kg)*

	Sembe			Rice		
Year	Official current price	SEFOMA current price	Official constant 1983–4 price	Official current price	SEFOMA current price	Official constant 1983–4 price
1972–3	0.80	0.98	4.88	1.65	1.64	10.07
1973–4	1.25	1.08	6.40	2.00	1.64	10.25
1974–5	1.25	1.62	5.06	4.00	1.82	16.20
1975–6	1.75	1.82	6.63	4.00	4.26	15.16
1976–7	1.75	2.82	5.94	3.50	4.74	11.89
1977–8	1.75	3.14	5.30	5.30	3.76	10.59
1978–9	1.75	2.60	4.69	3.50	3.98	9.38
1979–80	1.25	2.92	2.54	5.35	4.04	11.01
1980–1	2.50	3.36	4.10	5.35	7.26	8.76
1981–2	3.35	4.86	3.18	5.35	12.00	6.80
1982–3	4.39	5.00	2.50	7.20	16.54	7.20
1983–4	5.40	11.25	5.40	13.40	34.32	13.40
1984–5	7.60	10.50	7.62	14.50	30.31	8.04
1985–6	12.20	9.65	9.40	14.50	40.00	8.10
1986–7	12.20	10.34	9.20	19.00	39.00	30.00
1987–8	17.00	17.00	13.60	32.00	45.00	35.00

Sources: Marketing Development Bureau; K. Odegaard, 'Cash Crop versus Food Crop Production in Tanzania: An Assessment of the Major Post-Colonial Trends', *Lund Economic Studies*, no. 33, 1985.

Table 3.7 *Sectoral composition of Tanzanian imports (in percentages)*

	1974	1976	1980	1982	1984	1986	1987	1988
Consumer goods	30	29	15	10	9	7	16.6	23.0
Intermediate goods	43	36	40	42	45	38	30.2	42.0
Capital goods	27	35	45	48	46	55	53.2	35.0

Source: Economic Survey, 1980, 1987 and 1988.

Table 3.8 *Capacity utilization rates[a] in Tanzanian industry (in percentages)*

Year	1976	1980	1984	1985	1986	1987
Capacity utilized per cent	52	31	26	25	27	30

Note: a) Unweighted averages for 10 industries including beer, cigarettes, textiles, fertilizers, tyres, cement, corrugated iron sheets, hoes and dry cells.

Source: Ministry of Industry and Trade.

Table 3.9 *Excess demand for selected products by region, 1983–1984 (in percentages)*

Region	Cement	Cooking oil	Sugar
Arusha	98	80	77
Coast	93	92	78
Dar	93	98	41
Dodoma	98	92	54
Iringa	99	95	75
Kagera	98	95	74
Kigoma	98	93	74
Kilimanjaro	97	96	59
Lindi	99	97	73
Mara	91	95	64
Mbeya	96	97	79
Morogoro	96	96	73
Mtwara	–	97	78
Mwanza	99	88	69
Rukwa	96	94	82
Ruvuma	98	97	77
Shinyanga	86	93	75
Singida	98	94	68
Tabora	98	93	68
Tanga	93	93	75

Source: Board of Internal Trade.

Table 3.10 *Availability of consumer goods* in urban and rural areas, 1984 (in percentages)*

Item	Urban Times when product was available		Rural Times when product was available	
	Official	Unofficial	Official	Unofficial
Sugar	12	19	9	22
Salt	18	22	15	19
Cooking oil	17	15	19	15
Maize meal	30	60	40	42
Rice	14	30	21	51
Cement	9	15	5	9
Roofing sheet	29	28	10	17
Hoe	40	35	5	20
Radio	5	4	5	7
Khanga/Kitenge	6	15	3	12

Note: a) Unweighted averages for 10 regions including Arusha, Dar es Salaam, Kagera, Msoma, Mwanza, Mbeya, Kigoma, Dodoma, Coast and Ruvuma.

Source: Survey data, 1984.

Table 3.11 *Official and unofficial prices in selected towns*

	Beer ($\frac{1}{2}$ litre)	Hoes (1 piece)	Sugar (1 kg)	Washing soap (1 bar)
Arusha				
Official	30.15	37.35	13.75	7.00
Unofficial	45.00	75.00	40.00	25.00
Dar				
Official	30.15	37.35	13.75	7.00
Unofficial	50.00	50.00	25.00	18.00
Kagera				
Official	30.15	37.75	13.75	7.00
Unofficial	110.00	110.00	50.00	35.00
Mbeya				
Official	30.15	37.35	13.75	7.00
Unofficial	80.00	80.00	40.00	22.00

Source: Survey data, 1984.

Table 3.12 *Official versus unofficial consumer prices for selected items in selected towns, 1982–1984*

Item	Town (place)	Year	Unofficial price (T.Shs)	Official price (T.Shs)	Divergence percentage	Source of data
Minced meat	Tabora	Aug. 1982	25 per kg	15 per kg	67	*DN* 31.8.82, p. 3
	Dodoma	Aug. 1982	25 per kg	15 per kg	67	*DN* 16.8.82, p. 3
	Iringa	Oct. 1982	20–25 per kg	17 per kg	18–47	*Uh* 27.1.83, p. 3
	Bariadi	Jan. 1983	18–35 per kg	15 per kg	20–133	*DN* 1.12.84, p. 3
	Arusha	Nov. 1984	50 per kg	35 per kg	43	
Steak (meat)	Tabora	Aug. 1982	35 per kg	16 per kg	110	As in item 1
	Dodoma	Aug. 1982	40 per kg	20 per kg	100	As in item 1
Sembe/maize flour	Tanga	Aug. 1982	10 per kg	3/50 per kg	186	*DN* 28.8.82, p. 3
Beans	Tanga	Aug. 1982	8 per kg	6/50 per kg	23	*DN* 28.8.82, p. 3
A bar of soap	Zanzibar	Mar. 1983	25–40	5	400–700	*SN* 7.3.83, p. 3
Beer (Safari)	Mbeya	Aug. 1984	100	30/15	232	*DN* 15.9.84, p. 3
(Pilsner)	Mbeya	Aug. 1984	100	29/25	242	*DN* 15.9.84, p. 3
Kerosene	Tukuyu	Jul. 1984	320 a tin	159 a tin	113	*DN* 12.7.84, p. 3
Hoe	Tabora	Sept. 1982	90 to 100	37/35	141–168	*DN* 3.9.82, p. 13
Bucket	Shinyanga	Aug. 1982	220	82	168	*DN* 16.8.82, p. 5
Teapot	Shinyanga	Aug. 1982	120	51	135	*DN* 16.8.82, p. 5

Note: DN = *Daily News*; SN = *Sunday News*; Uh = *Uhuru*.

Source: *Daily News; Sunday News; Uhuru.*

Table 3.13 *Violation of TBS packaging and labelling standards*

TBS requirement	Percentage of sample items satisfying TBS requirements		
	Beer[a]	White bread[b]	Laundry soap[c]
Name of product	100	0	49
Name and address of manufacturer	0	0	35
Brand name and trade mark	100	0	72
Grade	0	0	0
Batch or lot number	0	0	0
Date of manufacture	0	0	0
Expiry date	0	0	0
Gross weight/volume/mass	100	0	0
Net weight/volume/mass	0	0	0
Specially marked wrapper	*	35	25
Nutrient and/or chemical composition	0	0	0

Notes: a) Sample of 14 crates (350 bottles) taken two each month.
　　　　b) Sample of 700 loaves taken 100 each month.
　　　　c) Sample of 700 bars taken 100 each month.
　　　　*   not a requirement.

Source: Survey data.

Table 3.14 *Minimum urban wage levels and their purchasing power*

Year	Minimum urban wage (T.Shs/month)		Purchasing power of minimum wage (kg staple/day's wage)		
	Nominal	Real[a]	Maize	Rice	Wheat flour
1973	240	1,985	10.0	4.8	4.8
1974	340	2,360	9.1	5.7	4.7
1975	380	2,085	10.1	3.2	3.4
1976	380	1,951	7.2	3.2	3.4
1977	380	1,748	7.2	3.6	3.4
1978	380	1,558	7.2	3.6	3.4
1979	380	1,380	7.2	3.6	3.4
1980	480	1,338	12.8	3.0	2.8
1981	600	1,331	8.0	3.7	3.5
1982	600	1,032	8.0	3.7	3.5
1983	600	913	8.0	2.8	2.5
1984	810	810	3.4	1.9	1.9
1985	810	832	2.0	1.9	1.6
1986	1,053	634	–	1.85	1.4

Note: a) in 1984 constant prices.

Source: Marketing Development Bureau.

Table 3.15 *Comparison of Tanzania's and international inflation, 1978–1987 (in percentages)*

Year	1978	1979	1980	1981	1982	1983	1984	1985	1986	1987	1988
Tanzania[a]	19.8	13.3	36.0	22.7	32.6	19.2	44.0	28.2	33.2	28.9	28.2
Worldwide[b]	9.7	12.5	15.7	14.1	12.3	13.0	14.9	16.1	18.3	14.2	10.9
Industrialized countries[b]	7.2	9.2	11.9	9.9	7.5	5.1	4.8	4.2	4.0	2.9	3.2
Developing countries[b]	20.4	23.4	28.2	27.7	28.5	41.6	51.8	60.6	66.5	49.4	6.3
	12	13.8	11.8	20.5	11.5	10.1	13.1	4.0	3.0	4.6	8.3

Sources: a) Annual rate of change in Tanzanian NCPI.
b) *International Financial Statistics*.

Table 3.16 *T.Sh nominal exchange rates in various markets[a] (T.Sh per $US)*

Year	1980	1981	1982	1983	1984	1985	1986	1987	1988	1989[b]
Official rate	8.2	8.3	9.3	11.1	15.3	17.5	32.7	70	120	145
Second economy rate	21.0	27.6	32.6	39.6	60.0	100	170	180	210	250
Gap (2:1)	2.6	3.3	3.5	3.6	3.9	5.7	5.2	2.6	2.8	1.7

Note: a) Period averages.   b) By Sept 1989.

Sources: *Pick's Currency Year Book* for black market rates between 1980 and 1983.
Own survey for rates between 1984 and 1989.
Bank of Tanzania for official rate.

Table 3.17 *Export goods seized by Tanzania Customs (in T.Shs)*

Type of product	1985	1986
1 Foreign currencies	400,078	336,347
2 Agricultural foodstuffs	167,489	199,261
3 Fishery and marine products	16,300	111,691
4 Agricultural produce	191,960	851,453
5 Livestock	4,510,000	800
6 Hides, skins and leather	27,320	46,348
7 Carvings and trophies	167,000	157,700
Total goods seized	5,480,147	1,703,605
Total exports	6,030,950,938	10,962,988,842
Total goods seized as percentage of total exports	0.09	0.02

Source: Tanzania Customs.

Table 3.18   *Imported goods seized by Tanzania Customs (in T.Shs)*

Type of product	1985	1986
1 Tanzanian currency	2,787,792	1,360,602
2 Foodstuffs (sugar, salt, cooking oil, margarine, milk, etc.)	21,696	214,117
3 Textiles, clothing and apparel, shoes and sandals	364,343	681,016
4 Used clothing	394,397	101,605
5 Soap, toothpaste, creams, perfumes, wigs, earrings, etc.	93,226	901,640
6 Beer, wines and spirits	49,900	118,885
7 Motor vehicles	1,529,298	2,704,229
8 Tractors	16,260,020	–
9 Spares	165,220	664,479
10 Fuel, motor oil and fluids	240,325	59,260
11 Bicycles, motor cycles and spares	1,800	55,200
12 Other manufactured and industrial goods and general merchandise	5,591,765	9,557,767
13 Medicines	55,320	6,424
14 Books, paper, etc.	438	108,110
15 Narcotic drugs and obscene publications	72,728	31,305
16 Radios, cassettes, TVs and VTRs	15,247,550	2,373,244
Total goods seized	42,875,818	18,937,883
Total imports	16,939,538,679	30,881,835,331
Total goods seized as percentage of total imports	0.25	0.06

Source: Tanzania Customs.

Table 3.19 *Estimates of recorded and unrecorded foreign trade (T.Shs 000)*

Year	1985	1986
1 Recorded exports	6,030,951	10,962,989
2 Unrecorded exports	109,603	34,072
3 Total exports	6,140,554	10,997,061
4 2 as percentage of 1	1.81	0.31
5 2 as percentage of 3	1.78	0.30
6 Recorded imports	16,939,538	30,881,835
7 Unrecorded imports	849,516	47,465
8 Total imports	17,789,054	30,929,300
9 7 as percentage of 6	5.01	0.15
10 7 as percentage of 8	4.77	0.153

Source: Tables 3.17 and 3.18.

Table 3.20 *Seized ivory trophies, 1982–1986*

	Number of tusks	Weight in kg	Value, T.Shs 000	$US 000
1982	1,480	7,997	2,797	337
1983	1,696	9,553	3,344	360
1984	1,379	6,144	2,150	143
1985	444	2,199	745	44
1986	772	455	159	9
1987	—	—	50,520	665
1888	—	75,305	1,373,730	13,468

Source: Ministry of Natural Resources and Tourism.

Table 3.21 *Estimates of illegal exports of cardamom*

Year	Official purchases (Tonnes)	Official exports Value ('000) $US	Official exports Value ('000) T.Shs	Official exports (Tonnes)	World market prices $US/kg	World market prices $US/kg Equivalent in T.Shs	World market prices $US/kg index (1974 = 100)	Domestic producer prices (T.Shs/kg) Nominal	Domestic producer prices (T.Shs/kg) Constant (1984 = 100)	Production estimates (Tonnes)	Second economy purchases (Tonnes)	Diversion of official purchases to second economy[a] (Tonnes)	Total available for export through the second economy (Tonnes)	(T.Shs '000)	($US '000)
1974	760	2,897	20,682	817	3.54	25.28	100.0	17.00	113.33	800	40	–	40	1,011	141
1984	424	3,153	38,656	371	8.50	129.98	240.1	63.00	63.00	700	276	21.2	297	38,604	3357
1985	127	1,153	21,649	106	10.87	189.92	307.1	80.00	56.52	700	573	12.7	586	111,293	6359
1986	211	366	6,145	61	6.00	196.19	169.5	96.00	50.24	700	489	63.3	552.3	106,531	3329

Notes: a) Diversion of official purchases to the underground economy is estimated at 5 per cent, 10 per cent and 30 per cent of official purchases for the years 1984, 1985 and 1986 respectively. See, for instance, MDB Reports, Cardamom, 1986, p. 1.

Source: MDB Reports, Cardamom, 1985 and 1986, and own calculations for estimates of production and the second economy.

Table 3.22   *Under- and over-invoicing of imports and exports*

Data source	Tanzanian imports from Britain (T.Shs million)		Tanzanian exports to Britain (T.Shs million)	
Year	1985	1986	1985	1986
Tanzania	1,896.0	3,744.1	890.0	1,360.4
Britain	2,299.5	3,464.4	894.5	1,640.1
Difference	– 430.5	279.7	– 4.5	– 279.7
Difference as percentage of UK data	– 18.7	8.1	– 0.5	– 17.1

Sources: Tanzania Customs; UK Department of Trade and Industry, Overseas Trade Statistics of the UK, 1985 and 1986.

Table 4.1   *Domestic and international interest rates, 1981–1986*

	Tanzania		International money market			
Year	Nominal time deposit rate[a]	Real time deposit rate[b]	Nominal LIBOR[c]	Real LIBOR[d]	Authorized investments LIBOR[e]	Illegal investments LIBOR[f]
	(1)	(2)	(3)	(4)	(5)	(6)
1981	5.00	– 16.40	16.13	30.48	15.08	– 7.63
1982	5.50	– 18.22	13.69	19.05	2.93	– 1.75
1983	5.50	– 16.93	10.18	12.89	– 6.51	– 7.50
1984	5.50	– 22.54	11.82	10.49	– 15.31	– 22.18
1985	7.50	– 19.35	9.11	14.61	– 3.37	– 30.89
1986	10.00	– 16.92	6.95	n.a.	– 39.62	– 34.23

Notes: a) 12-month time deposit rate (TDR)
b) 12-month TDR deflated by the inflation rate (NCPI = 100)
c) 12-month London Interbank offer rate (LIBOR) on $US deposits
d) 12-month LIBOR on $US deposits deflated by percentage changes in Tanzania's export price index (1980 = 100)
e) The sum of the 12-month LIBOR on $US deposits and the devaluation rate of the official Tanzanian shilling exchange rate. It signifies the profitability of authorized or official foreign exchange investments abroad in terms of T. shillings.
f) The sum of the 12-month LIBOR on $US deposits and the devaluation rate of the black market exchange rate of the Tanzanian shilling. It signifies the real opportunity cost for illegal foreign exchange resources invested abroad (i.e. in the form of flight of capital) in terms of T. shillings.

Source: Bank of Tanzania (1987) for nominal time deposit rate (column 1); IMF (1987) for nominal LIBOR (column 3).

Table 4.2 *Share of own-funded imports in total imports and exports*

	1984 Millions of shillings		1985 Millions of shillings		1986 Millions of shillings	
a) *Import licences issued under:*						
i) no payment basis	3,708.5	17.5	8,611.9	33.9	15,584.9	37.0
ii) loans and grants	6,888.6	32.5	3,282.8	12.9	6,530.7	15.5
iii) suppliers' credit	1,559.9	7.3	2,793.4	11.0	5,099.6	12.1
iv) import support	1,307.2	6.2	1,197.6	4.7	3,434.1	8.2
v) barter trade	819.2	3.9	910.3	3.6	476.2	1.1
vi) free resources	6,920.0	32.6	8,583.7	33.8	10,939.5	26.0
Total import licences issued	21,203.4	100.0	25,379.7	100.0	42,065.0	100.0
b) *Total imports*	12,961		17,962		30,270	
i) of which: own-funded imports	612		4,057		8,063	
ii) own-funded imports to total imports (percentage)	4.7		22.6		26.6	
iii) import licences under no payment basis to total imports (percentage)	28.6		47.9		51.5	
c) *Total exports*	5,750		6,031		10,963	
i) Own-funded imports to total exports (percentage)	10.6		67.3		73.5	
d) *Customs duty and sales tax on own-funded imports*						
i) Customs duty	25.9[a]		173.3		465.0	
ii) Sales tax	51.5[a]		234.1		613.2	
Total customs duty and sales tax	77.4[a]		407.4		1,078.2	

Note: a) Figures refer to July–December 1984.

Sources: Bank of Tanzania; Ministry of Finance and Planning, Hali ya Uchumi wa Taifa, 1986; *Daily News*, 17 July 1987.

Table 4.3 *Import licences issued in Tanzania*

Import licences issued under:	1980–1		1981–2		1982–3		1983–4		1984–5		1985–6	
	Millions of shillings	Percentage	Millions of shillings	Percentage	Millions of shillings	Percentage	Millions of shillings	Percentage	Millions of shillings	Percentage	Millions of shillings	Percentage
(1) No payment basis	–	–	–	–	–	–	–	–	6,619.4	26.6	10,396.7	42.3
(2) Grants, loans and import support	6,057.7	57.1	6,963.6	64.7	5,468.3	61.8	6,400	56.6	10,101.4	40.5	6,704.2	27.2
(3) Free resources	4,548.6	42.9	3,800.5	35.3	3,381.4	38.2	4,900	43.4	8,205.4	32.9	7,405.3	30.5
Total licences issued	10,606.3	100.0	10,770.1	100.0	8,849.7	100.0	11,300	100.0	24,926.2	100.0	24,596.2	100.0

Source: Bank of Tanzania, Economic and Operations Reports, 1980–6.

Table 4.4   *Attitudes towards liberalization in Tanzania*

	Unfavour-able	Percent-age	Favour-able	Percent-age	Total	Percent-age
Urban workers						
Agriculture	2	8.0	23	92.0	25	8.3
Professional	10	5.65	169	94.4	179	59.5
Trade	1	33.3	2	66.6	3	1.0
Business	0	–	4	100.0	4	1.3
Secretary	5	13.5	92	86.5	3.7	12.3
Unskilled	7	15.2	39	84.8	46	15.3
Other	0	–	7	100.0	7	2.3
Total	25	8.5	276	91.7	301	100.0
Rural households						
Agriculture	109	40.2	162	59.8	271	77.4
Professional	22	48.9	23	51.1	45	12.9
Trade	11	38.0	18	62.0	29	8.3
Business	0	–	5	100.0	5	1.4
Total	142	40.6	208	59.4	350	100.0
Transporters						
Kigoma	5	50.0	5	50.0	10	21.7
Arusha	6	46.2	7	53.0	13	28.3
Moshi	7	38.9	11	61.1	18	39.1
Misomni	5	100.0	–	–	5	10.9
Total	23	50.0	23	50.0	46	100.0
Traders						
Retail	18	19.6	74	80.4	92	33.0
Trade	14	36.0	25	64.0	39	14.0
Shop	34	23.0	114	77.0	148	53.0
Total	66	23.7	213	76.3	279	100.0
Combined groups						
Total	244	27.5	642	72.5	866	100.0

Source: *Survey Data*

Table 5.1   *Traders: Primary and secondary occupation and main income source*

	Number involved in primary activity	Number involved in secondary activity	Ownership of Primary Occupation					Employment					Non-family		Main Income Source		
			Individual	Company	Family	Co-operative	Total	Male	Female	Adult	Child	Family	Hired	Total	Primary	Secondary	Total
Shop	170	59	82 (48.2%)	21 (12.3%)	55 (32.4%)	12 (7.1%)	170 (100%)	268 (65.5%)	141 (34.5%)	390 (95.4%)	19 (4.6%)	123 (30.1%)	286 (69.1%)	409 (100%)	39 (78%)	11 (22%)	50 (100%)
Retail	127	52	88 (69.3%)	8 (6.3%)	29 (22.8%)	2 (1.6%)	127 (100%)	198 (63.1%)	116 (36.9%)	300 (95.5%)	14 (4.5%)	101 (32.2%)	213 (67.8%)	314 (100%)	33 (67.3%)	16 (32.7%)	49 (100%)
Trades	48	14	34 (70.8%)	2 (4.2%)	8 (16.7%)	4 (8.3%)	48 (100%)	51 (86.4%)	8 (13.6%)	59 (100%)	0	19 (32.2%)	40 (67.8%)	59 (100%)	8 (66.6%)	4 (33.3%)	12 (100%)
Total	345	125	204 (59.1%)	31 (9%)	92 (26.7%)	18 (52%)	345 (100%)	517 (66%)	265 (33.9%)	749 (95.8%)	33 (4.2%)	243 (31.1%)	535 (68.4%)	782 (100%)	80 (72.1%)	31 (27.9%)	111 (100%)

Source: Survey Data

Table 5.2   *Traders: Primary occupations by secondary occupations*

Primary	Secondary Agricul- ture	Trade	Retail	Unskilled/ Other	Total number engaged in secondary activities		
Shop	34	9	1	6	50	29.4%	Number engaged as a percentage of total number of shops
	68%	18%	2%	12%	100%		
Hawker	24	0	1	2	27	41.5%	Number engaged as a percentage of total number of hawkers
	00.9%	–	3.7%	7.4%	100%		
Bar/ restaurant	13	1	0	3	17	32.1%	Number engaged as a percentage of total number of bars restaurants
	76.5%	5.9%	–	17.6%	100%		
Tailoring	3	1	0	0	4	26.7%	Number engaged as a percentage of total number of tailors
	75%	25%	–	–	100%		
Shoe- dealer	4	0	0	0	4	26.7%	Number engaged as a percentage of total number of shoe dealers
	100%	–	–	–	100%		
Total other trades	4	3	2	1	10	37%	Total number engaged as a percentage of total numbers in all categories
Total 1st sector activity	82	14	4	12	112	32.2%	
Additional sector activity	5	4		4	13	11% of 112	
Total	87	18	4	16	125	36.5%	
	(69%)	(14.4%)	(3%)	(12.8%)			

Source: *Survey Data*

Table 5.3   *Ownership and employment in secondary occupations*

Ownership	Individual	Company	Family	Co-operative	Total
All secondary activities	66	18	37	4	125
Percentage	52.8	14.4	29.6	3.2	100

Employment	Male	Female	Adult	Child	Family	Non-family	Total
In secondary activities	205	87	281	11	80	212	292
Percentage	70.2	29.8	96.2	3.8	27.4	72.6	100

Source: *Survey Data*

Table 5.4   *Sourcing of all commodities by major groups (in percentages)*

Groups	Sources Other	Private	Public	Both	Total
Households	55	30	14.1	0.8	100
Workers	29.2	37.1	25.9	7.8	100
Traders	–	64.3	35.7	–	100
Transporters	–	18.9	76.5	4.6	100
Average	21.1	37.6	38.1	3.2	

Source: *Survey Data*

Table 5.5 *Primary by secondary occupations for households, workers and traders*

	Agriculture (all)		Business (all)		Trade: Retail (household) (traders)		Herbist: (household) Part-time (workers): Other: (traders)		Total number engaged in secondary activity	Number engaged as a percentage of total number	
Farmer	46	47.4%	33	34.0%	15	15.5%	3	3.1%	97	33.8%	Households
Teacher	16	100%	0	–	0	–	0	–	16	64.0%	
Fisherman	9	100%	0	–	0	–	0	–	9	90.0%	
Carpenter	6	100%	0	–	0	–	0	–	6	66.6%	
Doctor	3	75.0%	1	25.0%	0	–	0	–	4	50.0%	
Other	30	93.8%	0	–	2	6.2%	0	–	32	72.7%	
Total	110	67.1%	34	20.7%	17	10.4%	3	1.8%	164	42.8%	
Management	7	50.0%	6	42.1%	1	7.1%	0	–	14	51.9%	Workers
Accountant	15	78.9%	3	15.8%	0	–	1	5.3%	19	45.2%	
Agriculture	14	77.8%	3	16.7%	0	–	1	5.5%	18	72.0%	
Teacher	29	74.4%	4	10.3%	2	5.0%	4	10.3%	39	54.9%	
Doctor	7	70.0%	2	20.0%	1	10.0%	0	–	10	55.5%	
Economist	8	80.0%	1	10.0%	0	–	1	10.0%	10	100%	
Party	0	–	4	100%	0	–	0	–	4	50.0%	
Other	53	70.7%	14	18.7%	4	5.3%	4	5.3%	75	51.0%	
Total	133	70.4%	37	19.6%	8	42.0%	11	5.8%	189	54.3%	
Shop	34	68.0%	9	18.0%	1	2.0%	6	12.0%	50	29.4%	Traders
Hawker	24	88.9%	0	–	1	3.7%	2	7.4%	27	41.5%	
Bar/restaurant	13	76.5%	1	5.9%	0	–	3	17.6%	17	32.1%	
Tailor	3	75.0%	1	25.0%	0	–	0	–	4	26.7%	
Shoe-dealer	4	100%	0	–	0	–	0	–	4	26.7%	
Other	4	40.0%	3	30.0%	2	20.0%	1	10.0%	10	37.0%	
Total	82	73.2%	14	12.5%	4	3.6%	12	10.7%	112	32.5%	

Source: Survey Data

Table 5.6 *Workers' primary vs secondary occupation and major income source*

	Primary occupation	Secondary occupation	Major income source		
			Primary	Secondary	Total
Professional	208	–	61	68	129
Percentages			47.3%	52.7%	100%
Agriculture	25	133	11	7	18
Percentages			61.1%	38.9%	100%
Clerical	41	–	21	11	32
Percentages			65.6%	34.4%	100%
Sundry	65	19	24	17	41
Percentages			58.5%	41.5%	100%
Party officer	8	–	2	2	4
Percentages			50%	50%	100%
Trade		37	–	–	–
Percentages	–		–	–	–
Total	347	189	119	105	224
Column percentages			53.1%	46.9%	100%

Source: *Survey Data*

Table 5.7 Households' primary and secondary main income earner

	Primary occupation			Secondary occupation			Main income earner				Main income source			
	House-holds	Spouses	Total	House-holds	Spouses	Total	House-holds	Spouses	Both	Total	Primary	Secondary	Neither	Total
Agriculture based	300	264	564	109	20	129	214	50	34	298	27	67	14	108
Percentages	53.2	46.8	100	84.5	15.5	100	71.8	16.8	11.4	100	25	62	13	100
Professional	47	24	71	32	12	44	31	0	16	47	17	13	0	30
Percentages	66.2	33.8	100	72.7	27.3	100	66	–	34	100	56.7	43.4	–	100
Trades	31	4	35	18	3	21	17	7	7	31	15	3	0	18
Percentages	88.6	11.4	100	85.7	14.3	100	54.8	22.6	22.6	100	83.3	16.7	–	100
Business/trade	5	7	12	5	0	5	4	1	0	5	4	1	0	5
Percentages	41.7	58.3	100	100	–	100	80	20	–	100	80	20	–	100
Total	383	299	682	164	35	199	266	58	57	381	63	84	14	161
Column Percentages	56.2	43.8	100	82.4	17.6	100	69.8	15.2	15	100	39.1	52.2	8.7	100

Source: Survey Data

Table 5.8   *Household main income earner – heads and spouses*

	Heads	Spouses	Both	Total
Agriculture	214	50	34	298
Percentage	71.8	16.8	11.4	100
Professional	31	0	16	47
Percentage	66	–	34	100
Trades	17	7	7	31
Percentage	54.8	22.6	22.6	100
Trade	4	1	0	5
Percentage	80	20	–	100
Total	266	58	57	381
Percentage	69.8	15.2	15	100

Note: Household heads are 85 per cent male.

Source: *Survey Data*

Table 5.9 Transporters: type, ownership, source and employment

	Type of service					Type of ownership						Source of fuel				Source of tyres			Composition of employment				
	Bus	Taxi	Lorry	Other	Bus and Lorry	Individ-ual	Family	Com-pany	Co-op	Other	Miss-ing	Fuel Station	Other	Both	Miss-ing	Public	Private	Total	Males	Females	Family	Non-family	Total
Kigoma	4	4	4	6	2	12	6	1	0	1	1	6	6	7	3	16	1	20	75	0	2	73	75
Percentages	20	20	20	30	100	60	30	5	-	5	5	30	30	35	15	80	5	25.3	100	-	2.7	97.3	26.3
Arusha	6	7	3	1	2	8	5	6	0	0	0	18	1	0	0	8	11	19	74	4	15	63	78
Percentages	31.6	36.8	15.8	5.3	10.5	42.1	26.3	31.6	-	-	-	94.7	5.3	-	-	42.1	57.9	24.1	94.9	5.1	19.3	80.8	27.4
Moshi	7	7	3	1	2	9	6	5	0	0	1	19	0	0	1	10	10	20	77	5	15	67	82
Percentages	35	35	15	5	100	45	30	25	-	-	5	95	-	-	5	50	50	25.3	93.9	6.1	18.3	81.7	28.8
Musoma	4	8	8	0	0	15	3	2	0	0	0	20	0	0	0	20	0	20	47	3	0	50	50
Percentages	20	40	40	-	-	75	15	100	-	-	-	100	-	-	-	100	-	25.3	94	6	-	100	17.5
Total	21	26	18	8	6	44	20	14	0	1	2	63	7	7	3	54	22	79	273	12	32	253	285
Percentages	26.6	32.9	22.8	10.1	7.6	55.7	25.3	17.7	-	1.3	2.5	79.7	8.9	8.9	38	68.4	27.8	100	95.8	4.2	11.2	88.8	100

Source: Survey Data

Table 5.10   *Ownership of primary and secondary activities and major income source*

	Primary occupation				Secondary occupation			
	Individ-ual	Family	Com-pany	Co-opera-tive	Individ-ual	Family	Com-pany	Co-opera-tive
Traders	59.1%	27.6%	9%	5.2%	52.8%	29.6%	14.4%	3.2%
Transporters	55.7%	25.3%	17.7%	–	–	–	–	–

	Major income source		
	Primary	Secondary	Neither
Households	39.1%	52.2%	8.7%
Workers	53.1%	46.9%	–
Traders	72.1%	27.9%	

Source: *Survey Data*

Table 5.11a   *Participation in buying and selling by all groups (in percentages)*

	Selling		Buying		Price-controlled		Non-price-controlled foodstuffs		Commodities	
	Public	Non-public	Public	Non-public	Public	Non-public	Public	Non-public	Public	Non-public
Households	–	100	14.1	85.9	18.6	81.4	13.9	86.1	11.1	88.4
Workers	–	–	11.0	89.0	18.0	82.0	7.8	92.2	9.1	90.9
Traders	–	–	35.7	64.3	–	–	–	–	–	–
Transporters	–	–	80.1	19.9	–	–	–	–	–	–

Source: *Survey Data*

Table 5.11b   *Selling and buying to and from non-official sources (in percentages)*

	Selling to non-official sources			Buying from non-official sources						
	Adult	Child	Both	Male	Female	Both	Adult	Child	Both	Total
Households	96	2.6	1.4	51.3	34.6	14.1	77.5	21.5	1.0	100
Workers	–	–	–	35.8	59.5	4.7	–	–	–	100

Source: *Survey Data*

Table 5.11c   *Purchase of commodities by gender (in percentages)*

		Male	Female	Both
Controlled foodstuffs				
	Rural	55.7	34.2	10.1
	Urban	35.8	58.7	55.0
Uncontrolled foodstuffs				
	Rural	50.8	33.7	15.5
	Urban	37.2	59.6	3.2
Commodities				
	Rural	49.7	36.4	13.9
	Urban	38.8	55.1	6.1

Source: *Survey Data*

Table 5.12 *Gender of seller as reported by buyer for Dar es Salaam, Dodoma and Tanga (in percentages)*

	Maize flour	Maize	Sugar	Beans	Meat	Rice	Bread	Kerosene	Washing soap	Soap	Khanga
Dar es Salaam	38	41	65	55	56	48	65	56	59	34	26
Male percentage	76	76	45	75	100	69	34	91	86	82	81
Female percentage	21	17	49	23	0	27	60	7	8	12	19
Both percentage	3	7	6	2	0	4	6	2	6	6	0
Total percentage	100	100	100	100	100	100	100	100	100	100	100
Dodoma	11	27	19	21	46	7	7	95	92	46	33
Male percentage	64	93	79	90	93	57	100	86	85	74	55
Female percentage	31	7	21	10	7	28	0	9	10	24	42
Both percentage	3	0	0	0	0	1	0	5	5	2	3
Total percentage	100	100	100	100	100	100	100	100	100	100	100
Tanga	0	23	6	23	7	11	3	27	27	25	0
Male percentage	0	13	83	17	100	55	66	93	81	80	0
Female percentage	0	87	0	70	0	45	33	4	7	19	0
Both percentage	0	0	17	13	0	0	1	3	12	1	0
Total percentage	0	100	100	100	100	100	100	100	100	100	0

Source: Survey Data

Appendix II

Table B1   *Selected monetary ratios, 1967–1986 (in current prices)*

	Currency–demand deposit ratio	Currency–total deposit ratio	Currency–money ratio (C/M₁)	Currency–money ratio (C/M₂)	Currency per capita (Shs)	Shs 100 notes per capita	Less than Shs 100 notes per capita	GDP per capita
1967	0.75	0.50	0.46	0.33	41.70	14.60	27.12	549
1968	0.77	0.54	ˇ0.44	0.35	42.00	16.90	25.45	570
1969	0.66	0.47	0.41	0.32	46.80	20.40	26.26	577
1970	0.95	0.58	0.49	0.37	61.80	27.40	33.37	637
1971	0.92	0.60	0.48	0.38	72.40	37.40	35.21	668
1972	1.07	0.64	0.52	0.39	85.80	45.30	38.79	737
1973	0.76	0.49	0.43	0.38	83.40	46.80	34.69	737
1974	0.78	0.52	0.44	0.34	102.80	61.50	39.56	976
1975	0.69	0.46	0.41	0.32	114.70	74.30	39.48	1,156
1976	0.64	0.42	0.39	0.29	132.70	89.60	43.22	1,352
1977	0.59	0.40	0.37	0.28	147.90	107.90	41.59	1,583
1978	0.74	0.45	0.43	0.31	171.00	126.50	49.12	1,734
1979	0.64	0.42	0.48	0.34	225.50	174.70	57.28	1,854
1980	0.97	0.55	0.49	0.35	282.20	229.00	59.73	2,138
1981	0.97	0.55	0.51	0.36	312.60	291.70	61.96	2,423
1982	1.04	0.54	0.51	0.35	381.90	351.70	64.57	2,852
1983	1.01	0.51	0.50	0.34	445.80	347.90	60.98	3,060
1984	0.99	0.51	0.50	0.33	492.40	368.00	61.32	3,361
1985	1.05	0.52	0.51	0.34	503.77	492.20	80.45	4,685
1986	1.09	0.53	0.52	0.34	624.62	577.99	76.30	5,997

Source: Table 2.3.

Table B2 *Notes in circulation, 1967–1986 (values are in T.Shs million)*

	Total value of notes	Shs 100 notes		Notes less than Shs 100	
		Value	As percentage of total notes	Value	As percentage of total notes
1967	504.5	179.0	35.5	325.5	64.5
1968	526.5	213.5	40.5	313.0	59.5
1969	597.6	264.1	40.6	333.5	59.4
1970	801.2	364.0	45.4	437.2	54.6
1971	985.7	510.3	51.8	475.4	48.2
1972	1,177.6	634.6	53.9	543.0	46.1
1973	1,172.8	673.3	57.4	499.5	42.6
1974	1,497.9	908.4	60.6	589.5	39.4
1975	1,742.4	1,138.4	65.3	604.0	34.7
1976	2,081.8	1,398.8	67.2	683.0	32.8
1977	2,418.4	1,736.3	71.8	682.1	28.2
1978	2,986.5	2,156.3	72.2	830.2	27.8
1979	4,114.2	3,140.5	76.3	973.7	23.7
1980	5,336.1	4,254.9	79.2	1,081.2	20.8
1981	6,750.0	5,591.2	82.8	1,158.8	17.2
1982	8,196.0	6,956.2	84.9	1,239.8	15.1
1983	8,272.7	7,101.8	85.8	1,170.9	14.2
1984	9,007.8	7,750.7	86.0	1,257.1	14.0
1985	13,120.5	11,414.8	87.0	1,705.6	13.0
1986	14,329.8	12,658.7	88.3	16,711.1	11.7

Source: Bank of Tanzania.

Table B3   *Selected monetary ratios, 1967–1986 (in 1970 prices)*

	Currency per capita (Shs)	Shs 100 notes per capita (Shs)	GDP per capita (Shs)	Less than Shs 100 notes per capita	National consumer price index (NCPI)
1967	46.33	16.22	610	30.2	90.0
1968	44.68	17.97	598	27.1	94.0
1969	48.50	21.14	598	27.2	96.5
1970	61.80	27.40	637	33.4	100.0
1971	69.10	34.70	638	33.6	104.7
1972	75.50	40.20	662	34.4	112.7
1973	67.00	37.60	592	27.8	124.5
1974	69.30	41.40	658	26.6	148.4
1975	61.10	39.60	617	21.0	187.7
1976	66.10	44.70	674	21.5	200.6
1977	66.10	48.20	707	18.6	223.8
1978	68.60	50.70	696	19.7	249.3
1979	79.50	61.60	654	20.2	283.6
1980	76.40	61.90	579	16.2	369.4
1981	67.10	62.80	522	13.4	462.1
1982	60.80	59.90	477	10.8	597.3
1983	50.20	45.70	402	8.0	760.3
1984	49.30	40.70	371	6.8	905.1
1985	43.80	42.80	408	7.0	1,148.8
1986	40.82	37.78	391	5.0	1,529.9

Source: Computed from Table B1; deflated by NCPI.

Appendix III

Table C1   *Producer prices for maize and rice, 1971–1989 (Shs per kg)*

Year	Maize			Rice		
	Official current price	SEFOMA current price	Official constant 1984–5 price	Official current price	SEFOMA current price	Official constant 1984–5 price
1971–2	0.24		2.72	0.52		5.88
1972–3	0.26		2.70	0.56		5.81
1973–4	0.33		3.00	0.57		5.14
1974–5	0.55		3.66	0.65		4.76
1975–6	0.80		5.07	1.00		6.34
1976–7	0.80		4.64	1.00		5.80
1977–8	0.85		4.41	1.20		6.22
1978–9	0.85		3.94	1.20		5.56
1979–80	1.00		3.88	1.50		5.82
1980–81	1.00		2.95	1.75		5.16
1981–2	1.50		3.57	2.30		5.48
1982–3	1.75	4.00	3.15	3.00	4.00	5.39
1983–4	2.20	13.00	3.11	4.00	9.50	5.66
1984–5	4.00	8.50	4.00	6.00	12.00	6.00
1985–6	5.25	7.50	3.89	8.00	16.00	5.93
1986–7	6.30	6.50	3.18	9.60	25.50	5.69
1987–8	8.20	7.50	4.10	14.40	27.40	7.61
1988–9	9.00	8.80	4.50	17.30	29.25	9.14

Source: Marketing Development Bureau.

Notes

Prelude

1 *Daily News.* A Government daily newspaper from which most of the press reports were taken.
2 R. Young, *Canadian Development Assistance to Tanzania*, Ottawa: North South Institute, 1983, p. 22.
3 Arcado Ntagazwa, 'Mtindo Mbaya wa Ujangili Watisha Kumaliza Wanyama', *Uhuru*, Dar es Salaam, 1988, p. 1.

Chapter 1 pp 1–25

1 G. Frankel, in *The Washington Post*, 3 December 1984, p. 15.
2 G. Kahama, T. L. Maliyamkono and S. Wells, *The Challenge for Tanzania's Economy*, London: James Currey, 1986.
3 C. Legum, 'The Nyerere Years: A Preliminary Balance Sheet', in M. Hodd, *Tanzania After Nyerere*, London and New York: Pinter Publishers, 1988, pp. 3–11.
4 *Daily News*, 4 April 1989, p. 1.
5 World Bank, *Tanzania Country Economic Memorandum*, Washington DC: World Bank, 1984, p. iii.
6 United Republic of Tanzania, *Economic Survey 1984*, Dar es Salaam: Government Printer, 1983, p. 3.
7 ibid.
8 *Africa Today Journal*, London, 1981 p. 16.
9 R. Green, 'Malaise to Recovery: An Overview', *Journal of Development Planning*, Vol. 15, 1985.
10 A. Singh, 'The IMF World Bank Policy Programme in Africa: A Commentary', in P. Lawrence (ed.), *World Recession and Food Crisis in Africa*, London: James Currey, 1986; and 'Tanzania and the IMF: The Analytics of Alternative Adjustment Programmes', *Development and Change*, Vol. 17, 1986, pp. 425–54.
11 United Republic of Tanzania (URT), *National Accounts of Tanzania, 1976–1986*, Dar es Salaam: Bureau of Statistics, Ministry of Finance, Economic Affairs and Planning, 1987.
12 K. Odegaard, 'Cash Crop Versus Food Crop Production in Tanzania: An Assessment of the Major Post-Colonial Trends', *Lund Economic Studies*, no. 33, Lund, 1985; D. Bevan, A. Bigsten, P. Collier and J. W. Cunning, *East African Lesson on Economic Liberalization*, Thames Essays no. 48, Gower, 1987.
13 A. Coulson, 'Agricultural Policies in Mainland Tanzania', in Heyer *et al.*, *Rural Development in Tropical Africa*, London: Macmillan, 1981.

14   C. Legum, 'The Nyerere Years'.
15   G. Kahama *et al.*, *The Challenge for Tanzania's Economy.*
16   J. F. Rweyemamu, *Underdevelopment and Industrialization in Tanzania*, Oxford: Oxford University Press, 1973.
17   G. Frankel, *The Washington Post*, p. 16.
18   Earlier, in 1981, Government had hastily prepared the National Economic Survival Programme (NESP) in order to ease the foreign exchange constraint and improve capacity utilization. However, NESP was not a comprehensive programme of action, but a set of incoherent targets. Consequently the NESP did not achieve any of its objectives and a year later was abandoned in favour of SAP.
19   B. J. Ndulu, 'Stabilization and Adjustment Programmes in Tanzania 1978-1985', Helsinki: World Institute of Development Economics Research, 1986.
20   K. Odegaard, 'Cash Crop Versus Food Crop Production in Tanzania'.
21   ibid, p. 134.
22   A. Singh, 'Tanzania and the IMF', p. 436.
23   Economic Research Bureau (ERB) and Ministry of Finance and Economic Planning, *Tanzanian Economic Trends*, no. 1-3, 1988, p. 31. The emphasis is original.
24   World Bank, *Parastatals in Tanzania: Towards a Reform Program*, Report no. 7100 - TA (January), 1988, p. 85.
25   By 1980-1 National Milling Corporation had an overdraft of T.Shs 2 billion with the National Bank of Commerce. Recently the loss incurred by NMC rose from T.Shs 700 million in 1985-6 to T.Shs 1,840 million in 1986-7. Marketing Development Bureau (MDB), *Annual Review of Agricultural Marketing*, Dar es Salaam: Ministry of Agriculture and Livestock Department, 1987, p. 40.
26   M. Hyuha and N. Osoro, 'An Economic Analysis of Inflation in Tanzania, 1960-1979', *Journal of Economic Reflections*, 1981.
27   C. Brooke, 'The Heritage of Famine in Central Tanzania', *Tanzania Notes and Records*, Vol. LXII, 1967, pp. 15-22; K. Odegaard, 'Cash Crop Versus Food Crop Production in Tanzania'; C. Legum, 'The Nyerere Years.'
28   A. Singh, 'The IMF World Bank Policy Programme in Africa'.
29   P. Collier, S. Radwan and S. Wangwe with A. Wagner, *Labour and Poverty in Rural Tanzania*, Oxford: Clarendon Press, 1986.
30   Economic Research Bureau, *Tanzanian Economic Trends*, p. 6.
31   Green, cited by C. Legum, 'The Long Haul Back to Recovery', *Bulletin of Tanzania Affairs*, no. 32, January 1989, p. 4.
32   International Labour Organization, *Distributional Aspects of Stabilization Programmes in the United Republic of Tanzania, 1974-1984*, Report of an ILO mission, Geneva: ILO, 1988.

Chapter 2 pp 26-62

1   ILO, *Employment, Incomes and Inequality. A Strategy for Increasing Productive Employment in Kenya*, Geneva: ILO, 1977, p. 4.
2   Peter M. Gutmann, 'The Subterranean Economy', *Financial Analysts Journal*, Vol. 34 (November-December), 1977, pp. 24-7.
3   V. Tanzi (ed.), *The Underground Economy in the United States and Abroad*, Toronto: Lexington Books, 1982, p. 4.
4   ibid., p. 70.
5   D. Del Boca and F. Forte, 'Recent Empirical Surveys and Theoretical Interpretations of the Parallel Economy in Italy', in V. Tanzi, *The Underground Economy*, pp. 181-97.
6   This definition is similar to that used by Tanzi in *The Underground Economy*.
7   Economic Research Bureau (ERB) and Ministry of Finance and Economic Planning, *Tanzanian Economic Trends*, no. 1-3, 1988, p. 50.

8   V. Tanzi, *The Underground Economy*, p. 103.
9   R. Mirus and R. Smith, 'Canada's Irregular Economy', in V. Tanzi, *The Underground Economy*', pp. 273–83.
10 P. Wiles, 'The Second Economy, Its Definitional Problems', in S. Allesandrini and B. Dallago (eds), *The Unofficial Economy*, Brookfield: Gower, 1987, p. 22.
11 S. K. Ray, 'Profiteering: An Economic Analysis', *Eastern Economist*, Vol. 65, October 1975, pp. 732-4.
12 A. M. Tripp, 'Defending the Right to Subsist: The State vs. The Urban Informal Economy in Tanzania'. Paper presented at the African Association Annual Meeting, 28–31 October 1988, Chicago, Illinois, p. 24.
13 L. P. Shaidi, 'Legal Control of Surplus Labour in Tanzania's Urban Centres'. Paper presented at the Workshop on Social Problems in Eastern Africa, 9–14 August 1987, Arusha, Tanzania.
14 A. M. Tripp, 'Defending the Right to Subsist', p. 19.
15 M. S. D. Bagachwa, 'The Dar es Salaam Urban Informal Sector Survey', in ILO, *Tanzania Basic Needs in Danger*, Addis Ababa: ILO, 1982, p. 83; A. M. Tripp, 'Defending the Right to Subsist'.
16 M. S. D. Bagachwa, 'The Urban Informal Enterprise Sector in Tanzania: A Case Study of Arusha Region', *Economic Research Bureau Paper*, no. 81.4, University of Dar es Salaam, 1981, p. 83; B. J. Ndulu, 'Investment, Output, Growth, Capacity Utilization in an African Economy. The Case of Manufacturing Sector in Tanzania', *Eastern African Economic Review* (New Series), Vol. 2, 1986, pp. 14-30; A. M. Tripp, 'Defending the Right to Subsist'.
17 D. Del Boca and F. Forte, 'Recent Empirical Surveys and Theoretical Interpretations of the Parallel Economy in Italy', p. 182.
18 See for example the classic works of W. A. Lewis, 'Economic Development with Unlimited Supplies of Labour', *The Manchester School of Economic and Social Studies*, 22, 1954, and H. Myint, 'Organizational Dualism and Economic Development', *Asian Development Review*, Vol. 3, 1985, presents a good survey on this.
19 D. Mazumdar, 'The Urban Informal Sector', *World Development*, Vol. I, 1976, pp. 655-79.
20 S. Acharya, 'The Informal Sector in Developing Countries – A Macro View Point', *Journal of Contemporary Asia*, Vol. 13(4), 1983, pp. 342-445.
21 ibid.
22 ILO/JASPA, *Informal Sector in Africa*, Addis Ababa: ILO/JASPA, 1985, p. 11.
23 ibid., p. 13.
24 United Republic of Tanzania (URT), *National Accounts of Tanzania 1976-1986*, Dar es Salaam: Bureau of Statistics, Ministry of Finance, Economic Affairs and Planning, 1987.
25 ILO/JASPA, *Employment Promotion in Tanzania: Prospects in the Rural and Informal Sectors*, Addis Ababa: ILO/JASPA, 1986.
26 R. Bromley and C. Gerry, 'Who are the Casual Poor?', in R. Bromley and C. Gerry (eds), *Casual Work and Poverty in the Third World*, Chichester: John Wiley, 1979.
27 D. Cornuel and B. Duriez, 'Local Exchange and State Intervention', in N. Redcliff and E. Mingione (eds), *Beyond Employment, Household, Gender and Subsistence*, New York: Basil Blackwell, 1985.
28 Hernando de Soto, 'The Informal Economy in Peru'. Paper presented to the Conference on Micro-Enterprise Development in the Third World, Ontario, 24 April 1985.
29 K. Odegaard, 'Cash Crop Versus Food Crop Production in Tanzania: An Assessment of the Major Post-Colonial Trends', *Lund Economic Studies*, no. 33, 1985.
30 D. F. Bryceson, 'Household, Hoe and Nation: Development Policies of the Nyerere Era', in M. Hodd (ed.), *Tanzania After Nyerere*, London and New York: Pinter Publishers, 1988, pp. 36-48.

31   J. F. Rweyemamu, *Underdevelopment and Industrialization in Tanzania*, Oxford: Oxford University Press, 1973.
32   World Bank, *Parastatals in Tanzania: Towards a Reform Program*, Report no. 7100 – TA, January 1988, p. 6.
33   A. M. Tripp, 'Defending the Right to Subsist'.
34   Marketing Development Bureau, *Price Policy Recommendations – Maize, Rice and Wheat*, Dar es Salaam: Ministry of Agriculture and Livestock Development, 1986.
35   D. Ghai, 'Economic Growth, Structural Change and Labour Absorption in Africa: 1960–85'. Discussion Paper no. 1, United Nations Research Institute for Social Development, 1987.
36   B. J. Ndulu, 'Economic Stagnation and Management of Change: Adjustment and Reduction of Macro–Micro Conflict of Interests', Dar es Salaam, mimeo, 1988.
37   A. M. Tripp, 'Defending the Right to Subsist'.
38   National Productivity Council (NPC), *Productivity and Operations Report for the Year Ended 30 June 1986*, Dar es Salaam: NPC, 1986.
39   F. Ellis, 'Agricultural Price Policy in Tanzania', *World Development*, Vol. 10(4), 1982.
40   K. Odegaard, 'Cash Crop Versus Food Crop Production in Tanzania'.
41   G. Hyden, *Beyond Ujamaa in Tanzania: Underdevelopment and an Uncaptured Peasantry*, London: Heinemann Educational Books, 1980.
42   ibid.
43   A. M. Tripp, 'Defending the Right to Subsist'.
44   ibid.
45   M. S. D. Bagachwa and B. J. Ndulu, 'The Urban Informal Sector in Tanzania', Dar es Salaam, mimeo, 1988.
46   A. M. Tripp, 'Defending the Right to Subsist'.
47   M. L. Swantz, *Women in Development: A Creative Role Denied?*, New York: St Martin's Press, 1985, pp. 129–30.
48   A. A. Aboagye, 'An Analysis of Dar es Salaam's Informal Sector Survey', Addis Ababa: ILO/JASPA, 1985; M. S. D. Bagachwa, 'The Urban Informal Enterprise Sector in Tanzania'; 'The Dar es Salaam Urban Informal Sector Survey'; 'Structure and Policy Problems of the Urban Informal Sector in Tanzania', *Economic Research Bureau Paper 81.4*, University of Dar es Salaam, 1983; M.S.D. Bagachwa and B. J. Ndulu, 'The Urban Informal Sector in Tanzania'; M. A. Bienefeld, 'The Informal Sector and Peripheral Capitalism: The Case of Tanzania', *Bulletin of the Institute of Development Studies*, 7(3), University of Sussex, 1975; A. M. Tripp, 'Defending the Right to Subsist'.
49   K. Mporogomyi, 'Industry and Development in Tanzania: The Origins of the Crisis', in M. Hodd, *Tanzania After Nyerere*, pp. 51–63.
50   K. Odegaard, 'Cash Crop Versus Food Crop Production in Tanzania'.
51   P. Wiles, 'The Second Economy, Its Definitional Problems'.
52   *Daily News*, 6 April 1983.
53   R. Green, 'State, Magendo and Class Formation in Uganda'. Paper presented at the 25th Conference of the American–African Studies Association, Washington DC, 1981.
54   ibid.
55   Actual economic performance is understated as the rate of economic growth is measured only in the official economy. Savings and consumption are understated because the underground sources of income are not recorded. Inflation may be overstated or understated depending on the relative factor prices in the two economies.
56   A. G. Keeler, G. Scobie, M. Renkow and D. L. Franklin, 'The Consumption Effects of Agricultural Policies in Tanzania'. Report to USAID. Raleigh, NC: Sigma One Corporation, 1984; Marketing Development Bureau (MDB), *Preliminary Report on the Parallel Market for Grains in Tanzania*, Dar es Salaam: MDB, 1983.
57   K. Odegaard, 'Cash Crop Versus Food Crop Production in Tanzania'.
58   Maliyamkono, using data on cash impounded during the 1983 Government

crackdown on economic crimes, estimates the volume of the second economy in Tanzania to account for 10 per cent of GNP. T. L. Maliyamkono, 'Ulanguzi: Emergence of a Second Economy in Tanzania', ERB Seminar Paper, University of Dar es Salaam, 1985.

59 For a more detailed description and evaluation of the various methods used in estimating the second economy and their applications see S. Allesandrini and B. Dallago (eds), *The Unofficial Economy*, and V. Tanzi, *The Underground Economy in the United States and Abroad*.

60 P. Wiles, 'The Second Economy, Its Definitional Problems'.

61 ibid.

62 V. Tanzi, *The Underground Economy in the United States and Abroad*.

63 P. Cagan, 'The Demand for Currency Relative to Total Money Supply', *National Bureau of Economic Research, Occasional Paper 62*, New York, 1958.

64 P. Gutmann, 'The Subterranean Economy'.

65 E. Feige, 'The Anatomy of the Underground Economy' in S. Allesandrini and B. Dallago (eds) *The Unofficial Economy*, Brookfield: Gower, 1987.

66 P. Gutmann, 'The Subterranean Economy'.

67 This was also the year in which the currency–demand deposit ratio was lowest. Incidentally, it was a boom year for Tanzania: coffee prices quadrupled; real GDP grew by 8.8 per cent, and terms of trade improved by about one-third between 1975 and 1977.

68 In Uganda, *Magendo* or the second economy is reported to constitute about two-thirds of GDP (R. Green, 'State, Magendo and Class Formation in Uganda'), while the estimate for Zaire in 1971 was that 60 per cent of the state's ordinary revenue was lost or directed to purposes other than the official ones (J. Peemans, 'The Social and Economic Development of Zaire since Independence: an Historical Outline', *African Affairs*, Vol. 74, 1975.

69 M. O'Higgins, 'Measuring the Hidden Economy: A Review of Evidence and Methodologies', in V. Tanzi, *The Underground Economy in the United States and Abroad*, p. 14.

70 T. L. Maliyamkono, 'Ulanguzi: Emergence of a Second Economy in Tanzania', p. 22.

71 ibid.

72 M. O'Higgins, 'Measuring the Hidden Economy'.

Chapter 3 pp 63–108

1 J. de Vries and L. P. Fortmann, 'Large Scale Villagization: Operation Sogeza in Iringa Region', in A. Coulson (ed.), *African Socialism in Practice*, Nottingham: Spokesman, 1979.

2 M. T. Schultheis and L. Seshamani, 'Rural Development and Incentives', Dar es Salaam: Economic Research Bureau (ERB) mimeo, 1982.

3 D. F. Bryceson, 'Household, Hoe and Nation: Development Policies of the Nyerere Era', in M. Hodd (ed.), *Tanzania After Nyerere*, London and New York: Pinter Publishers, 1988, p. 44.

4 P. Collier, S. Radwan and S. Wangwe with A. Wagner, *Labour and Poverty in Rural Tanzania*, Oxford: Clarendon Press, 1986, p. 5.

5 A. Coulson, *Tanzania, A Political Economy*, Oxford: Clarendon Press, 1982.

6 L. Putterman, 'Is a Democratic Collective Agriculture Possible?', *Journal of Development Economics*, 9, 1981.

7 A. Coulson, *Tanzania, A Political Economy*.

8 United Republic of Tanzania (URT), *Economic Survey 1984*, Dar es Salaam: Government Printer, 1983.

9   K. Odegaard, 'Cash Crop Versus Food Crop Production in Tanzania: An Assessment of the Major Post-Colonial Trends', *Lund Economic Studies*, no. 33, 1985, Chs. 4 and 5.

10 *Sunday News* (Tanzania), April 1984.

11 K. Odegaard, 'Cash Crop Versus Food Crop Production in Tanzania'.

12 See, for example, K. A. Malima, 'The Determinants of Cotton Supply in Tanzania', ERB paper no. 69.14, University of Dar es Salaam, 1971; C. T. Gerrard and T. Roe, 'Government Intervention in Food Grain Markets: An Econometric Study of Tanzania', *Journal of Development Economics*, Vol. 13, 1983; K. Odegaard, 'Cash Crop Versus Food Crop Production in Tanzania', and M. Lundahl and B. Ndulu, 'Market Related Incentives and Food Production in Tanzania: Theory and Experience', in S. Hedlund (ed.), *Incentives and Economic System: Proceedings of the Eighth ArneRyde Symposium*, London and Sydney: Croom Helm, 1987.

13 K. Odegaard, 'Cash Crop Versus Food Crop Production in Tanzania'.

14 ibid.

15 World Bank, *Tanzania Agricultural Sector Report*, Washington DC: World Bank, 1983.

16 Y. Suzuki and F. Benard, 'Effects of Panterritorial Pricing Policy for Maize in Tanzania', International Food Policy Research Institute (IFPRI), June, 1987.

17 E. Temu, *Marketing, Board Pricing and Storage Policy with Particular Reference to Maize in Tanzania*, New York: Vantage Press, 1984.

18 A. G. Keeler, G. Scobie, M. Renkow and D. L. Franklin, 'The Consumption Effects of Agricultural Policies in Tanzania', Report to USAID, Raleigh, NC: Sigma One Corporation, 1984.

19 K. Odegaard, 'Cash Crop Versus Food Crop Production in Tanzania'.

20 D. Bevan, P. Collier and P. Horsness, 'Supply Response Under Goods Market Rationing in Tanzanian Peasant Agriculture', paper prepared for the OECD Development Centre, 1988.

21 Marketing Development Bureau (MDB), *Preliminary Report on the Parallel Market for Grains in Tanzania*, Dar es Salaam: MDB, 1983, p. 1.

22 K. Odegaard, 'Cash Crop Versus Food Crop Production in Tanzania'.

23 A. G. Keeler *et al.*, 'The Consumption Effects of Agricultural Policies in Tanzania'.

24 NMC sales of maize, rice and wheat have been directed mainly at meeting urban sector consumption needs. The rate of urban sector population growth between 1967 and 1978 was 9 per cent per annum and is estimated to have prevailed during 1978–88. The annual increase in demand for the predominant staples has been estimated to be in that magnitude while official procurement of these staples declined sharply between 1979–80 and 1984–5. It is also suggested that the increase in demand for the predominant staples is partly attributed to shifts in urban consumption patterns from traditional coarse grains (millet and sorghum) to maize, rice and wheat (V. Jamal and J. Weeks, 'The Vanishing Rural–Urban Gap in Sub-Saharan Africa', *International Labour Review*, Vol. 127, no. 3, 1988, pp. 271–92; Y. Suzuki and F. Benard, 'Effects of Panterritorial Pricing Policy for Maize in Tanzania').

25 F. Ellis, 'Agricultural Price Policy in Tanzania', *World Development*, Vol. 10, no. 4, 1982.

26 V. Jamal and J. Weeks, 'The Vanishing Rural–Urban Gap in Sub-Saharan Africa.

27 ILO, *Distributional Aspects of Stabilization Programmes in the United Republic of Tanzania, 1974–1984*, Report of an ILO mission, Geneva: ILO, 1988.

28 V. Jamal and J. Weeks, 'Getting the Crisis Right: Missing Perspectives on Africa', *International Labour Review*, Vol. 127, no. 6, 1988, pp. 655–78.

29 J. F. K. Mongi, 'The Development of Price Control in Tanzania', in K. S. P, Rwegasira and L. A. Kanneworff (eds), *Inflation in Tanzania*, Dar es Salaam: Institute of Finance Management, 1980, p. 101.

30 State Trading Corporation – STC, 'On Socialization of Trade and General STC Status', Report 17/11, Dar es Salaam (mimeo), 1971.

31 S. M. Wangwe, 'Industrialization and Resource Allocation in a Developing Country: the Case of Recent Experiences in Tanzania', *World Development*, Vol. II, no. 16, 1983, pp. 483–92; B. J. Ndulu, 'Investment, Output, Growth, Capacity Utilization in an African Economy. The Case of Manufacturing Sector in Tanzania', *Eastern African Economic Review* (New Series), Vol. 2, 1986, pp. 14–30.

32 D. Bevan, A. Bigstein, P. Collier and J. W. Gunning, *East African Lesson on Economic Liberalization*, Thames Essays no. 48, London: Gower, 1987.

33 M. S. D. Bagachwa, 'The Urban Informal Enterprise Sector in Tanzania: A Case Study of Arusha Region', *Economic Research Bureau Paper no. 81.4*, University of Dar es Salaam, 1981; 'Structure and Policy Problems of the Urban Informal Sector in Tanzania', *ERB Paper no. 83.1*, University of Dar es Salaam, 1983.

34 Bevan, Bigsten, Collier and Gunning, *East African Lesson on Economic Liberalization*.

35 Bevan, Collier and Horsness, 'Supply Response Under Goods Market Rationing in Tanzanian Peasant Agriculture'.

36 G. K. Galbraith, *A Theory of Price Control*, Cambridge: Harvard University Press, 1952.

37 C. D. Msuya, 'Policies and Strategies for Economic Recovery', Address to Workshop on Economic Recovery, Dar es Salaam (mimeo), 1986.

38 ILO, *Distributional Aspects of Stabilization Programmes in the United Republic of Tanzania, 1974–1984*.

39 S. M. H. Rugumisa and J. J. Semboja, 'Productivity, Incomes and Prices in Tanzania', Dar es Salaam (mimeo), 1985.

40 B.J. Ndulu, W.M. Lyakurwa, J.J. Semboja and A.E. Chaligha, 'Import Tariff Study', report to the Ministry of Finance, Economic Affairs and Planning, Dar es Salaam (mimeo), 1987.

41 Marketing Development Bureau (MDB), *Annual Review of Cardamom*, Dar es Salaam, MDB, 1987.

42 Bevan, Collier and Horsness, 'Supply Response Under Goods Market Rationing in Tanzanian Peasant Agriculture'.

43 For example, up to 1987 the state had monopoly power over the marketing of gold and gemstones. This led to a thriving second economy market at more than double the official price. Our interviews with unlicenced small scale gold miners revealed that about 70% of their production is not sold to licenced dealers. Licenced gold buyers claimed that over 80% of small scale gold mining is sold in the second economy markets. It was also pointed out by the State Mining Corporation (STAMICO) officials that over 50 per cent of gold and gemstones is not marketed through official channels. At the same time it is being reported that security measures at Williamson Diamond's mines in Shinyanga have become lax and theft of diamonds has become very common. Roughly it appears that perhaps about half of the potential official foreign exchange earnings from the minerals sector is lost through black market deals. On this basis, it can be assumed that the Government has been losing about $US10 million from unofficial sale of precious minerals per annum between 1985 and 1988.

A large amount of unrecorded foreign exchange is similarly generated in the services sectors especially in tourism street banking, medical services, education and housing. In the tourist industry for example, an average tourist spent about $US29 per bednight between 1980 and 1985 (This compares unfavourably with $US50 spent by a tourist in Kenya). Interviews with a sample of tourists in Tanzania revealed that this was about 30 per cent of the amount of foreign exchange actually spent per day. Between 1985 and 1988, daily official tourist expenditure averaged $US52.0. Government officials in the Ministry of Lands natural resources and tourism strongly believe that the actual daily expenditure per tourist is about $US100.00. Since official tourist receipts averaged $US18 million per annum between 1980 and 1985; and $US27 million per annum between 1986 and 1988, it would appear that during the former period about $US36 million was spent annually on unrecorded tourist services while in the latter period about $US27 million of tourist earnings escaped government notice.

Another important second economy earner of foreign exchange is private housing services. It is a well known fact that private land lords demand to be paid in foreign exchange for housing services provided to expatriates. In 1988, rent paid by expatriates ranged from $US800 to $US2,500 with $US1,500 being fairly typical. In 1988, Tanzania had an estimated expatriate community of 6,154 persons. Of these 2,133 were in the executive high income category, 1,707 in the middle-income professional category, 2, 314 in the general (low income) category. If about half of the members in the executive category rent private houses at $US24,000 per person per annum, each of the half of the families in the professional category pay house rent of $US14,500 per annum while about a third of the expatriates in the low income group rent private houses at $US6,000 per person per annum; then an estimated $US42.6 million was spent on private housing in 1988. This amount of foreign money was mostly banked in overseas accounts. However raw these estimates are, they clearly suggest that there is still considerable potential for further officialization of parallel exports of both goods and services within Tanzania. In the case of gold and other precious stones it might be pragmatic for the Government to allow licenced private dealers to buy these items at market prices, export them and then allow these exporters to retain a substantial portion of the foreign exchange earned in foreign account for importation of essential inputs and spares or incentive consumer goods. In the 1989/90 budget Government has extended the export retention scheme to cover landlords leasing houses to expatriates which are being paid for in foreign exchange. However the retention percentage of 35 which is allowed under this scheme appears to be too low to attract potential landlords into this scheme.

Chapter 4 pp 109-117

1   According to Wangwe, overall industrial output continued to decline by 4 per cent from the 1985 level in spite of capacity expansions which resulted in low levels of capacity utilization. Since 1987 some industrial activities have recorded increases in output, mainly as a result of the retention scheme and import support arrangements. S. M. Wangwe, 'Recovery of the Industrial Sector: Some Lessons from Experience', *Tanzanian Economic Trends*, Vol. 1, no. 3, 1988, pp. 34–44; A. R. Ngemera, 'The Performance of Industrial Sector and Prospects Amidst the Trade Liberalization Policies', Paper presented to the Sixth Seminar on Planning, Arusha, 1988.

2   For example, in 1988 'own-funds' import licences opened and were valued at $US450 million. This was about 38% of total imports and 12% of the total merchandize exports in that year. Import financing from retained foreign exchange earnings was $US7.8 million in 1988 (about 1.7% of 'own-funded' imports). Clearly this suggests that the bulk of 'own-funds' imports are financed by foreign exchange earned from second economy sources, eg. smuggling, black market purchase of foreign exchange, over- and under-invoicing.

3   R. H. Bates, *Markets and States in Tropical Africa*, California: Berkeley University Press, 1981.

4   M. Hodd, 'Africa, the IMF and the World Bank', *African Affairs*, Vol. 86, no. 344, 1987, pp. 331–42.

5   A. Lawnsley, 'MP Plans Role as Africa's Go Between', *Guardian*, September 1988.

6   Ministry of Foreign Affairs News Release on telex reaching Tanzania High Commission's Office in London on 22 September 1988.

7   *Tanzanian Economic Trends*, 1988 Vol. 2: no. 4.

8   *Africa Analysis*, no. 47, March 1988, p. 5.

Chapter 5 pp 118-138

1   R. Green, 'State, Magendo and Class Formation in Uganda'. Paper presented at the 25th Conference of the American-African Studies Association, Washington DC, 1981.
2   G. Kahama, T. L. Maliyamkono and S. Wells, *The Challenge for Tanzania's Economy*, London: James Currey, 1986.
3   T. L. Maliyamkono, 'Ulanguzi: Emergence of a Second Economy in Tanzania', Economic Research Bureau Seminar Paper, University of Dar es Salaam, 1985.
4   D. Belshaw, 'Agriculture-led Recovery in Post Amin Uganda: The Causes of Failure and the Basis for Success', in H. Bernt and M. Twaddle, *Uganda Now*, London: James Currey, 1987, pp. 111-25.
5   E. Gargan, 'Tanzania Economics: First, a Cow', *New York Times*, November 1985.
6   A. M. Tripp, 'Defending the Right to Subsist: The State vs. the Urban Informal Economy in Tanzania'. Paper presented at the African Association Annual Meeting, 28-31 October 1988, Chicago, Illinois.
7   H. K. R. Amani, S. M. Kapunda, N. H. I. Lipumba and B. J. Ndulu, 'Effects of Market Liberalization on Food Security: The Case of Tanzania', *Proceedings of Southern African Food Security Conference*, Harare 1987; B. J. Ndulu, 'Economic Stagnation and Management of Change: Adjustment and Reduction of Macro-Micro Conflict of Interests', Dar es Salaam, mimeo, 1988.
8   A. M. Tripp, 'Defending the Right to Subsist: The State vs. the Urban Informal Economy in Tanzania'.
9   V. Jamal and J. Weeks, 'The Vanishing Rural-Urban Gap in Sub-Saharan Africa', *International Labour Review*, Vol. 127, no. 3, 1988, pp. 271-92.
10 R. W. Richardson and D. S. Ahmed, 'Challenge for Africa's Private Sector', *Challenge*, January/February 1987, pp. 16-25.
11 The limited impact of prices on production has been asserted in various studies. See, for example, D. Ghai and L. Smith, *Agricultural Prices Policy and Equity in Sub-Saharan Africa*, Boulder, Colorado: Lynne Rienner, 1987; M. Faber and R. H. Green, 'Sub-Saharan Africa's Economic Malaise', in T. Rose (ed.), *Crisis and Recovery in Sub-Saharan Africa*, Paris: OECD, 1985; ILO, *Distributional Aspects of Stabilization Programmes in the United Republic of Tanzania, 1974-1984*. Report of an ILO mission, Geneva: ILO, 1988; V. Jamal and J. Weeks, 'The Vanishing Rural-Urban Gap in Sub-Saharan Africa', and J. Shao, 'Politics and the Food Crisis in Tanzania', in S. K. Cummins et al., *Africa's Agrarian Crisis: The Roots of Famine*, Boulder, Colorado: Lynne Rienner, 1986.

Index